Sunshine Sketches of Nizwa

By John Eacott

This work is the effort of John McBride Eacott, who with his wife Donna lived in Nizwa, Oman from September 1996 to June of 1999.

The ISBN information: 978-0-9878227-1-0

Copyright 2014 by John Eacott, all rights reserved

Orders for copies of this book, or permission to quote or reproduce may be submitted to the publisher, John Eacott at eacott@execulink.com or to his current address.

My web sites www.eacott.info Or eacott.weebly.com

Sunshine Sketches of Nizwa, Oman
An Oman Adventure

Our Lives in Oman 1996 -1999

These impressions are of the people, the place and the culture and how we changed our view of the world around us. It was a most exhilarating time in a most fascinating place. This book is a collection of writings, some in real time, some after the fact, and all designed to convey the essence of what it was like to be living in an oasis on the edge of the great Arabian desert in a culture just confronting the modern world.

Readers will find I have written a period piece of places now much changed and things which no longer exist. Such is the speed of change in Oman.

Sunshine Sketches is dedicated to our grandchildren: Aven, Tessa, Mackenzie and Nathan so they may know.

John Eacott
Curries Ontario
2014 (Arabic year 1435)

SUNSHINE SKETCHES
Table of Contents

Adventures Happen	1
We Arrive in Oman	11
The Drivers Licence	24
What's It All About?	30
Making a Home	40
Television	41
Getting an Automobile	43
The Pajero	49
How to Build a House	53
Life in Our Palace	56
Our Daily Bread	65
National Day	68
The Tourists Nizwa	72
On Raising a Glass & Other Things	74
An Evening Walk	77
January 27, 1997	79
Something of History	82
Education Day	89
The Embassy Party	98
Love and Marriage	102
Dates	111
Critters, Creature and Things in the Night	114
A Trip to Masirah Island	116
Secret Bases	124
Musandam	126

A Trip to Salalah	130
Meetings and Cultural Oddities	138
Ablutions	141
The Hoti Cave	144
Christmas 1998	150
A View of Indian Culture	155
One's Persona	160
Camel Races	163
Gardening	169
Our Social Group	171
Omanization	178
A Camping Trip to Madrakah	182
Easter 1999	192
Ancient Times	194
Picnics	198
Wanderings in the Heat	202
A visit to the Empty Quarter	208
The Fernandez, Lily and Little India	215
Religion	219
The Omani Student	230
The West and Islam	234
Two Cultures in a Day	238
Wadi Bani Khalid and the Wahiba Sands	242
Sea Turtles	248
The Wadi's Coming!	252
Banking and Finance	255
The College Changes	257
Who's your Boss	265
The End of the Journey	274

Adventures Happen

Oman is the center of the world. Well, if you live there that may seem true! Look at the typical wall map of the world and put your finger at the center. You will likely have put it on Oman. Practically nobody has heard of it. Even fewer people have heard of Nizwa where we lived. For three years it was the center of our world. While we lived there, we felt as if we were observing the middle ages coming to an end and the dawning of a new modern world, a world of huge cross-cultural currents. Also, we felt we were in the quiet eye of the epicenter of world events. I was there not as a tourist but as a working resident living in the Omani Arab world. Here is the story of how two Canadian expats were altered by life in an ancient desert.

Adventures happen! Is it because we want them or is it something else? Either way this is a story of the adventure my wife, Donna and I had. For three years we lived in an entirely different world. As you read, you will come to understand just how surreal such an adventure can be.

It was a fine spring afternoon and I set off to till the earth for a new garden. There was brilliant sunshine and a pleasant aura as I worked. Gradually my head filled with an awareness, a portent that I was about to experience something remarkable. From time to time I have had these premonitions. By and large this awareness is not unsettling but when it happens, it tends to throw empirical process and scientific astuteness off track. I frequently never said anything about having these moments because I really don't like the idea of the paranormal and the expectation of funny looks from people if I mention them.

However in this instance the message was really intense that I was going on a journey and things were going to change in our lives. I felt compelled to stop my hoeing and go in the house and tell Donna what had just happened. I got a blank look.

In addition to this initial experience I had a series of smaller less intense ones during the following three years. I felt like I was periodically consulting a mental road map of what was unfolding and I was just going along for the ride although I also felt I could have gotten off at any time.

For the next couple of days I went about my business which included at the time being a trustee with the Oxford County Board of Education. After the agenda had been sent, it was the habit of the Director to pass out several sheets of additional information before the board meeting. These were usually pieces of general information or advertising that usually went into the recycle bin on the way out. A Toronto consulting company, ECS, Educational Consulting Services, was soliciting opportunities to provide services to the Board if they were planning any building or reorganization activities. Two lines at the bottom indicated that they were seeking people with experience in educational administration or teacher education to serve as Deans at colleges in Oman. They had been awarded a new contract.

I wondered if this was the experience that had been foreshadowed. The paper did not go in the recycle. It went home. The next day, May 2, 1996, Donna and I discussed this notice and as I had these exact qualifications, I thought I would send off a short email to the company. I wrote the briefest of notes simply saying I had the qualifications and I provided my telephone and email address.

Less than an hour later a phone call came from the company.

Could I provide a full resume and did I have any questions? By the time that call came in I knew where Oman was and that it was a warm desert country and I didn't know much else. I was so taken off guard that I really had no questions formed in my head. I sent in my resume. My career over the past few years had been mostly contract work with the federal government as a chairperson for different projects. Prior to that I had been a teaching master at the Ontario Teacher Education College and before that, an elementary school principal. The college job vanished when the college was closed and my credentials were good enough for me to apply for a superintendent position with a school system. Unfortunately, there were few of these openings and when there were, I was always able to make the short list. The short list and interview resulted in a half dozen disappointing phone calls. So I applied my skills in self employment.

I did not get very excited when ECS called and invited us for an interview a few days later. An interview is one thing and a job offer is another. The interview was in an office in a high rise on University Ave in Toronto on Thursday, May 9 at 2:00 p.m.. That meant I had to take a full day off work and drive into downtown Toronto for another exercise. I had other things to do. Did we want to be bothered? "Nothing ventured nothing gained" came to mind so off we went.

The chrome and glass walled office was pleasant and we sat by a coffee table covered with several books on Oman. We spent a few minutes looking through them. Then Tim Hore and Margot Thompson introduced themselves to us and led us into an office. They asked a couple of questions about my resume and proceeded to tell us in great detail about the plans they had for Oman and how they visualized the work of the Deans they were entrusted to appoint. ECS was working under contract with the Ministry of Higher Education for the Sultanate of Oman to supply six administrators to reorganize six teachers' colleges which were completing their first year of operation. The young man had just returned from Oman and had all sorts of information to tell us about his wonderful time there.

In turn we had a lot of questions ourselves. Some of them they could not answer. Was this for real? What will we do with the house? Will we come out ahead financially? What about the kids? Am I too old for this sort of stuff? How will Donna handle the isolation? We are not sure we like the money or the conditions or the foggy nature of the job.

I felt like I was getting a sales pitch and when Donna and I stepped into the elevator to leave my first words were, "Who was interviewing who?" I had no doubt in my mind that they were going to offer me a position. The pay and perks we decided were good enough and an adventure to a warm country was a plus. However, in spite of the fact we were told there was a J.C. Penny and a McDonald's in Muscat, we really had no idea what life style we were going to experience. We had been in Kenya in the 70's and were guests of some teachers in a rural area. They had a cistern, windows with no glass, and some simple furniture. It takes a certain adaptability to go off into the unknown.

The wheels were in motion. The information package about us was to be taken to Oman by Margot on May 23. A final decision was to be made by the Director General of Higher Education.

We needed more information, a lot of it. If there was a chance we were going to this place, we had to learn what we were getting into.

We tracked down a recent National Geographic magazine with an article about Oman. The library had very little but there was a travel guide with an Oman section and a couple of other books. I chose "Arabian Sands" by Wilfred Thesiger, an explorer who went to Oman in 1948. I was eleven that year. Thesiger had to disguise himself so he would not be found out as an Englishman. He had wanted to visit Nizwa but the local imam there had proclaimed that any Christian found in his town would be shot. The country was described as a desert with a few communities all still living in the middle ages.

"It is a bitter, desiccated land which knows nothing of gentleness or ease... Men live there because it is the world into which they were born; the life they lead is the life their forefathers led before them; they accept hardships and privations; they know no other way.

Life moved in time with the past. These people still valued leisure and courtesy and conversation. They did not live their lives at second hand, dependent on cinemas and wireless."

- Wilfred Thesiger

Each time Thesiger and his companions encounter others, they stop, invite them to share their food and look forward to exchanging the latest news. The Bedu love to talk and gossip.

This was the stuff of adventure from my youth. It was alluring and concerning at the same time. Oman in 1948 was not yet part of the modern world. It was very undeveloped and especially isolated.

Donna didn't read that book. Things appeared to have improved according to Fodor's travel guide. Oil had been discovered and the old ruler Said Bin Taimur had been deposed by his son Quaboos bin Said Al Said, a very progressive person. Westerners, mostly Dutch and British oil workers, lived in Muscat. There were a lot of Indians brought in for manual labor.

June 1, a Saturday afternoon call from ECS tells us that Muscat has approved me for a position. But where? We think Salalah. ECS wants another interview. We still have a lot of questions and uncertainty about accepting.

June 6, Thursday, 1:30 p.m. we are scheduled for a one hour meeting with senior members of ECS, Steve Lichty and Tim Hore. This turns into a two hour plus dialogue session. The apartment furnishings include a gas canister and a hose. What are these for? Will this be some God awful place? That night it's back to the internet and we find photos from NASA guys who went to Salalah. One photo of an apartment building conjures up thoughts of noise and heat. Salalah appears pretty backward. Still, it looks intriguing.

June 13, an offer of employment arrives. Jonathan and I were busy digging up the septic line and suddenly it's decision time. Our son, Jonathan, has gotten admission to McGill for September. Our daughter, Erin, is preparing to go to Minsk in eastern Europe to do a summer of Chernobyl rehabilitation with kids. What a family! And Donna and I have to decide on going to Oman. I go to a board committee meeting that night and say nothing. We are also preparing to go to Halifax for a school board convention.

Our life is getting a little surreal as this is one of the last weeks we will all be together here at the same time as a family.

We had decided that unless something came up that we really didn't like, we would agree to go. There were six colleges: Sur, Sohar, Salalah, Ibri, Rustaq and Nizwa. Salalah was a city in the south of Oman farthest away from the capital Muscat and had a unique climate and location on the water. Salalah had beaches, a green season, and was a town with amenities. The dean was to have a furnished apartment upstairs on a busy street. We were quick to indicate that as we lived in a rural area, we would not be happy living in a second floor flat over a shop on a busy street. There was some restlessness across the table.

We deans would be empowered by the Director General of Higher Education to reorganize and structure as best we saw fit the operation of the colleges so they would meet western standards of education. Oman was bringing in a new curriculum for their schools based on Canadian methods and Canadian designed curriculum. There was another Dean at each college who would be arabic speaking but not an Omani. His role was to do liaison with the parents, the local schools, and student discipline. The arrangement sounded reasonable.

ECS would pay us but we would report to the Director General, Dr. Rawya bint Saud al Busaidiya. The perks of the job included air fare home each summer for both of us. I would get six weeks vacation. The accommodations were basic but paid for. Our contract was for 18 months but it could be extended. If we completed the 18 months, there would be a nice cash bonus. Return home included shipping all our goods up to 700 pounds of freight. The Sultanate paid for medical care. The salary was roughly the same as a school superintendent in Ontario. To all of this was added abundant sunshine.

Our contract approval, Tim informed us, would have to come from the Director General. She had the final say. We reiterated the fact that we did not object to Salalah but we did not like the accommodations. Tim said that he had only two weeks to line up the places and realized some might not be ideal. He did not know if he could make any changes. Since there seemed no room for negotiation on the contract details, I made the accommodation the point to negotiate. It was really clear they really wanted me to sign up and I reasoned that there likely were not many people around who had teachers' college experience who would want to, or be able to, take on such a challenge.

I did not want to accept until I knew where we were going. Margot called to tell us they wanted us to go to Nizwa. The person who had gone out for ECS to Nizwa in April would not be returning in September. He had said that he found the apartment to be acceptable and quiet. We agreed to go. Nizwa was the old capital of the interior of Oman, the place where no Christian was allowed in the town as recently as 1948. Nizwa was a palm tree oasis at the base of a mountain and a two hour drive by car from Muscat.

Our next trip to Toronto was to meet our colleagues who were also going off to be Deans. One was currently at Rustaq. The rest of us were new. We had a pleasant orientation session. Details of the furnishings and working in Oman were provided. We would leave September 8 and the college classes would begin the 15. At the same time the job description had been tempered to make it even more vague. Another prospective dean, Norm, speculated it was a cross between a high school VP and a consultant. I think the Arabic and the English versions of the job description were very different although the telling feature was that both deans got the same pay and benefits. Who was the boss? Who was responsible for what? It was a recurrent problem at all of the colleges. I sensed later that it was part of the Arabic way. Always keep things a little off center, a little off balance, a little unclear, just in case! In case of what? Who knew?

The company provided an interesting document of pointers about the sensitivities of the Arab world. We digested this material carefully. Women were to dress modestly in long skirts or slacks and sleeves to the elbow. Men were to wear jackets and ties at work. It was customary to leave small portions of food and liquid after a meal to show you were satisfied and full. A hand over a glass indicated no more. When seated on the floor, one was to be careful not to expose the soles of the feet to others sitting there. Sitting like this took some skill to master so as not to show rudeness. I spent most of the next three years carefully arranging my feet. Then one day while having kawa, the Omani coffee with cardamon, with several of the office staff, we got into a cultural discussion. One of the secretaries, Gamoodi, said he had been told that the Jordanians had a custom where you were to keep the soles of your feet away from exposure. I asked if that was true for the Omani people. There was laughter because they had no such custom and what was more they had asked the Jordanians they knew and the Jordanians never heard of it either. Three years I had spent rearranging my feet!

For the next two months we went about our business. Our son

Jonathan was preparing to leave home to go to University at McGill just as we were planning to leave for Oman. I had empty nest problems when our daughter left for university and now our son was going as well. I thought that it was good we were also going away as it would be hard not having any kids around the house. I dreaded the empty nest. I did not tell any of the school board members of our plans because there was enough about the endeavor that left me feeling ECS was quite sketchy about some things and it could all fall through. I was vice chair of the school board and would have been the chair come December. At the same time it was looking like the next chair would have been the last as the county boards were to be merged into regional boards. I hated to see that happen. My last year as school principal had been the first year of this same board so I could easily have seen it in and out. Some distinction that would be!

At the end of August I announced that I was resigning from the school board to accept an appointment abroad.

Before we could enter Oman, we had to have a visa and a work permit. We could not depart without the visa. September came but the visa had not. A couple of days before we were to depart the photocopy of my visa arrived but Donna's did not. I informed them that I would not depart until hers also arrived. My resistence caused some consternation but I held my ground. Sept eight passed without us departing. We were thankful we had time to go visit an ailing friend who unfortunately died a couple of months later. On the 10th Donna's visa arrived and our flight was quickly booked for the 12th of September. We had been packed for several days and our house was set for shutdown, prior to it being rented out.

We Arrive in Oman

The adventure was about to begin with a British Airways overnight flight to London and then a 5-hour stopover in London before the flight to Dubai and Muscat. We did not cross the Atlantic in first class. We sat in the middle of a five across row of seats, crammed in, sitting up, sleepless. Heathrow got explored but we had been there before. The Muscat bound flight was much better. We sat side by side in two seats with tv sets in the back of the seat and lots of leg room. I got the impression that passengers bound for the Middle East expected better treatment than those crossing the Atlantic.

We flew across Europe and went farther east than I expected for reasons I could not understand. Later flights took a totally different route over Cyprus. However, this time we flew over The Black Sea to eastern Turkey where out the window I saw the gigantic cone of volcanic Mt. Ararat off to the west. The clear air afforded fine views of a rough desolate landscape in hues of brown. We flew on over Iran and across the Persian Gulf. As night descended, we approached Dubai. The lights of the city were seen far off and we were anxious to get off and stretch our legs before completing the final hour of the journey to Muscat.

Dubai airport was busy and the duty free area where we had a few minutes was most impressive because of the Lexus car they were raffling. It seemed more like a casino than a duty free shop. Once back on the plane we were eager to complete the journey as it was now nearly 24 hours since we had left home. Peering out the window in the darkness we saw little clusters of lights but nothing else of our home to be. We never ever saw the runways of Oman airport in the daylight as all the flights we ever took were always in the middle of the night. Someone said it was because the Americans had defense equipment there and didn't want people to see. That was a reasonable explanation because I was later to discover there were such facilities around the country.

Once we landed in Muscat we were to clear customs and show our documents and pick up our actual visa after which we would be met by Florence Seroggie who was another Dean already in Oman.

We landed and stepped out into a hot muggy night. There was some anxiety while we waited, seemingly forever, for our luggage as they were almost the last bags off the plane. Bags in tow, we were nearly at the back of the custom's line and we patiently waited our turn. A customs agent called us out of line. This action perplexed us. He went to a box of documents and verified our visas were not there. After some shuffling he went off to speak with another agent. Two agents came to say that yes our papers were in order but the Ministry of Higher Education had not yet brought the original documents. It was now well after midnight. We told them someone was meeting us beyond the opaque sliding doors. By this time the other passengers had all departed and the airport looked like it was about to shut down. We were led into an office where we discussed our situation after which apparently someone went to speak to Florence. She called the Ministry and got some functionary out of bed.

In the meantime we were asked if we would like a cup of coffee since we would have to wait.

The coffee arrived in English bone china cups and we sat alone in the arrivals area on a couple of chairs that had been provided. Here we were all alone having a pleasant drink. The place got ever more quiet until only one person was left working in the airport. This individual could not go home until we could leave.
I was concerned that I might get my documents but Donna might not get hers. Would she be back on the next plane or what? After an hour or so there was some commotion and we were called to the counter where our documents had arrived. They were stamped and we headed toward the sliding opaque doors to see who Florence was and to find out how we were to get to the hotel.
Florence was instantly upon us and eagerly welcoming us to Oman. With her was an Omani in his white dishdasha and turban. He looked rather groggy. He said he had not been advised that we were arriving that day and apologized for the delay in a tone that suggested it was our fault he had not been advised. We were to get used to that attitude when things went wrong.
Florence called a taxi to get us to the hotel and so we exited into the steamy hot sauna like night air. A few people were standing around. They were an eclectic bunch. Some were in Pakistani shirts, some in dishdashas some in western clothes. We left the airport and entered a brightly lit road with a roundabout containing what looked like a large monument. It was a head turning view. Then we drove into an underpass with blue mosaic tiles that blended into a community mural before emerging into an expressway that was lit up like midday. There were flower beds, shrubs, trees and monuments all over the place. We had no idea about what to expect but it had not been an opulent roadway. It was very surreal and dazzling. I had never seen a highway so magnificent.

We arrived at the Al Falag hotel about 2:00 a.m. and wasted no time in getting to bed.

The next morning we met Norm Hunter another new dean with whom we had breakfast. There was lots to eat from a large buffet. Most of the staff spoke English and looked and sounded like Indians. We could have stayed at the hotel for a couple of days but as the college was about to begin, I was anxious to get there. Norm was in no hurry to get to his post which was even more remote than mine. As for me, Muscat could wait. Our clothes and belongings were all packed except for an overnight bag and we would have had to open them up if we lingered. The college was sending a driver to meet us at ten. The few hours of sleep had refreshed us and anyway we were running on adrenaline. The hotel seemed a decent place and as we were only two hours drive from Muscat we could easily come back. Norm and another dean Lee were going to stay another day before heading off to Ibri and Salalah.

The driver arrived with a white Toyota pickup truck. Our luggage was tossed in the back and Donna and I climbed into the cab.

Every building was painted white. We drove along a multilane road sided by rows of eight to ten storey buildings. The streets were spotlessly clean and here and there flower beds and watered lawns could be seen. The driver negotiated off the street and parked beside an office building. There was neither parking space nor parking lot. He simply pulled up over the curb. I asked where we were and he said, "Ministry, come." We got out and I protested about our untended luggage in the back of the truck, sitting in the open on a busy street. "They will be ok," he said.

We didn't have a choice but to walk off leaving all our possessions exposed in the back of a pickup truck. I fully expected to return and find it all gone. We would have nothing but the clothes on our back. Donna stays in the truck.

We headed into the building and entered an elevator that took us to the 7th floor. The building was built in a square with an interior walkway all around an open court. We walked halfway around and it was clear our driver was looking for someone. I did not know who. It could have been a personal visit for all I knew. He spoke in arabic and was redirected to another office and from there to the 5th floor. Finally in the elevator I was able to discover that he wanted to introduce us to the Director General but she was not to be found. She was not on the 5th floor and apparently he learned she was away. We got back to the truck. Nothing had been touched. The driver said that no one would steal our stuff. This was Oman. It was to be a couple of months before I actually met the Director General, my boss.

The journey resumed and we passed the airport. At each roundabout was a huge fort like monument with lawn and flowers. We passed one with a giant clock tower and soon after that one we turned away from the manicured gardens that lined the road. A dual lane expressway was headed toward some low lying craggy hills. There was a scattering of shrubs and the occasional building with a palm tree or two. Otherwise, it was blue sky and brown rocks. I was suffering from a great thirst and the air conditioning in the truck was doing a poor job of cooling. I asked if we could stop for a drink. We pulled into a roadside store. I had a few Omani currency notes but they were fairly large and the store clerk could not cash my smallest. The driver bought each of us a large Pepsi. It was the best pop I ever had.

We were back on the road. There were fewer and fewer buildings. The dual highway turned into a two lane road. It was very hot and extremely bright. The sun blazed out of a totally blue sky. To the right of us was an enormous mountain, a slab of rock that tilted up for thousands of feet. This was the edge of the African plate jamming into Asia and it looked exactly that way. It was a great slab many miles long jutting into the sky. On the right the formations looked like black slag heaps punctuated by stretches of flat pebbles and beyond that there were small ragged rocky hills. It looked like it would be difficult terrain to walk over. It looked like an entrance to hell.

An old fort tower was perched on an outcrop and not far away there were some palm trees and a few houses. This scenario would be repeated every few miles usually with some evidence of a stream or a rock strewn wadi. It did not look very prosperous although there were pickup trucks parked here and there. They were mostly white, mostly Toyota. Clothes were hung up on lines but also sometimes spread out on rocks to dry. The buildings were uniformly tan and looked like they were made of mud.

As the journey continued, the landscape kept looking less and less inviting and ever more foreboding. The mountain was grey and in shadow, barren except where rocky gorges broke its uniformity.

The left side kept looking like some hideous moonscape. This land seemed incapable of growing even a cactus plant. I had never seen such an ugly landscape and I was having visions of living like these people in these small villages. What on earth had we gotten ourselves into? My apprehensions grew by the mile.

About two hours into the trip the driver pointed forward and said, "There is the college. You can see it from here." I looked out into what appeared to be a large level plain on my left side. There were buildings scattered about and some more than a story. A huge stadium caught my eye and the driver said the college was just past the stadium. As we approached, it was clear this was a brand new elaborate stadium that could seat 20 thousand or more people. It was impressive. Just past it the driver announced we were at the college and pulled the truck off the road. We entered an open gate and went past a small empty gate house. There were several buildings in distinctly arabic styling. We drove up what looked like a side walk and pulled up before the steps of a two story building. Donna commented how nice the flowers were around the college. The driver got out, motioned for Donna to stay in the truck, and took me up to the door.

I barely got my foot in the door when I was greeted by a delegation. How did all these people know I had arrived? We shook hands all around and exchanged greetings but I could see they were quite upset. There were problems. Questions were asked. Answers wanted.

The college was due to receive students almost immediately and the timetables had not been approved. There were issues as to who had authority. Authority conveyed an unwritten right. That right was to award class scheduling on the basis that the authors and their friends got the best positioning for class times. Some did not like that so there was an uproar. The most senior ranking member of the faculty in the absence of a dean was theoretically in charge. He was an Egyptian. I soon learned that most of the faculty was from Egypt. The Jordanians, Moroccans, Tunisians and assorted other nationalities were badly outnumbered. These lesser nationals all seemed to get classes late in the day or Friday afternoon. Everyone had a view as to how they had been slighted in the timetable process. While I was trying to figure out what they were telling me, there were others standing around with other urgent issues about the preparation of the first day, the organization of students into classes, the registration and the welcoming activities.

I arrived knowing that this was the second year of operation and that the college was about to open. That was about the sum of my information. Now I was there and decisions had to be made.

However we still had a truck load of luggage and no idea where we were going to be sleeping that night. We picked up the apartment key and I left promising to come right back as soon as Donna had been dropped off.

The faculty who spoke English could clearly lord it over the others since that's all I understood. I sat down with Anwar, the head of the Science department, who was the senior staff member. I heard him out then received the committee charged with creating the timetable. Anwar kept interjecting and I got the impression he was not very popular as he had a lot of late day classes. Since I recognized the problems of altering a timetable that had taken weeks to assemble, I asked to go see the actual master timetable. I was led to a room covered with sheets of paper to which had been attached bits of paper with arabic writing. I asked if any of this had been done with a computer and got negative nods. It was obvious without asking that this was a tedious awkward way of laying it out. I wanted to know if each department had been given a copy or a right to inspect. They had

not. So all the department heads were sent for and were told to verify that each of their department faculty had the prescribed number of lessons and a classroom for each and to tell me by noon the next day. The timetable committee seemed anxious and I told them it was necessary that each department had a clear understanding. They would have the next afternoon to make any corrections. I would deal with the favoritism issue another time.
As the room was about to be full of department heads, I went out to meet with the student welcoming committee who seemed proud of the fact that I wanted to meet with them. They were exuberant and full of arm waving and assured me they had their act together. I asked if they wanted me to speak to the students. That sounded good to them and I had two days to learn an Arabic greeting. The remainder of my few words would be through a translator. They left and I had only the organization of student classes committee to report on their issues. That was a pretty routine matter that simply required my confirmation to proceed.
By five o'clock I had collected my wits, landed on the ground running, made decisions and called a faculty meeting for the next day. There was no sign of the other dean and I never had time to ask. An Omani secretary offered to drive me home as he knew where I lived. That was fortunate since I sure had no idea where I had been a couple of hours earlier.

ès

The college was outside of Nizwa and some miles from our home. There were fields of stone. Stone-covered ground punctuated by various buildings bearing Omani Flags. Most were two or three stories high. We came to a roundabout where there was a group of shops most bearing English signs. We continued on a dual roadway with more white apartment buildings. As we approached Nizwa proper, a dry river bed separated us from what looked like a shopping area, a majestic old fort and a roundabout with a park and monuments on a smaller scale than we had seen in Muscat. We crossed a modern bridge and came to another roundabout that gave a better view of the downtown. I thought it looked like a set from Disneyland. It was so incredibly clean and other worldly. After another mile we turned at the police station and continued on a few more blocks. I would need a car and soon. The college was a good 20 minute drive from our home.

We pulled up by an eight foot wall and drove into a courtyard covered in gravel. The only plant was a red Bougainvillea growing against the courtyard wall. There were four apartments and ours was upstairs overlooking the street. The building appeared unfinished and sat in a barren field. The apartment was not clean. The telephone didn't work. The toilet was broken. There was little pressure in the bathroom taps. Luxury it was not! Donna had set about washing down the wardrobes and began the process of unpacking.

The Omani who brought me home waited while I got Donna. We went shopping. Donna said it was an unusual array of goods. Lots of paper products were available but not cheap. The fresh meat did not look good. There were vegetables and fruit and spaghetti but no sauce. Fresh bread was sold at a bakery nearby. Our Omani guide bought us each a Yop yoghurt drink that tasted delicious. We drank it on the way back home. It had been a long time since breakfast. He would pick me up in the morning. Our bed was a decent king size.

We were both too wired to sleep much and rose at six a.m. and went for a walk about the neighborhood. Children were heading off for school. Some boys in white or purple dishdashas were waiting for a bus. The girls wore white pants and black or yellow tunics and had a scarf over their heads. The kids gawked at us. Some said, “good morning.” Little girls giggled and smiled. Western people were a novelty especially at six a.m.

By the end of our first day in Nizwa the apartment was pretty much in working order and we went up on the roof to look around and have a drink and read the paper. Supper was made from frozen spicy chicken fingers, fried onions with peppers, zucchini, tomatoes and black olives served with pita bread. We had completed our first full day in Nizwa and were starting to feel at home.

❧

During out third week in Oman I began writing some recollections of our daily lives. Donna kept a daily diary. These were composed at the time and were designed to capture the essence of how we lived. Several of these “at the time” accounts are included in this book and are italicized. The first of these was composed -

October 1st, 1996. It is 8:30 p.m. and the temperature is 94f. A hot dry wind is blowing. It feels like heat coming from an oven. I am sitting on the roof surrounded by a meter high crenellated wall resembling a fort. All the houses seem to have a variation of this wall around the flat roof. The stars are dim because of the lights of the town. The gravel faced mountain opposite isn't visible tonight. A couple of nights ago the moon came up like a giant spotlight over it. The higher wall of the Jabel Akbar mountain to my left has one little light on it about half way up. There is not a road there and I don't know what is there. To my right the ancient defensive tower on a small knoll is floodlighted but I can't make out the small artificial waterfall which is beside it. Life size models of small deer are placed here and there on the rocks around the tower.

Next door the chicken vendor's birds are quiet. Cars hum up and down the street. They don't beep as much in the evening. Across the street the older homes nestle among the date palms with the green gardens growing under their shade. This land is watered by the ancient canals from the mountains. The Falag Daris, built three thousand years ago, is a famous long falag and its clear waters irrigate this land. The green palm tree oasis is in stark contrast to the red brown of the hills.

I can hear kids playing on a balcony. It is too dark to be out now. Just after sunset they leave the dirt patches that they use for soccer. The key to go in is the call of the mullah for prayers. Even in the heat of the evening they change from their dishdashas into sports clothes and have a great time until the prayer call.

I walk across the warm tiles to feel the water tank, hot to the touch after a day in the sun. My eyes feel scratchy from the dust or the dry heat. The heat is dry for I never feel sweaty, even at 40 plus Celsius.

A couple of women draped from head to toe in bright colors have gone into Bijou's little store. His sign proclaims "Foodstuff for Sale" in English and Arabic. It is one small room perhaps 15 by 15 at most. There is lots of stuff there for sale, especially for the raft of kids living nearby. He is Indian and never seems to have enough change for my small bills.

It is nice up here on the roof, especially at sunset. The ring of hills takes on different colors and the few clouds seem to glow. Dusk comes quickly and five or ten minutes after sunset we begin to hear the mullahs calling the faithful to prayer at the several small mosques among the date palms across the road. First one then another and yet another even louder chimes in. Allah, Allah Akhbar is repeated but it does not sound much like that to me. It sounds more like a hog or moose calling competition. I read where there are two mosques in Nizwa that are 1300 to 1400 years old.

People have lived here a long time. Evidence of that fact is the large cemetery behind me. Here stones are set on their edge to mark the graves. There must be thousands of nameless bones in this field. The stones and earth are burned to a dark red and brown by the centuries of sun. Beyond the cemetery is a row of street lights marking the road leaving town. Someone said we will have street lights on our road soon. I wonder when they will give the streets names. Perhaps they have them but no one seems to know what they are.

The wind is away from the garbage bin so there are no smells from there. There is no smell of smoke from the evening fires but a cloud of dust hangs in the air and like a giant balloon passes by.

Some boys in their blue dishdashas and embroidered caps stand by a car. There are no Indians about just now. Some went by earlier carrying water from the tap. They wear shirts and pants.

It is nice to have these plastic chairs up here. I must be careful not to break another one. They are two rials each and not sturdy. The wind is picking up again. It is odd to feel it so hot. Yet it is not as hot as when I walk from one college building to another. It is more windy tonight than most nights and it is from the north, over the mountains as well. It is not late but 6:00 a.m. comes early. I'll go in now.

The Drivers Licence

The next morning was a perfect example of how the pressures of daily life would totally derail my duties at the college. We had arranged for a rental car until I could find a four wheel drive that suited us. I was using my Ontario driver's licence but as a resident of the Sultanate of Oman I had to obtain an Omani driver's licence.

October 2nd.1996

Today I got my Omani drivers licence. I was quite pleased but it took about eight hours of running back and forth to the police station and hospital along with frequent instructions to come back later.

Day one... I take the young college office clerk Mahommed Al Gamoodi to pick up my papers and get them filled out. I have my passport, drivers licence and photo with blue background. We arrive at the licence area, a dusty field beside the usual slag heap mountain. There are some mobile huts mounted on pylons. The windows are screened. At the windows business is transacted as the fly screen opens and closes. We get the papers and the processing begins. This takes some time.

I find I must go for an eye test at the hospital.

The next day we go to the hospital. The other dean decides he wants a licence also. It is more difficult for him as he is an Egyptian and must take a driver's test which is not needed for Canadians. I arrive to find the eye test is closed. "Come back one hour from now." We sit and wait. A Bedu woman, in black with her head covered, is there with four girls. Another older lady comes and squats. There is lots of room on the benches but they are hard. She prefers to squat. Some women have the birka or black mask over their faces.

The other day I saw a lady with a black shawl over her face and she saw so poorly that another lady had to help her with the stairs. Most Omani women just cover their hair with black shawls or sometimes a brightly colored shawl.

A young father is playing with his infant child. Omanis really seem to pay a lot of attention to their kids. It shows. The children are polite and happy and often I see an older child with a younger one in tow. Groups of kids all seem to get along well.

An old fellow in white robes who is holding a thin cane whacks on the door for the benefit of the person who approaches. In the green door there is a small window hole which enables one to speak to those inside. It is a joke amongst us sitting there waiting as he whacks for each visitor. Another person goes to the door and the old gent leans over and whacks the door sharply several times.

Ah, the door opens and we line up to get our eye test. I read the sign, Room #1 Eye Testing.

They call my name. They always get it right. In Arabic it is phonetic. The balding Indian doctor sits at his desk and begins filling in my paper. He turns on the eye chart. I start reading. He tells me to wait. "Take off your glasses." I'm basically blind in one eye without glasses. "This line please." I read. "Cover your right Eye." I easily read "Z P D G " "OK" left eye next. I guess at the letters. " Z R N." "OK " he says. I think to myself, "I can't read that line." He hands me back my papers stamped 6/6 and 6/6, passed. Well that took about a minute and a half. We head back to the police station. The desk man studies my Canadian photo card and a discussion ensues. He has never seen one before. "When does it expire?" "Permanent," I say. Forewarned, I don't give him the second part because it is renewed every three years and in Oman you must have three years proof of driving. I'm learning to play the system. Finally he wants a letter from the college. The other dean is sitting next to me but we don't have paper with the college letter head. We drive back 20 km to the college. The Egyptian dean writes a letter in arabic on college letterhead paper saying I need a licence. He writes himself one. We drive 20 km back to the licence camp. It looks like a camp. Another person is at the desk. He asks the same questions but starts filling out the final details. Somebody had called Muscat or said they did to see if it was okay to give me a licence. The paper work is done. I must take it to another building along with 75 dollars (20 Rials) and my blue photo. It is 12:30 and we are told that it is closed for today. "Come tomorrow."

The next day, day three, we arrive at 9:30 a.m.. Neither dean has spent much time doing college work. The little man in the window tells us to leave the papers as he is busy and has no help. The other guy is on vacation. Come back in one hour. We see he is busy and we've been there 45 minutes to get this far so we leave. Mohammed, my office clerk, takes me to his uncle's son's house which is nearby. This person is also married to his sister. Mohammed is the youngest child of his father's 3rd wife. His father is about 80. Mohammed has a brother over 50. He says he is 24 and strikes me as a very smart fellow. He is a graduate in journalism and politics from the University and speaks perfect English. We enter the men's living room after he speaks with his sister. I get a glimpse of the lady as she vanishes into the back of the house. We enter a nearly bare room with only carpets on the floor. There is a TV on a stand and on the TV a bottle of lotion. The walls are painted half way up with enamel paint and then a less glossy paint above. This time the walls are in yellows as opposed to the greens in our apartment. Soon a big bowl of dates arrives along with some small cups and a thermos of coffee. A pitcher of orange Tang comes later.

We squat on the floor and discuss mid east politics. Mohammed is well informed.

His brother-in-law is a Sargent in the military and is a good runner. He has won many medals for racing. Mohammed lives in Tanouf, a village near Nizwa, and his father fought in the civil war there in the 1950's. I learn about the prices of dishdashas and caps. From Mohammed I learn a lot about Omani society.

The dates are red and short. The best ones are nearly all brown. The red part is quite astringent indicating that it is not ripe. Soon the longer dates will be in season. The coffee has no sugar and the cups are small without handles. It is explained the other arabs use sugar but since the dates are so sweet none is needed. Omanis like to add cardamon to their coffee which is drunk black. I find I like the coffee and date combination.

While we drink our Tang, some kids come in. The oldest boy is four and quite curious. The girl, three, is dark haired and has a dazzling smile. She is cute as a button and brightly dressed. The youngest lad just grins and tries to show off like any two year old. The TV program changes from western girls in track suits doing an exercise class to Omanis in turbans talking about some paintings. We finish our juice and I ask that the lady be thanked and we go back to get the licence, perhaps, Inshalla (God willing).

We are informed that the fellow who must sign has gone to the police station. It is now well past 11:00 a.m. We sit for a time. Nobody comes. Mohammed speaks in the window. He asks for my 20 rials which I hand over. Still nobody comes. Suddenly my name is mentioned and Mohammed jumps to the window. I stand bewildered and there it is ... my plastic card with my picture and in English it says "valid till 2006." I have my Omani licence.

I wave it around the office at the college in triumph and get a round of applause and some comments about having a party. The next day I treat the office staff to a cold drink.

In the meantime the other dean, Ahmed Naggar, has to take a driving test. Canadians, Americans and most westerners and citizens of the Gulf states get a reciprocal licence. Most of the time this applied to the Brits but the head of the Oman police got a ticket while in England and could not get it fixed. So for some months all the Brits who wanted a licence had to take a driving test.

Omanis do not care much for Egyptians. Omanis are not big in stature while many Egyptians are. The Omanis think Egyptians tend to be loud and boisterous and like to get their own way. The ones with authority are liked even less. The other dean grumped around and finally admitted he had failed the test. He has lost face which is an insult in the Arab world. Worse, it appears, he failed a second time. That was discerned because you could only take the test once a week and he took more than two weeks to produce his document. There was some subtle glee among the Omani staff members over this state of affairs. Doctor Naggar mentioned quietly to me that he had finally obtained the licence and hinted at the fact that he was abused and that there was nothing wrong with his driving.

What's It All About?

It had been nearly a month since we left home and so far we had not contacted people so I decided to send out a letter.

October 9, 1996
To friends, relatives and others,

It is almost one month since we arrived late, one hot night. Oman was for a day or so a dazzling array of new sights. Now that we have things in better focus, I can tell you a little of our experiences. I apologize for the photo copy letter but work is busy and there is so much to tell.

Oman is hot, very hot, 40c or more every day. We had one little shower of rain. It is also dusty. It is mountainous of a unique nature and there are gravel plains. Where we live it is all mountains from here to the coast.

Muscat has grand expressways, in the old style, with flower beds and plantings of trees along the roads. It is very clean, tidy and fresh looking. Outside the city the land is a panorama of barren rocks interspersed with the occasional village. The central part of the village will have a date grove and older buildings. Outside the core there are large interesting looking buildings usually with a satellite dish on top.

The main roads are excellent.

Nizwa is a historic old city. Some mosques go back 1,400 years. The Nizwa fort is 500 years old although it has been rebuilt in recent years. Nizwa's skyline is impressive across the dry river bed. There are old parts of town that resemble the pueblo buildings of New Mexico. The new residential areas are totally unlike residential areas at home.

Nizwa is safe and friendly and it includes 43 small villages. The main part of town is a small shopping area about the size of Norwich, Ontario. It has the same atmosphere. In under two weeks I could walk the streets and know half the people, mostly students or staff at the college. The people of Oman are quiet, friendly and courteous. Everyone I meet from abroad feels the same way about the Omanis.

I think the new Egyptian faculty members had more culture shock than I did. They all came from huge cities like Cairo and were bewildered at small town Nizwa.

Our accommodation is not great but liveable. My college office is well equipped, excellent in fact, and I am enjoying my work greatly. Of course I have lots of confusion since most of the staff speak little English. I speak only a few words of Arabic. Yet we manage to figure things out. It is excellent mental exercise to keep up with the demands of a multilingual workplace.

Donna has a much more limited social life. There are only two or three western women in Nizwa. She stands out in dramatic contrast when we go out. She will tell her own story in time.

I have decided to write little anecdotes which illustrate our experience. I hope they give you a feel for our life here.

We got a letter this week which took 18 days by air mail. We have a phone 968 425 177. The best time to call is at 11:00 p.m. EDT as this gets us at breakfast at 7 a.m. It really is not our phone. We were told it takes weeks to get a phone hooked up. So to the telephone company when I pay my bill, I am Mr. Woods, my predecessor. He had the service hooked up. I just pay his bills.

Our mail address is c/o Teachers' College of Education, PO box 699 postal code 611 Nizwa Oman.

While we posed as Mr. Woods because we dwelled in the same apartment that he had used during his four months in Oman, we were trying to make the furnishings and decor more appealing to us. We had met Dr. Jim Woods who was a former English professor at the University of Toronto. He came to our house on his return from Oman and filled us in on what he considered the situation to be at the college. Four months had been long enough for him. In order to prevent getting malaria he had taken Mefloquin which was a potent antimalarial drug. The drug has serious side effects for some people. After a few weeks one might begin to hallucinate and have other psychotic reactions. In his case it appeared to be true. He was convinced he was being constantly watched, spied upon, and his phone calls monitored. Woods said every time he made a call from his office he could hear a click as if someone was listening in on his calls. He guessed it was the senior Omani who was the business administrator at the college. It set me on my guard.

We found a ledger left in the apartment that was full of his thoughts. Many of them despaired of the situation and some were simply garbled and incoherent. If we were being watched and spied on, so be it. I was not going to be bothered by such things although I was inclined to believe it was true sometimes. I was the foreigner here! It was clear Woods could not stay longer than he did. I was glad Donna was with me.

There were not a lot of mosquitoes around. It was a desert. Our neighbor, an Indian, was head of public health for Nizwa and he told us that there was an active campaign to eradicate malaria and that it existed only in a few places up in the mountains. The last case diagnosed in Nizwa resulted in a quarantine of an area. People with sprayers went round spraying mud puddles. Periodically in the middle of the night a fogger truck drove around the neighborhood. Still every night we seemed to have just one mosquito buzzing around the bedroom and we could not settle down until it had been swatted. We never took any medication. Some friends who came out did and one of them began to have problems after a couple of weeks on Mefloquin.

We were very concerned about sanitation and at first drank only bottled water and washed all our vegetables in a weak bleach solution. Finally I decided to take one mouthful of tap water. The next day I took two mouthfuls. The third day I had a glass of water and I was fine. We stopped washing with bleach. Gradually we relaxed and realized the food and water were safe.

The apartment came with a gas stove that strongly resembled a camp stove. In the parlance it was the cooker described in our literature. It was small and flimsy. The propane cylinder was downstairs and outside and hooked to a copper line that went through the building up to our kitchen. After two weeks the tank was empty and we had scarcely used it. I called for another tank but I was somewhat perplexed at how much propane we had used. Another two weeks and it was again empty. These were large 60 pound tanks. I checked the third tank for gas leaks and found none. I then realized the open valve was letting gas flow up to our apartment which meant that gas was leaking into the walls. The whole place could have gone up in a fireball. From that day on every time we wanted to use the stove one of us had to go downstairs and around to the side of the building and open the valve. Then afterwards we had to go turn it off.

Making a Home

The living room had a view up a side street on one side and a view away from the mountains that also included the live chicken sellers shop on the corner. We had a small low wattage bulb in each room near the ceiling. These were green or blue Christmas tree type lamps. It took a long time to find out that these were to be left on to keep the gins (genies) away. There were outside lights for the same purpose. Superstitions die slowly.

We needed more furnishings than what the company gave us. At first we read with only a ceiling light at night. Donna sat in a chair and I on the sofa while we tried to find some non existent English language station on the shortwave. If it had not been for the newspaper, we would have had no news at all. The Egyptians were amazed that we had no TV. Their lives seemed to depend on it. What did we do at night? They asked. We agreed. By Christmas we had a TV and roof top dish and even better Oman had just hooked into the internet so we soon had a computer at home to help us keep in contact with the outer world.

It was interesting to be able to read local Canadian newspapers and listen to Canadian radio stations live on the internet when at home. It made the remoteness seem less. We had no English language radio at all in Nizwa so in the car we listened to tapes we bought in Muscat. I think most were illegal copies. Now and then I listened to the local radio which seemed to use the familiar format of talk shows, music and news on the hour which you would expect to hear in Canada. I even began to recognize the top music hits of the day.

One aspect of the local radio was the sound clip that was played before the news. It seemed like an ancient recording of chickens squawking although in reality it was a human voice that sounded like it had come from an Edison Victrola. What is was or said I never learned. One of life's little mysteries!

Television

You could tell by the direction a satellite dish was pointed whether the occupants of the dwelling were Indian or Arabic. The Arabsat carried BBC and French TV and various Arab nation signals. The other satellite was Indian and carried BBC, CNN, and Indian channels. The local Oman TV had a considerable amount of English including an eight p.m. news broadcast followed by an English language program. At seven on Friday night they showed the CBC's Anne of Green Gables series (read Friday as Sunday). The English news was often presented by a blonde English woman who wore no head cover and wore dresses with deep cut cleavage. The Omani men must have enjoyed watching the English news. Omani news was presented by men and women but the women had head scarves and high collars. Canadian TV programs were shown more often than TV from the US or UK. I am not sure why. We also got the TNT classic movie channel. Dr. Zhivago seemed to be on at least once a week. I knew it pretty well. That music and the music of Lawrence of Arabia kept haunting me all the time I was there.

Indian TV was also available and I was fascinated to see the modest maidens singing across the mountain meadows pursued by a lovelorn singing male. The game shows were fascinating amalgams of Hindi and English. "@C%&@" then "Come on down" followed by more Hindi and "We have a winner!"

India detonated their first atom bomb and there was exuberant excitement for days over this, to me, a sorrowful event. The TV was full of Indian supremacy of the sort that leads to foolish belief. To me India was only number one as a future target for someone else's bomb.

TV from Pakistan, Iran, Egypt, Syria, Saudi, Syria, France and other countries gave glimpses into their cultures. When I went for a haircut, the station would be changed from Urdu to English by the barber. I told him I wanted to see what was being shown to Pakistan. This impressed him no end and from time to time he would explain what the program was about.

Syrian TV had programs that looked more western. Their news showed domestic scenes that might be in a western country.

Yemen TV was very rigid with lots of military parades and men's talking heads. Saudi TV included lengthy prayers and speeches by Imams as well as science instruction classes from the University of Waterloo.

There were several Egyptian channels. Al Jazeera, a new station from Qatar, was the choice of nearly all the faculty and the daily faculty chit chat was often about what had been seen there. It was considered to be free of national bias and politics.

When I tired of the Arab selection, I would go to the roof and tilt my six foot dish toward the Indian stations. Since this took a bit of time, I would do this only once in awhile. Either way we got the BBC but only one satellite had CNN.

Getting an Automobile

We met an Indian family which had been living in Nizwa since 1974. At the time there was no road from Muscat to Nizwa. In our time we left Muscat on a four lane highway and traveled about a third of the way to Nizwa before changing to a two lane road which was designated to become four lanes. The scenery along the road is spectacular as it crosses or travels along the base of the mountains. One has little time to enjoy the scenery as the two lane section is heavily traveled and the trucks move slowly along the curves and hills. Passing and tail gating are constant problems for the cautious driver. There are numerous accidents.

As one travels about, it soon is apparent that Omanis prefer white vehicles, especially Toyotas, and especially four wheel drives and pickup trucks. At the other extreme they seem to also like big expensive luxury cars, especially in Muscat.

We started out with a rental car and following the advice of the experienced began to search for a good used four wheel. Used car buying is a high risk activity here. Even recent models of used cars seem heavily used and in poor condition. Dust is everywhere and the filters are plugged, the battery lasts for a few months, and the seats are bleached by the sun. On top of this, the rural roads are extremely rough. While there is no rust, a three year old car otherwise looks 10 years old. There is one exception, the vehicles of the Western workers. Expatriates are thought to take better care of their vehicles than local drivers. Hence a premium is placed on obtaining a car from an Expat. There are used car dealers but the good stuff is advertised on supermarket bulletin boards in Muscat. After touring the used car lots, the only vehicle of interest was a used blue dodge which although devoid of a set of plates contained under the hood some live oak leaves and long pine needles that said Florida. Then under the seat was a scrap of paper that referenced the university of Florida. I suspected it was a hot car. Stolen cars were regularly shipped from the US to the middle east for resale. I kept researching the supermarket boards until I found a few four wheel drives we could afford.

Expats like four wheel drives for wadi bashing, the off road weekend activity of exploring the country. Expats own four wheel drives of all sorts but the Mitsubishi Pajero and Land Rover seemed to be quite popular. After two months of searching we found a Pajero we could afford, equipped with altimeter and inclinometer and the rarest of all an automatic transmission but there were no pollution devices since the gas was still leaded.

Buying a car is not an easy proposition. The new car show rooms are modern and glittering places enticing the buyer with specials and promotions. We attended a new car unveiling. There was a live band, free dates and pop, special draws and loads of hoopla. We sat down with a salesman and a cup of tea and learned we must have permission to buy a car from our employer and in addition we must have an Omani drivers licence. We must have two photos, a letter of agreement from our employer, a work permit, and a bank statement. The real hurdle is the Omani driver's licence. Some nationals can convert a licence. As I wrote earlier, the Egyptians and Pakistanis and most others must pass a test even after taking the compulsory driver education course. There seems to be a lot of very tricky exam questions and driver requirements for these people.

The agreement to buy a Pajero was made in the supermarket parking lot by a Canadian and a Scot and sealed with a handshake. The buyer and seller agreed to meet at the police station to transact the sale. The police carry out the job of transfer of ownership. There must be passport photocopies which we don't have. With a sinking feeling it looks like we can't get the transfer done in one day. Across the property I dash to beat the 12:30 p.m. closing to get a photocopy. They also want the front page ... another dash for another photocopy. Now there isn't any other thing the clerk can think of so I get the ownership which includes the balance of the insurance. We own a 1991 Pajero made by Mitsubishi. We are off to see Oman.

Everywhere on the road we see the little red and white striped driver education cars. These training cars are very distinct. They are most visible on the roads in the morning hours. Close observation indicated that most of the people learning to drive are

Omani ladies. Yet in practice there didn't seem to be any women drivers on the road. Fortunately I did not need driver education.

In Nizwa a car is not really a great necessity. There are lots of taxis and mini buses. One does not call a taxi as many of the passengers don't have telephones. Getting a ride requires standing along one of the paved roads and waiting a few minutes. A wave of the hand gets the driver to stop. For 100 baisas (35 cents) a ride to the souk can be made. At the souk another vehicle can be obtained and the driver will take you to any location you want. Around Nizwa the fare is not over 200 baisas. For a few rials you can have a shopping trip to Muscat for the entire day either by taxi or mini bus. Some families need a mini bus for the trip to the city.

The road from the college into Nizwa is something of a showplace. The desert is pushed back by a strip of flowering bushes and trees along the roadside. At the several roundabouts there are tended lawns and pruned shrubs. Fountains, monuments and green lawns decorate these roundabouts. Here and there along the roadside are decorative monument like items. Urns, models of coffee pots, sculptures, scenic paintings and motifs give the roadsides charm and uniqueness because past the road is an ugly gravel field. Litter is never seen along the roads. There are street cleaners always at work. The skyline of Nizwa across the dry wadi bed is impressive with the fort, souk and mosque against the rugged hills.

Nizwa pales beside the miles of larger and more impressive roadside program that exists in Muscat. Here one is impressed by the beauty and the extent of the flower beds, pruned shrubs and flowering bushes backed by palms and other trees. Each of the three to five bands of planting is higher than the previous. Past the last band of trees is gravel and sand and perhaps buildings.

Away from the highways lead numerous trails and roads. It is hard to sort them out for they are universally rocky and rough. There are teeth jarring travels across dusty miles. Around the mountains there are mighty canyons with precipitous slopes. Trails winding at dizzying angles to villages and viewpoints give reason for driving a four wheel vehicle. The wide tires used for sand and stone often soften the ride and the four wheel gearing is needed on the rough ground and steep slopes. The altimeter shows us over 2000 meters. We have been climbing. There isn't time to view the inclinometer as we lurch around a curving dip in the road.

We have picked up fellow Canadians, Denis and Florence. Denis is fresh off the plane. We take him up a wadi heading for the mountains. There is a village up there we want to visit. We lurch over river boulders before snaking up the side of the canyon wall. The trail meanders up and down but mostly up. We crest a ridge and the incline down has everyone putting their arms out for support to keep from pitching forward. Then the tires are grabbing at the stones as we climb up at such an angle I can only see the sky. The trail is so narrow we could not pass another vehicle if there was one. There is no road to my left. I cannot see the shoulder. I glance down to my left and estimate it is hundreds of feet straight down. I can only see a wall of rock past Donna. Denis and Florence are totally silent. The village is visible, dead ahead, across at least a mile of space. We have to meander in a huge semicircle to get there.

Denis is pale. He is one day in the country and we have terrorized him. My only solace is the fact that there are tire tracks ahead proving it is a real road and probably navigable.

We are greeted by an English speaking student. Not many cars come that route we just took. We know why. Most come over the mountain from the other side where there is a better road. The few houses and a small shop comprise the village. The shop has a four foot florescent lamp over the door. There is a phone booth with a solar panel and an antenna. We take our leave as time is short and we refuse the invitation to tea. The alternate route would take us too long to get back to Rustaq so we head back the way we came. Everyone is relieved when we get back to the wadi bed. Lurching over the boulders was better than plunging off a no lane cliff trail. The Pajero would take us on many such adventures.

The four wheel does give us the pleasure of seeing the grandeur of Oman away from the foundation planting. High in our seats with a grand view we bounce happily about. That is when it's not white knuckle fear gripping us.

Even the two lane Nizwa Muscat road is an opportunity for terror. Passing a lumbering slow truck means edging into the oncoming lane to see if it's safe. Then as I decide to go, I am passed on my left by the vehicle behind me who decided to pass me as I am passing the truck. Every oncoming truck must be studied to see if a vehicle should emerge from behind it and every vehicle coming up behind me must be studied to see what it is going to do. Since God determines when a Muslim is to meet his creator, reckless driving is fine. More than once I was able to take to the gravel shoulder to save my neck. Fortunately it was always where I could leave the road. For that matter you could drive most of any journey beside the highway if you wanted. It was just a gravel plain.

Sadly, I knew several staff and students who met their maker in head on crashes out on the wide open two lane highway.

The Pajero

The Mitsubishi Pajero was the source of some grief and some memorable incidents. My first problem was an incident with the muffler. The tail pipe had separated and needed to be welded back. The separation was directly under the gas tank. I was directed to a subdivision of shops near Firq, a village near Nizwa. Here there was a mini mall with a series of open front repair shops. I pulled up to the first and explained the nature of my problem. The Omani proprietor had a look and summoned an Indian fellow dressed in shorts, sandals and a dirty white tee shirt. He looked at the situation and walked down to another shop to fetch the welding cylinders. Two low metal ramps were provided and I was asked to turn the car around and back up the ramps. This was a great opportunity to show my driving skills because the ramp had a one foot platform on which to stop.

The so-called welder produced a couple of welding rods, ignited the torch and was about to crawl under the car when I asked where his face shield was. He didn't understand. I pointed at my glasses and he said, "No need, no need." Flat on his back, his nose inches from the tail pipe he proceeded to weld. Sparks and drops of metal were flying all over. He would pause to swat at his chest where hot metal bits burned holes in his shirt. I expected to see him scream as he went blind or, considering his proximity to the gas tank, to blow himself up. I could not stay there. I had to walk away as I was probably going to be partly responsible for him blinding himself and could not bear to see it.

Finally he crawled out. The job was finished except for his swatting at burned spots several of which were on his face. I told him he was foolish for not wearing goggles. " No have, no have," he shrugged. I would find another mechanic for next time.

The brakes were acting up as we had been driving through some large puddles created by recent rains and I drove into the same industrial area to find a proper garage. This time I found one on the side street. There were bays and hoists and benches and equipment. The Omani, who sat in an office with a telephone and a wooden desk and a chair, was the boss. He sponsored all the Indians who worked in his shop and took a cut from their salary for himself. The system for all expatriates in Oman was the same, including me. An Omani sponsored every expat who came. The Omani paid the way to Oman, backed them in a job, provided accommodations and a return ticket home. Some were more elaborate like mine but for the Indian workers it was a cross between indentured servant and slave. The master got a good income for sponsoring. In this case I was talking to a man who had 100 sponsored employees and they all paid for the privilege of having a job in Oman. It was still a better wage than back in India, Pakistan, Egypt or the Philippines.

The tires came off and the Indian worker sat on the ground performing some activity. He was cleaning the surface of the brake shoe. He had a pen knife to do this task. I asked if he knew what sandpaper was. He looked at me and at the knife and got up and left, shortly returning with some emery paper. I walked away shaking my head. However, I thought I better not stray too far away as I wanted to see if there would be any brake parts left over. I pointed out the grease cover cap that had rolled aside as he was going to put the tire back on.

Miles from Muscat on a weekend tour heading toward Sohar along the coast road we blew a head gasket and had to have the vehicle towed back to the city. It was a long way and took two hours but the tow charge was not very much. The vehicle was taken to Edward, a Philippino, who worked as a mechanic for the city and did moonlight work on the side. He did a competent repair job and a tune up including replacing the spark plugs.

Soon thereafter I had problems with misfiring when the car slowed to enter a roundabout. For the next six months we endured this while taking the vehicle back to the Philippino, then the Mitsubishi dealer and finally the local Nizwa repair shop. Nobody could tell me what was wrong. Finally I changed the spark plugs again and matched the code with the plugs called for in the service manual. The plugs were not the same. I then set off to find the correct plugs but absolutely no one had any. There are lots of Pajeros in Oman but no correct replacement plugs. They only had plugs that happened to fit but none that met the specifications for the vehicle. So like any good Canadian I checked with Canadian Tire and had some new plugs brought out from home by a visiting friend. After six months the car finally performed exactly as it should have even though the Indian who installed them without adjusting the gap insisted that the plugs came correctly gap spaced from the factory. In any event he could not have set them as he had no gage. However the car now ran well. Six months I spent cursing the unknown wrong plugs!

Batteries have very short life spans in the hot desert. When mine died, I went to a local car wash and garage. The cheap battery had little warranty and the good battery had several years. The Omani owner beamed when I chose the far more expensive battery with a warranty. The new battery was placed on the ground and the Indian worker sat down in his shorts and sandals and proceeded to pour the battery acid free hand into the holes. A lot of the acid ran off and some splashed all over his shorts and legs. I told him it would burn him and that it would also ruin the pavement. He got a rag and wiped up the acid then cleaned off his legs with the same rag. I think he was feeling the heat of the burn by then. I pointed out that the acid had to cover the plates in the battery. We peered down into the holes to see the plates still not covered. He had no more acid so he got water to pour into the battery. I said this would weaken the battery and it would not last very long. Sure enough about two months later I was back. The Omani owner tried to charge the battery and conceded that it was not able to take the charge. He was unhappily on the hook for a warranty replacement.

A new under warranty battery was produced. Before the Indian worker started, I told him to get a funnel and not spill the acid. He had some ingenuity as he produced a cut off plastic water jug for a funnel. I told him if he did not do it carefully this time I would tell his boss why the battery failed so soon. He kept nodding his head "yes" and this time I think he knew how strong the acid was.

How to Build a House

After a year in a flat we were able to move into a new house not far away. The flat, we discovered, was in a building that was not actually on the road. There was a building lot available between us. A house was constructed in our last months in the flat. We could see the daily progress from our living room windows. The construction techniques differed little from the techniques used to build the learning resource center at the college. Oman has no wood. It does have cement and apparently lots of it.

The foundation was excavated a couple of feet and a perimeter foundation wall was built along with bases for the support for the interior walls. Drains, water pipes and electrical conduit were installed. The outline of all the rooms could be determined pretty easily from the foundations. The next step was to fill the space to about 3ft above ground level with gravel and dirt after which the cement floor was poured and left to set. It looked like a raised platform for several weeks.

Cement blocks walls were built. The Indian construction workers wore shorts, shirts and flip flops. Work boots and hard hats did not exist. Some worked in their bare feet. I found that interesting as I had a running confrontation about the nails that were constantly scattered on the ground that I used as a driveway. My complaining about the nails did not register as a nail in a tire or a foot was just something that happened. I would take a walk along my driveway which abutted the building and pick up the nails which were used in the wood cribbing for the cement. I would throw them back into the site or hand them to any worker present while shaking my head no.

Once the block walls had risen to the level of the next floor all the interior walls had been blocked in with holes left for doors and windows. The next step took some considerable organizing as this was the creation of a plywood platform that was supported with a dense network of cribbing pipes. This scaffolding was so dense it was not possible to walk through the building. Once in place more cribbing was built around the edge of the new ceiling and steel rebars were laid out. Now it was time for the cement truck to arrive and pour the second storey floor. The preparation took days but the truck was there for only a few hours. The workers troweled the surface to a fine smoothness. The floor was about 6 inches thick and held up by the plywood shell and the supporting scaffold. Then all work ceased for some time as the cement had to cure.

When work commenced for the second floor, the cement blocks were added for the rooms and exterior walls still leaving the doors and windows open. When that was completed, the scaffold supporting the ceiling/second floor was removed. The plywood was taken down and the whole affair began again to put on the roof. This time the scaffolding rested on the cement slab that had been made for the upper floor.

Thus the weight of the roof was supported until the cement there set sufficiently to complete the small retaining wall around the roof as well as the cement stairwell to the roof.

Next the wood cribbing for the stairs was created, the rebars installed and the cement poured for the stairs.

The electrical conduits were installed by marking the walls with red paint and chopping holes in the cement blocks so that the pipes and wires and outlets could be installed.

The plumbing was installed the same way. Once it was installed and checked out, the walls were cemented back to cover up the holes.

The next stage was to tile all the floors and then tile the bathroom and kitchen walls right up to the ceiling. The kitchen counter was also poured cement with a marble slab for the counter. Steel framed windows were installed usually with metal barrier bars. The kitchen shelving and drawers under the counter were also metal.

As for wood the men's and women's front door were made of elaborately carved wood. The interior doors and frames were also wood, mostly mahogany. The roof door would be metal. Pillars and other cement decor were added to the exterior and the court yard would have a seven foot wall surrounding the entire property. Metal gates for vehicles and pedestrians were installed.

The interior of the house was usually painted in vivid colors. The lower half was painted in a hard enamel and the upper half a semi gloss. Sometimes fancy plaster work was put in as a form of crown molding around the ceiling.

Bathrooms were accorded special status with highly elaborate decor. In our house the shower had no doors or curtain. The water stayed mostly in the elevated stall area but what ran out simply ran down a drain. The wooden bathroom door had a metal plate across the bottom to protect it from water being sloshed around. Since everything was cement, hosing the bathroom and kitchen floor with water was as good a method as any to clean it.

Our court yard had an area to wash your feet or get water for the plants. The enclosed courtyard area was all surfaced with bricks although in the case of the house which we were to rent, I requested that there be a two foot space for some gardening along the wall.

Life in Our Palace

Our new house looked like a miniature Indian palace. Pillars, fancy curves, and ornate decor all were enclosed with high walls for privacy.

When we arrived back after our summer break, we were to move into our own house. It was unique in that unlike most Omani homes it had only one storey. The landlord, Saud Al Mazouri, had designed it for himself but with limited funds he decided the second floor would be an addition at a later date. Saud was a very practical fellow. When he discovered he could rent the house, his plans to move in were changed. I'm not too sure what his wife thought about his renting out her new home as it meant she would be living in a rental flat over some stores or back with his parents and sisters.

The house was supposed to have been ready but he had run out of money. My company agreed to advance several months rent to him so he could install the windows. We also insisted that he connect us to the city water line. He had intended to have water hauled in and put in our rooftop cistern. The city mains were not far away but it was an added cost. Interestingly, the city mains went to the roof and filled our 5ft x 5ft galvanized tank. From there we had gravity feed pressure. The reason we had a cistern was because there was always the chance the city well pumps might not be working. The city water well and pumping station was visible on a hillside from our house so we were near the source. Most of Nizwa was not on the city line and so people had the truck come weekly with a load of water.

Water trucks were blue and sewage trucks were green. It was hoped that they never confused these trucks. That was not a certainty. If the trucks were late or you used too much water, you had a day or two with an empty cistern. We knew all this and that's why we demanded to be hooked up to the mains.

The cistern sat in the blazing sun. Down below inside the house we had a pleasant 25c air-conditioned home. Each bathroom had a small five gallon electric hot water tank on the wall. It did not take long to realize that the water in the hot water tank was room temperature and the cistern water was often 40c. So when we wanted cool water we took it from the hot tap. This practical step, hot water out of the cold faucet and cold out of the hot faucet, worked just fine.

We had three bathrooms. The master bath off of the bedroom had fixtures that were highly ornate Victorian style and purple pink. The next bathroom had an unusual tub that could best be described as a reclining tub with a hand held shower. Both of these bathrooms had normal western toilets.

The third bathroom was outside the front door. It was a two piece for guests and featured an Arab or eastern toilet. A porcelain pad with two foot places and a hole to perch over was fine for persons who wore dishdashas or skirts but a trouser wearing westerner would have to wrap his pants around his neck. We turned the outside bathroom into the laundry room. The washing machine fit nicely over the porcelain pad and the hole served well for the discharge hose. We had to have a power outlet installed. The electrician arrived and was befuddled because he could not put the line inside the wall as I would not let him hack up the cement blocks. I had no idea how that would ever get fixed properly. I presented him with a solution in the form of a tube of Goop adhesive and some masking tape to hold the wire until the glue set. He was incredulous at the simpleness of this. Ten minutes work had replaced several hours of chipping away and who knows how much time to plaster and paint the wall back together.

We had only a washing machine. There was no need for a dryer. On the roof we had rigged up a clothesline and when a load came out of the washer, it went in the basket and was carried to the roof to be hung. By the time the next washer load was ready to go up, the clothes on the roof had already dried in the desert heat and low humidity.

The living room was a light lavender color and we had a blue Turkish carpet on top of the terrazzo tiles. To house the TV we bought a Sauder do it yourself kit to make an entertainment center. It came all the way from Ohio and once we had it assembled, our room took on the ambiance of a more comfortable place.

The dining room was seldom used and its original purpose was to be the ladies living room. There was an elaborate carved entrance door and a fine carved wood tympanum over the door. Unfortunately the back side of the tympanum was a blank unfinished space over this door. We had moved in before it was completed and it just remained that way.

The three bedrooms were turned into a guest room, a combination computer room store room and thirdly our bedroom with a king size bed and a wardrobe.

The kitchen had a table and chair set that we usually sat at for meals. We could look out the open back door at the cemetery and distant highway by the hills. When closed there was no view outside from the table. No screen door had been installed and while there were not a lot of bugs having a screen door made us feel better and allowed us a view. I set off to the now familiar workshop area near Firq to find a carpenter who could craft a screen door for us. I had learned to call the screen, fly screen, otherwise the workers would have no idea what I wanted. Nobody around Nizwa seemed to have screen doors. However I had careful measurements and a drawing of what I wanted so a door was made in a couple of days. It was the carpenter's first such effort and he was quite proud of his effort. The door worked perfectly. From then on the kitchen door was usually open.

Our fridge was okay but with the new house we wanted an electric stove. A year turning the propane tank off and on had been enough. Electric stoves were not sold in Nizwa as there was basically no demand. The reason for this was the nature of the electric supply. In the year we arrived, the Nizwa electric gas generating plant was closed down and the city was connected to the grid of a major new power supply. In the months before we arrived constant and sometimes lengthy power failures were the norm. Under those conditions who would want an electric stove. However after the new hook up we experienced only a couple of power outages in all the time we were there. An electric range was brought in from Muscat. It was possibly the first ever installed in Nizwa.

Another appliance we wanted was a toaster. The one we brought home from the shop would only toast on one side. We took it back and the Indian clerk could not comprehend our problem. Finally he had to produce another toaster and hook it up so we could show him how it was supposed to work. Wires glowed on both sides of the machine. We got our replacement. This leads us into our corn popper story.

The same shop had, on a top shelf, a hot air corn popper. "Twelve rials," (about 45 dollars) the clerk said. I reviewed the toaster problem and he agreed that if the popper did not work they would give us another. I headed home with the expectation that I would have to take it back as well. Sure enough! We plugged in the hot air popper and a wisp of smoke rose from out of the element cone and that was that. I went back to the store with the corn popper. By now I was convinced that everything sent to sell in Oman was defective, second class, crap.

The clerk had no idea what the problem was. He had never seen a popper used. The old machine sat on the counter and we plugged it in. Nothing happened. I explained that heat and air blew up from this thing. He climbed up and brought down another machine and sat it on the counter and walked out of the store. I stood there wondering what was going on. Was he getting the boss, some help or what? He came back holding a tin of popping corn which he opened. The clerk poured the whole can of corn into the machine. I got him to remove most of it. He plugged it in and a small crowd gathered to watch. There were three Indian clerks, four mixed nationality customers and me. The corn bubbled away uncovered. Suddenly it began to pop and I went for the plastic cover and told him to get a bowl. Pop corn was flowing all over the counter and the crowd was enthralled at the spectacle. Everyone was happy. This machine worked. We were all eating popcorn. The clerk said they had never sold one before because they did not know what it did. I never checked back to see if sales had perked up.

ɾ⋅

From a little park I picked a clip off of a vine and rooted it in a bottle. I placed it alongside the north wall of the compound and hoped it might climb a bit up the wall. I bought a pretty potted vine with blue flowers and planted it in the bed by the front window. Other plants went into pots and we planted a tree outside the gates. A banana plant from the market produced a few small bananas for us. Beans and tomatoes were easy to grow but corn would not do well. Petunias grew very well. But what most impressed me were the two vines. That little pot of purple flowers grew to the top of the roof and covered the entire window area in weeks. The railroad vine I planted along the north courtyard wall was over a hundred feet long in six months.

I came home to find a goat herder and his flock by the house. He was trying to get the goats away from the railroad vine. I told him it was ok to eat it as it was growing so fast it needed to be eaten. I just asked that he keep the goats away from the Vinca flowers by the entrance. The herder said he took the goats out of the pen every day for some exercise and food and just followed them around for a few hours. Here was a man whose day began with sunrise and ended at dark. He wore no watch and had no need to be preoccupied about time. He would sit and watch the goats snoop around my compound and then he would wander off down a lane where the goats grazed at bits of grass. Then he would urge them to go right at a road fork. A few days later they would reappear and he would pass the time of day before the goats found a new route to follow. His ancestors had lived the exact same life. They tended a herd like it was family. At night they were all gathered in some place I never located.

ஃ

Oman is not always arid. It does rain. Our barren field of unbuilt housing lots once turned into a lake 5 inches deep. The water lasted for some hours not soaking in or running off. An occasional vehicle would churn up the water but otherwise it was still, blue and like glass.

Any thunderstorm would flood our roof and when it did we had to roll up the carpets and get out the brooms because the water would pour under the closed door on the roof and flow down the stairs like a miniature Niagara. By sweeping madly we would try and guide the water into the drain in the bathroom which was directly across from the stairs.

On a hot day we would sit on our lawn furniture under the unused carport. We entertained here in the privacy of the high walls and enjoyed our gin and tonics. The courtyard was red brick. The pots of flowers and edge flower beds with bougainvillea made this a pleasant area. Under the carport floor was the septic tank.

When we first moved in a small child had been buried behind the house in the cemetery. A man came there once or twice to visit the site. The body is scarcely buried. It is but inches under a small mound of dirt with rocks placed at the head and feet. Not long after the child was buried we began to get an overpowering stench outside the house. It was revolting. At first I thought it was the rotting child that we smelled. Later I decided, somewhat relieved, that the smell was actually originating inside our property. After some discussion with the neighbor it was decided our new septic tank was not yet working. My neighbor advised me it needed food. It needed fresh meat. Excrement was not good enough. I went to the meat market and bought a couple of pounds of cheap hamburger and tossed it into to the tank. Sure enough within two days the smell vanished.

The roof was where we went in the evening. The mountains on three sides, the distant Jebel, the sun set, the moon rise, the stars on a dark night, the homes along the road nearby, the highway on the backside in the distance, the palm trees of the oasis all became familiar and part of our lives. A few plastic chairs, a low table, the six foot antenna dish, the water tank, the A/C and the clothesline were up here on the roof.

ૈ♦

Not far in front of the house was a large gravel hill that would be a challenge to climb because it was impossible to get a foothold in the scree pebbles. On that hill there were a few scruffy bushes that had managed to grow.

Oman is a land of biblical proportions. Job's tomb, Jonah's home, the queen of Sheba's palace and gold, frankincense and myrrh are all in Oman. In many ways it feels biblical as well. On one hot late afternoon I sat looking at the gravel hill with its scattered little bushes. Suddenly fire erupted in a bush more than 3/4 of the way up the hill. I used my binoculars and there was no sign of any living thing near that blazing bush. It had no leaves but the twigs were burning merrily. The thing was a ball of flames. There was nothing to cause this fire other than spontaneous combustion or an act of God. Moses could have appeared and I would not have been surprised. God could have spoken and divulged the unknown to me. The heavens could have parted. I was in awe. There it was, the burning bush blazing biblically before me. Finally it died away leaving a blackened corpse still rooted to the hill. It's not everyday one witnesses such an event. What if anything could it mean? My binoculars could find nothing to indicate a cause. I decided I needed a gin and tonic.

❧

Donna had left for the summer. It was hot. I decided to sleep on the roof and dragged my gear upstairs. The rising moon prompted me to do this. Under a sheet it was fairly comfortable. The moon to my left was clearing the burning bush hill. Above were stars in massive abundance, little specks of light in a dark sky. To my right over the Jebel Akdar was a thunderstorm with pops of lightning leaping from cloud to cloud or perhaps to the mountain itself. The light flashes would outline the clouds. The storm did not seem to be moving and it was too far away to hear the thunder. Only the moon was moving, slowly advancing to the center of my field of view. I was a speck in this universe. I came up here to sleep but the scope of the sky and the majesty of the night left me awake until the moon was almost touchable above me. There is something special about the desert night in summer. The heaven above is a wonder, mysterious and unfathomable. Suddenly it's the middle of the day or so it seems and the sun is up and it's still hot on the roof. It's time to get moving and go out to the Pajero and head off to work. The metal door of the gate clangs behind me.

Our Daily Bread

Shopping in a new place is always interesting. Getting our groceries meant a trip to the local Al Reef grocery store located in the center of the main downtown area. There were two other general grocery stores that were not as busy and did not have the range of goods. Al Reef had a meat counter but we chose not to buy much there. The meat had a distinct blue color, not red, perhaps because it was halal. (Killed according to religious methods) . Of course there was no pork sold. We did buy frozen chicken from Brazil, McVities Hob Nob Cookies and John West salmon from Britain. The store was small and space was a premium.

I watched the little Indian clerk filling the shelves with bags of potato chips. He carefully stuck a pin into each bag so as to remove the air so he could push more bags into the space. The shelf could hold a lot more that way. I suggested that it was a bad idea to do that. He looked at me and the near empty box and ceased. The power of the western sahib prevailed.

There was a limited selection of cereals, paper products and other staples. Fresh fruit was better bought elsewhere. Still, we did buy a lot of our staples there. The Muscat supermarkets were the preferred markets for us.

At the check out we paid our bill and collected points. From time to time we turned the points in for pretty little 24k gold wafers. Over time we collected enough to turn them in to buy Donna a substantial 22k gold necklace.

The checkout clerk was always glad to see us. We would be greeted as we entered. I'm not certain why this was as not many other customers got this welcome. Perhaps it was our supposed status or because we were aliens like him. Or perhaps it was only because we were friendly back.

The bakery was next door and featured a store front oven that turned out the typical Arab flat pita bread on a conveyor belt. As the bread turned past the window, it arrived before the customer where it was presented still warm or it was stacked off to the side. They also sold small loaves of conventional western style bread. They said they baked them there as well but all I ever saw was the oven conveyor with flat bread.

Fruits and vegetables were sold at the petrol stations. Here there were small crates of apples, oranges, mangoes, grapes and from time to time strawberries. The vegetables were usually peppers, potatoes, melons, cucumbers and cabbages. All were stacked by the door. Most every thing was one rial or about four dollars and all was imported, often from Iran, but also many other places. The quality was good and the fruits and vegetables sold quickly. It was fun to shop at the gas station on the way home from work but the family sized containers were often too much for us to eat before spoiling.

Our heavy duty grocery shopping was in Muscat. There were many super markets. We liked one in an affluent area near the British Council which was an educational and cultural organization based in the UK. It operates around the world. The supermarket was part of a pleasant strip mall which had a nice park beside it.

The store featured a pork room and sold frozen turkey at Christmas time. They also sold artificial Christmas trees and had a range of British goods. Later we discovered another store near where the oil company expats lived that featured Dutch goods including nice Gouda cheese. In the main shopping area of Muscat was a huge emporium that had an attached restaurant. The French hypermarket Carrefour sold everything from furniture to soup. There was little a consumer could not buy in Muscat.

The expat shopping stores all had pork rooms. Away from the rest of the store in a small room clearly marked as "Pork Room" was a world no Muslim would enter. Pork roasts, hams, Kenyan bacon, tins of pork and beans and anything with a hint of ham or pork or lard was sold from this room and carried an extra hefty price tag as well. We pork eaters bought here anyway. Nizwa had no pork for sale, period. Muscat had enough infidels to make a rial or two off the sale of pork.

Our favorite grocery store was on the sea in the diplomatic area. Al Fair was where we usually shopped after a weekend in Muscat. It was on the way out of town and we would first have lunch at the seaside patio of the Oasis By The Sea, a very nice restaurant. The waters of the Gulf lapped at the broad sandy beach. We gazed out from under our patio umbrella enjoying our last sip of tea before crossing to the market. Australian beef that looked far more palatable than Nizwa beef was available. Frozen peas and cakes and french fries were McCain from Canada. Cheerios came from Ontario. I was randomly searching for a nice jam, just the right size and color and picked the most appealing jar I could find. It was by sheer chance made by E.D. Smith, Winona, Ontario. Peppers, tomatoes and fresh cut flowers came from Holland. On balance we ate as well as we ever did in Canada. But why not, as half the stuff we bought came from Canada.

To get back to Nizwa was a two hour drive in searing heat so we packed the freezer chest and filled the back of the Pajero with our loaded plastic bags of goods and headed directly for home so nothing would thaw.

National Day

The Egyptian dean and I are invited to attend the National Day celebrations on November 18 in Nizwa. The college has a delegation of 60 students to march in the parade. We arrive at 8:00 a.m. and sit in the second row of dignitaries under the shade of a red, white and green canopy. Glancing about I see that I am the only westerner in the entire official delegation of about 200. Only we two deans wear business jackets. The rest are Omanis in their best dishdashas and turbans. Our college administrator is wearing a very nice khanjar dagger with a fine handle of ivory or horn. His girdle belt is silver embroidered into leather. When I admire it, a staff member also wearing a khanjar says that Nassar Khomenis is worth over 1000 rials ($3,500). At least I can tell quality when I see it!

Our stand is opposite the great wooden doors of the Souk. The ground between is a well cleaned parking lot. The doors open and I am totally unprepared for the sight I am about to see. There is a full regalia Scottish marching band emerging through the doorway. There are pipers and brass in the best British tradition. Boy Scouts follow carrying a bevy of flags followed by the Cubs and Brownies. The Brownies wear white shawls over their heads. School boys in dishdashas and caps and girls in their yellow and grey uniforms with white shawls pass by. One girl has a shawl which will not stay on her head or perhaps she just won't wear it. Groups in sports outfits representing soccer teams are followed by a Pakistani social club. A large group of men, traditional dancers waving swords and carrying small leather shields, supposedly of rhino horn, gesture in dance as they go around the parade circle. They chant as they go. Women in green and other bright colors are led by a large lady with a bull horn. She sings into the horn a refrain picked up by the other women.

The women spectators and dignitaries sit at the end of the parade square also under a canopy of the national colors. Across the parade square which is the parking lot of the souk, we can see the impressive skyline of the souk, mosque and fort all decorated with colored lights.

During the speeches cups of Tanouf water are passed out. I think they are handing out cups of ice cream or yogurt. Next a large bowl of halwa, an Omani sweet made of sugar, butter, nuts, flour and spices, is brought. It resembles a bowl of very thick caramel pudding . I dig my fingers in with some effort to get a small blob. Next the coffee man comes along with a thermos bottle and small, handleless, china cups. The coffee is black and flavored with cardamon. Only about two spoonfuls in a cup. I have two. It is not considered polite to have more than three. I hand it back shaking the cup as an indication that I do not want more. The cup is now rinsed out in a bowl and passed on to another person. I estimate that about 30 others have already drunk from my cup that morning. A teapot of cool water follows the coffee. Now I can wash my sticky hand as the *water is poured over my fingers.*

The speeches over, the band strikes up again and leads everyone off in much the same manner as when they came on the field.

We adjourn to the wali's garden. The Wali is the mayor. Under the trees are mats and on the mats are large silver platters covered with foil. Bowls of fruit sit next to the platter. I take off my shoes and sit cross legged with a group from the college and some others. The Wali and visiting deputy minister sit down and we uncover the trays to discover a huge pile of rice with saffron and raisins. On top of this is a large section of meat, part of a shoulder of a goat I think. We dig in using our fingers to eat. I pull at some meat and try eating rice with my fingers. It is a little messy and I get some rice on my pants. We hardly put a dent in the food and when the Wali rises, we all stand and go wash at the trough nearby. In a sea of mauve and white dishdashas only the other dean and I and the Sultan's minister stand out. The dean and I are in jackets and the minister is in a black and gold robe over his dishdasha. It is about 11 am when the Wali greets his guests and to me says, "Welcome." I respond, "Salam Alykam" and we exchange greetings in Arabic.

After the meal the huge amount of excess food is piled onto the back of a pickup truck to become "gatant." The custom is to have more food than the guests could possibly eat.

We return to the college to find the students have chosen to skip classes. National day is not a holiday although the shops were closed in the morning. It turns out the holiday will be two days some where in the future at the end of November. This makes a nice long weekend in which many people go to Dubai. It is a good move to separate the official day from the actual time off work as otherwise there would be nobody around to carry out the ceremonial duties.

In the evening we watch the official televised celebrations at Sur. A new stadium was built for the event. When the celebrations were in Nizwa two years earlier, a new stadium was built next to the college. It seats 25 000 and cost 25 million dollars. It is 20 km from town and I have yet to see it used for anything. Anyway at Sur there was a 2 hour presentation worthy of the opening of the Olympics. It concluded with the annual message from the Sultan. Sur will be the site of a natural gas export facility with additional industries tied to the gas. Forward planning like this should help prolong the oil boom.

The festivities seemed to go on for another month or so. The flags flew along the entire 80 km Sultan Quaboos Highway from the royal stables to Muscat. The entire 80 km with flags 20 meters apart. Only with the end of the 4 day holiday did things get back to normal. The decorations all came down a short while before Christmas. Having colored lights hanging up at Christmas might have sent the wrong message.

Around the same time the Indian community celebrated Diwali, the festival of lights. It was also held a few weeks before Christmas. Hindu events also got confused in the celebration mix. While in a small Indian café, I noticed a string of lights hung up and I thought it was early to have

Christmas decorations out. When I asked, I learned about Diwali. A small music box attached to the lights played Jingle Bells, Santa Claus is Coming to Town and other Diwali classics. Whatever works, I guess.

The Tourist's Nizwa

Whenever I see a travel program about Oman, Nizwa is always the place that one visits to see the Friday Morning animal auction. The fact is the auction is for the locals to sell goats, cows and sheep and it draws a nice crowd of rural Omanis including some women with full burkas(black face masks) who poke and prod at animals they may be intent on buying. The creatures are walked in a circle while the auctioneer stands in the center of the ring and takes the bids. We always took our guests there and while there were tourists there, we were far outnumbered by the locals. The tour groups would hang around for a few minutes and head off to see the souk and the stalls selling Omani silver, frankincense burners and Omani dishdashas. After that they would head for the Fort which stands beside the great mosque. The fort dates to the 1600's and is a large mud building offering a splendid view of the date oasis and the mountains. After Nizwa the tour might head off to Bahla to see the ruins of the old city, now a United Nations heritage site. They would pass by the village of Tanouf which was bombed by the British in the 1950's uprising. Small irrigated farm plots dot the area at the foot of the mountains.

The more adventuresome would want to go into the mountains to wadi Misfa located high on the side of the Jebal where there was a spectacular view. Then they would travel on the winding road that takes you past the trees where the goats climb up into the higher branches to nibble the leaves. I never saw goats that could climb trees at any other place any where. The gravel road leads to the base of a huge cliff face where it veers and commences to ascend up the side of the mountain for several miles. Eventually it climbs over a mile to arrive at a supremely spectacular gorge that drops straight down for several thousand feet. The tourists will drive along the gorge to stop for scenic views both down into the gorge and off into the blue haze of distant landscapes comprised of jagged rocks. Down below small settlements can be seen with their green patches of farm. It's like a view from an aircraft. The locals will be on the lookout for the tourists and will come to offer their homespun rugs and trinkets in the hope of making a sale. Young children and their mothers and perhaps an old man who wants his picture taken for a coin will be wanting to meet the visitors.

In our time these were dusty gravel roads but now they have been well paved and no doubt there are amenities for the tourists as well. While the Jebel is a day trip for us from Nizwa, the tourists would be hard pressed to fit it all in without making camp.

The trip I have just described is one I have taken with every guest who has come to visit. It is so spectacular it could never be tiring. One cannot become blase about such grandeur. Yet something in me says I was lucky to experience all this when it was still primitive and undeveloped.

A day trip anywhere from Nizwa is a trip into spectacular landscape and biblical looking settlements. There were two local hotels catering to the tourists. The older Falaj Daris Hotel sold memberships to western residents so we could go and use the pool and have supper afterward or just laze by the pool after work. The newer hotel a little farther from town was a palace of marble and polished stone. We only attended special events there. The cozier Falaj was our hang out. On my way in after work I would check the large humidity indicator by the thermometer. Since the temperature at 4 p.m. was usually 42 to 49C (115-120f), it was the humidity that really told how uncomfortable it was. Most of the time it would be 20 to 25% and when it got to 30% it was almost humid enough to feel sweaty. The pool was usually around 100 to 104f and so was more like a hot tub experience. The tourists were never very abundant and most of the guests were business folks. They would adjourn to the bar after supper and sit with a few Omanis who were ignoring the fact that alcohol was haram in Islam.

On Raising a Glass and Other Things

Alcohol is an arabic word. The religion has some ambivalence about its use. In the first years of Islam it was okay but later its use was forbidden. We found out that while westerners could have a pass book to purchase alcohol, Muslims could not. However the hotel bars served anyone. We had Omanis at various parties and when there were only a few among us, they would have a beer or two. We learned that the military mess served alcohol and also the police had alcohol privileges. I believe it was a way to sort out those whose loyalty to the Sultan was greater than their loyalty to Islam. It was concluded that a person of moderate views would indulge but a strict practitioner would not. The same logic applied to the military and police about being clean shaven except perhaps for a mustache. A full beard indicated a more radical Islamist. After a time I began to understand the undercurrent of unease among the more educated and liberal minded people I met. The unease was an undercurrent of pressure from those who would force others to abide by their version of strict Sharia laws. Islam is a religion with rules to live by and deviating off of the straight and narrow is not easy when you are being pressured to conform. The Sultan appears to be pushing for an enlightened form of Islam but a society that is still largely in the middle ages takes time to make the accommodation.

We soon learned that the dehydration from the desert heat gets an extra boost when more than a couple of beers have been consumed. A two beer party was enough for most as any more would result in a horrendous headache as the reward.

Most of the time we would be happy with the fresh fruit juices sold at the roadside shops or a Pepsi. Pepsi was the preferred soda and Mountain Dew was second. I kept a case of lemonade pop and bottles of water in my office fridge. No one went anywhere without a bottle of water handy. Staying sober was not an issue in a climate where water went down so easily. I suspect the same was true for the Omanis who never ever seemed to serve any alcohol. They only drank when at a party with westerners. As dean I never served alcohol to any Omanis. The Omanis on staff were by and large pretty pious.

Whenever I went looking for an absent secretary, I would be told he had gone to pray. Perhaps he had or perhaps he had just gone shopping. While I was learning about their culture, I was often surprised by their odd views of life in the west.

About the middle of February I was approached and asked about that festival where we all got naked and made love and sent each other red hearts and flowers. Try and explain what Valentines day is all about with a straight face when you are sure they don't believe you. Another time I was asked to explain about the models (statues) of people in all the old cathedrals in England. For that matter try and explain any of our customs and traditions. They must seem like incomprehensible babble.

I asked about fasting in Ramadan if one lived in Northern Canada or Norway where the sun never sets or rises for days. That was the question of the day for several days. Finally an answer was produced. Observe the day as if one was living in Mecca.

During Ramadan when everyone was supposed to be fasting all day, I found I had to lock myself in my office to enjoy my lunch. This was not usually a problem because few people came at that time of day. A rattle of the knob would not last long and I could digest my ham sandwich in peace. I was asked one day before lunch if I had been fasting. I honestly replied that I had had nothing to eat since breakfast. I was told that was good because I was a nice person and deserved to go to heaven when I died. The Muslim gets to heaven by following the rules.

In fact a secretary once asked what I was having for lunch and when I replied ham, he gagged at the thought of eating pork. I asked why it was haram (forbidden)? Such a question usually gets kicked around because nobody knows why. The reasons are lost in tradition. I suggested it had to do with trichinosis, a disease in pigs that could be spread to humans. Just why God told Peter it was ok to eat pigs is unclear.

My driver, when I needed one, never listened to the radio but always played tapes of recitations from the Koran. These reminded me of medieval Gregorian chants. While he might be sedated by the drone of the recitations, at least I could be sure he wasn't drunk. These undulating chants were very soothing, which considering the reckless high speed driving he constantly used, did help calm me down. On the other hand it was also hypnotic and I was afraid he might go into a trance. Moreover he believed whatever happened would be God's will. Fatalism in driving was not my idea of safe driving. He assured me that God did not want me to be killed with him. As if! Whenever possible I would drive my own car.

An Evening Walk

Often we went for a stroll about 6 p.m. Sometimes we choose to walk into the hara, the old section of Muddah, our local village. This area has old homes, small plots of garden, tall date palms, walls, newer homes and a few scattered shops. Mostly the streets are paved but can be pretty narrow and are all crooked. We took visitors back here when they came because it is quite picturesque.

The signs over a shop advertises "Foodstuff for Sale" in English and Arabic. Another offers "Luxury Goods" in a grungy little windowless shop.

In the old sections there are the remnants of archways over the road. These are possibly the outer wall of a fortified location. There are mud houses with sections of wall that have collapsed and some walls with iron gates. Some mud home windows have an air conditioner poking out. The falag water system runs through the area. Little cement streams a foot deep snake along the walls and beside the small fields of cilantro, lettuce, and other veggies all shaded with date palms. It has the feel of the middle ages, exotic and timeless. The falag runs under the road and then forks. A barrier is inserted so the water goes only one way. Later the barrier will be switched so the water distribution will be equitable.

There is a bath house and water is diverted into it. Some boys are inside washing themselves in the presence of their father. The house has no door and has a low tin roof. The walls are mud bricks.

Other boys are taking a class with an older man who is coaching them in the protocols of the daily prayers. They are sitting on the floor of what was once a mosque. Their recitations are earnestly repeated. Soon they will be able to go to the mosque prayers with Dad. The building's walls have fallen and the roof is long gone but the wall with an alcove facing Mecca and the entrance door still stand.

We meet up with some children who are very eager to practice their English which they start to learn in grade four. It happens quite frequently, but, of course, their English consists of "Hello, How are you?" And sometimes "Goodbye," and we hear the numbers from 1-10. However one night they decided to follow us. Each one took a turn talking proudly and as we went, we picked up more smiling, talkative little people. There didn't seem to be any adults about. Perhaps they were watching out of the windows. We felt like the Pied Piper as we collected about twenty five kids who finally dispersed as we walked away.

January 27 1997

Three times in 6 months a wandering low pressure system brought some cloud banks up against the mountains and caused rain and grey skies for a day or two. The most recent one left us feeling housebound and so when the sun came back out, the clear skies prompted us to go exploring. It was Ramadan, and the College closed early at 2:00 p.m .

We climbed aboard the Pajero and headed up the street directly toward the Jebal Akhdar mountain. The base is 6 km from the house. After leaving the suburbs we drove across a flat gravel plain covered with baseball size river bed stones. We noticed stakes placed at regular intervals and decided there must be a plan for a subdivision. Nizwa in time will grow right to the base of the mountain.

Rounding a small hill, we drove into a wide short valley that marked the end of the gravel plain. After parking at the end of the drivable land we set off on foot to climb the mountain. The stones here were much larger although still rounded from abundant water rolling over them. The stones end abruptly at the point where the mountain slope rises. It is quite distinct. Now the climbing begins.

It is easy going over the rocks which are fairly smooth and at a steady, regular incline. The whole face of Jebal Akhdar is like this. The sea bed is tilted up at a 45 degree angle and on this side presents itself as a smooth face broken by small gorges and at intervals great fractures. The Afro Asian plate shoves up against the continent of Asia lifting the ancient sea bed. The other side of the Jebel has towering cliffs.

Now the rocks are sharp edged, jagged stones in black, red-brown and sometimes white. The black rocks are etched by water and sand. In 20 million years since the upheaval, enough rain has fallen to carve groves across the rocks. Strange patterns in rows and of varying depths and size create an unusual effect as if fingers had been dragged through mud. Where the rocks are flat there are little pock marks eroded leaving jagged edges between them.

We continue to climb. At this low level we are still in the shade of the adjacent low ridge. Above us the sun shines on the higher slopes and the peaks to our right and left. We see no sign of habitation or animal life. No birds fly. Below is our 4 wheel and some debris. It is hard to think we are ten minutes from home.

Higher we climb past small plants with small pink flowers and leaves flat to the ground. Other plants are a foot high and the small leaves are interspersed with lots of thorns. Most of the desert plants are thorny. None are very interesting and they are not abundant on this hillside of barren rock.

The vehicle is getting pretty small now and the air is quiet. Our walking moves some flat stones creating a metallic sound, almost bell like. It is cool this day and we approach the line of warmth where the sun is shining again.

A small tree ahead, perhaps 10 ft tall, has leaves which are reminiscent of long pine needles. Otherwise it looks like a bush. From the vicinity of the tree we begin to notice a low moaning, whooshing sound. It increases in volume as we approach the tree. A breeze is blowing and the place is so quiet the sound of the wind in this lone tree seems quite loud. We pause to take in this experience before continuing our climb.

Some white quartz stones attract our attention as they lay among other stones of dark red marble. A cluster of stones by themselves seem arranged. I am reminded of stones gathered to make a small fire shelter and indeed there are some old ashes in the center. They are a reddish burned color and when I bend down to touch them, I am surprised. These aren't ashes. They are rock. Are these ashes so old they have fossilized? How old are they? A short distance away on a level spot the stones have been moved to leave an area large enough for a person to lie down comfortably. There is a small raised ridge of rock to break the wind. A bit of skull, white, very light in weight, is probably that of a goat. There are some other tiny bone remains. Someone's ancient supper? Here several hundred feet up the mountain I recall that the Persians were here thousands of years ago and Nizwa itself is 4 thousand years old. How old are these evidences of mans presence?

We climb up more but despair of reaching the top before dark. We set our eyes on a set of large boulders as our final destination. Now we can see across the ridge where the sun is rapidly setting. The houses on the outskirts of Nizwa are visible as white specks contrasting with the green palms. We go no further.

The trip down is more difficult and we pick our footing

carefully among the stones which are inclined to slide under our feet. Back at the Pajero we see a pile of broken glass and some tin sheets. We drive across the gravel plain with its scattered Acacia trees. Here and there pop bottles, some broken, plastic bottles and tin cans litter the ground. Modern man has brought these things only in the past 30 years to this part of the world and now the landscape is littered with debris that will last as long as the fire stones on the mountain. Perhaps when the houses come this far they will just bury this garbage.

Ten minutes from home we go mountain climbing! On the roof the next day I scan the hillside with the binoculars to see where we had been. The boulders we reached were not very far up after all. We hadn't gone as far as we had thought. Perhaps another day.

Something of History

It does not take very long after arriving in Nizwa to get a sense of the antiquity of the place. It's old, very old. Oman is littered with the debris of a long history. I tried to piece together something of the past to make more sense of what I was seeing.

Once upon a time, say 10 to 15 thousand years ago, these mountains and their foothills were wetter and greener places with an abundance of wild game. Gazelles, oryx, wild goats, and ostrich supplemented the human diet of berries and fruits. Arrow heads, knives, scrapers and other tools have been found in surrounding towns like Izki and Bahla. Ruins of 5000 year old tombs and towers link the early culture to lands to the north,

Sumeria and the Indus valley. Clay tablets tell of trade with Magan as the local people were then known. Copper, carving stone, onions and dates along with timber from Jebel Akhdar formed the bulk of the trade. This time was prosperous and progressive but something happened and with the changing climate a time of unknown occurred leaving a gap in history.

Omanis began to look to the sea about 2500 years ago and traded with India, Africa and into the Mediterranean where frankincense was much in demand. Pliny in the first century AD mentions Omana, a land populated by the Al Aribs.

Nizwa's famous falag, the Falag Daris, was built in the time of Darius, the King of the Persians, who had captured and invaded the land around 500 BC. The camp of Darius was located along this falag toward the mountain. The Persians were occupying land held by the Azd tribe who had also come earlier from Persia. Their leader, Malik ibn Fahm and his son Hnat founder of the important Bani Hina tribe, was a leader of the 6000 man army they assembled on the plains of Nizwa to do battle with the troops of Darius.

I tried to find out where this flat area was but no one seemed to have any idea except that it was somewhere around Nizwa. Memories of events over 2000 years ago is thin. However Malik on his horse, in full armor, a red robe over his shoulders and a yellow turban on his helmet, charged into the Persians with his cavalry. Over three days the Persians on elephants withheld the Azd until Malik himself slew the General of King Chosroes 531 -578 BC. The Persian Baluchis withdrew to Sohar. This attack left the interior controlled mostly by the Bani Hinai tribe. It also set up a long standing tugging over the land between the coast and the interior.

A thousand years later, Nizwa remote and deep in the interior, becomes linked to events happening across the empty quarter in western Saudi Arabia. It is an early outpost in the founding of Islam.

In 630 AD while Mohammed was still alive, he sent a letter inviting the joint rulers of Oman to embrace the new religion. The letter still exists. However, even before that letter there were converts to the new religion. The first convert was a Samail man named Mazin ibn Ghadhuba whose tomb still exists in the town of Samail. However Islam was also evident in Nizwa where 2 mosques date earlier than the conversion of the rulers to Islam.

The Shuadhna (2 AH) 623 AD mosque first faced Jerusalem as it predated Mecca. It is behind the Nizwa Souq past the fort. The Second mosque Si'al (8 AH) 629 AD has a defense tower and is across the wadi from the Souq. Neither of these very historic buildings seems to evoke much public interest which is a fact I found most unusual. In fact I had trouble finding anyone who could point them out. These mosques go right back to the very foundation of their religion and they are just out of the way mud structures of no great interest or concern.

During the first half century of the new religion Omanis were involved in both local and foreign military efforts to establish the faith. Nizwa was the center of the believers. After being defeated on the coast by others holding differing views on Islam, the Omanis who had supported the early concepts of the faith had formed their own version of the true Islamic state. This concept was to become the Ibadi concept. By 750 AD the Omanis elected an Imam based on the Ibadi view of Islam. This view held that Imam were chosen because of their worthiness and not through inheritance. When an Omani faculty member gave a lecture at the college on this idea, he met with reproach by Egyptians and others present who did not share this Ibadi view. However, the Ibadi version of the faith is strongly held to this day in the interior. A key feature of it is the election of the religious leader, the Imam.

Such an election was held on the plains of Nizwa in the 700's to elect Rashid ibn Walid. Four eminent men of virtue and probity met in Rashid's house under the chairmanship of the sheikh. They agreed on the principles of government and they gave their allegiance to Rashid. A great crowd representing many towns gathered on the plains. The Sheikh addressed the crowd and called for them to give their allegiance. In pairs and singly they did so. The new Imam appointed governors over all the towns and districts as well as collectors of the voluntary alms for the religion. He led the prayers at Nizwa the next Friday.

Another early Imam is buried by the river bank outside a small pink mosque sandwiched between the main road and the wadi. There is a solitary tombstone under a tree. The story is told that this Imam had arrested and jailed several men for some crime. They were held in a cell by the Wadi and a large flood came and the prisoners were trapped. The concerned Imam went to free them and in so doing was also swept away in the flood. His body was found where he is buried.

Other Muslims took an uncharitable view of the Omanis and their Ibadi ways. The calif of Islam, a successor of Mohammed, from the area which is now known as Saudi Arabia, assembled an army of 25 000 men in chain mail who marched on Oman and instituted a reign of terror. The falags were blocked, eyes gouged, hands and feet and ears cut off and the books of the Ibadis were burned. Still in the interior their views survived although no more Imams were elected for several centuries.

A traveler of 1228 AD, Yaqut Al Hamawi said of Nizwa "Nizwa means to jump or leap...Nizwa is famous for its gowns adorned with silk. These are good quality robes which have no equal anywhere in the Arab world. The inhabitants also make a coverlet in the same style as the robes and these are costly and exported to many destinations." He went on to say that the Omani were the most learned people of all the Arab lands.

A century later, in the year 1331 Ibn Batu, a famous Arab explorer visited a prosperous seafaring Oman and commented. " The coast is subject to the wrath of the interior inhabitants who frequently raid." However things in the interior appeared quite tranquil during his tour.

Ibn Batu writes about the many mosques and makes note of a custom still very much alive. Ibn Batu noted that there was a custom of shaking hands with all around, before and after prayers both morning and afternoon. The shaking of hands is still carried out with much formality and enthusiasm today. He commended the Omani modesty, good nature, generosity and hospitality that still mark their character.

He was especially impressed with Nizwa, the capital, with its many gardens and aflaj and describes the inhabitants as courageous, heroic, and steadfast. He observed that people eat communally in the courtyard of the mosque with each person contributing according to his ability for the benefit of any guest who might come. In front of the door of his residence the Wali, the governor, would sit alone without guard, companion or minister and dispense charity to passers by. Such was Nizwa in those days.

Yet, even today, the ladies of Nizwa are distinctive in their colors and fashion and the nature of the people is still much as described centuries ago.

The Imams were restored in the 1400's at Bahla. Today the old quarter is a huge mud complex which is being restored. Bahla is a designated United Nations historic site. Also during the 1400's the Portugese occupied the coast of Oman. There are several Portugese ruins and forts. In 1624 Nadir ibn Mushed who was invited by Nizwa and other towns took control of the interior from his fort at Rustaq. Sultan bin Said who followed him drove the Portuguese out of the coast and established the great fort at Nizwa and restored the falags around Nizwa and Izki. His son Bil'arub succeeded him in 1668 and built the fort-palace and a college at Jibrin. After a struggle his brother Said took control and went on to drive the Portuguese out of East Africa and parts of India bringing these lands into Omani control. With the new wealth he built new falags and planted thousands of date trees. This action accounts for the great oases seen today in Omani towns like Nizwa.

The civil war of the 1700s resulted in Said, the son of Said, who was only a small boy, being made and unmade the leader several times during his life. This poor fellow was usually supported by the interior tribes who on six different occasions proclaimed him leader. At one point a great battle at Firq near Nizwa saw him reclaim his title. Finally a truce was arranged at Nizwa in 1724 at the great fort and it resulted in various places being held and controlled by different tribes. Said brought in Persian (Iranian) mercenaries to help him but they decided to take over themselves. When he died, Ahmed ibn Said, ancestor of the current Sultan, continued the fight to get the Persians out. He invited their leaders to a great lavish feast billed as a truce and in the midst of the feast proceeded to ambush the lot of them. For his success of riding the land of the Persians, he was elected Imam. However there was still internal division and a plot against him became known. He went into hiding and spread the word he was dead and when the opposition celebrated, he knew who his enemies were and took an army from Sumail to Firq to defeat them. It was another battle in the plains before Firq! Our college was in the plain near Firq.

Ahmed ruled from Rustaq and his son Said was Wali (governor) of Nizwa where he made a fortune dying indigo cloth at Firq. The indigo industry vanished sometime before 1996. The vats still exist but are in ruin.

Knowing the history of the area gave me new insight into Nizwa and I realized the place was ancient and full of extremely historic remnants of the past. I could visualize the ancient battles along the road to the college.

Education Day

April 29 was Education Day in the Interior Region. We Deans were among several hundred guests who were crowded into the covered court yard of a girls secondary school. We arrived to be greeted by various education officials, some of whom I had come to know.

The school was quite new and had the most pleasant garden of any school I had visited. The school garden is an area usually in the entrance area inside the walls. Trees, vines, shrubs and flower beds and walkways make these attractive sites in every school.

The school corridors like most Oman schools were decorated with paintings of local scenes or with a Koranic verse painted on sheets of plywood. The corridors are not interior but are open on one side with classrooms on the other. The classrooms have low windows looking out on the corridor and often out the other side as well.

Most schools I visited are all on one floor and all tend to be organized around a courtyard. All have terrazzo floors and well painted walls. The schools are always tidy and well kept. The general impression is pleasant.

Classrooms are crowded and lack a teacher's desk. There are no shelves or storage. Desk tables are frequently grouped in pairs. Chairs are detached. Most walls have no decoration on them but there are some exceptions both in schools and classes.

To reduce dust, chalkboards have been replaced with white marker boards.

Students dress according to certain standards. Schools are divided with boys and girls sometimes working in shifts. There are primary, preparatory and secondary schools that are all state funded. Money is given for school uniforms and running shoes are provided. Boys wear dishdashas and caps like their elders. Under the dishdasha may be sweat pants, shorts, or gym clothes. White shoes and socks are provided for physical education classes but on other days most wear sandals. Every child carries a sack full of books to and from school. Nothing is left at school.

Girls in primary wear a yellow tunic over white slacks and have a white scarf. Prep girls wear a grey tunic and secondary girls wear navy blue. At a glance they all look the same but up close the style is there. Some girls have pleated skirts; others do not. Some have a patterned scarf; others do not. Some have tight slacks at the ankle and others are loose. It seems to be the color that counts.

Teachers, mostly Omani in the primary, mostly Egyptian or other Arabic nationals at secondary, wear whatever clothes are accepted in their homeland. Omani men wear a turban and dishdasha. Egyptian men wear shirts and slacks. Egyptian women wear loose fitting outfits and head scarves. Some men teachers carry a thin cane.

Photocopiers, computers, science equipment and manipulative materials are almost none existent. It is not hard to see why the lecture method is virtually the only method of instruction.

We all gather in the courtyard. This school, like some others, has layered green mesh stretched over the entire area creating a gymnasium like effect. School openings and meetings take place here . There is also a stage. The sound system is quite elaborate but squeals. A great red velvet curtain hangs across the stage.

Being a dignitary I am escorted to the second row and identify my seat by the card (in Arabic). The front row will be occupied by several of the regional walis (mayors) and the Vice Minister of Education. The audience is made of representatives from all sorts of educational and other groups but not parents. Next to me is a representative of the Nizwa water authority.

I think we two deans are the only people in jackets. There are fans and some portable air conditioning units. Ours blows the hot air vent at us. I wonder how an air conditioner system that has input and output in the same room can achieve anything. The sun shines down through the green netting. It is easily well over 90f but not unbearable.

The program could come right out of any school back home. There is the national anthem and a recitation from the Koran by a boy about 10 who is seated with the Koran in his lap. He does a creditable job of chanting the verses.

A teenage girl, rehearsing her lines, sits directly in front of me. At the other end of the stage a boy sits. He wears a splendid kanjar (ceremonial dagger) and his neatly pressed white dishdash shines. The girl wears a dark green head scarf over which, in Cleopatra style, was a gold head piece composed of several strands of real gold beads that hung down either side of her temples. The gold would be pure 22 karat and worth a bundle. A grape colored sequined dress and silver and green leggings made her quite a showpiece. They were the announcers.

The first skit was a yarn I recognized from the Arabian nights. Of course, Ala Ad- Din (Aladdin was Omani). The boys had a good time with the acting. There were scenes and props and painted backdrops. There was lots of work here from the school that contributed to this play.

Poetry recitations were given. Omanis like poetry. It is a national pastime. Even on TV there are poetry sessions. People sit about in groups reciting poetry from memory. Even though I don't understand the poem, I can appreciate the message. One is about the importance of being a teacher.

A choir sings with boys on the left and girls on the right. I think the songs are patriotic. A keyboard backstage is the accompaniment.

There is another skit with boys and girls. Since there are no mixed schools yet I wondered how they managed that. This skit was about a boy who was lazy and didn't want to learn.

Then there are more choirs. The children are all dressed the same, boys in red turbans and girls in red and gold sequins. Money would be provided to the school from the Ministry for the special things needed for this day. Whether it included the clothes or not, I don't know.

The front rows were distracted during a skit on keeping Oman clean when glasses of water were passed out. Later the big bowl of halwa (a sticky oily sweet) was passed along and next the handiwipes. Then extra hot kawa was served from tiny communal cups. The cup holds about two mouthfuls of this coffee and cardamom drink.

Senior girls with wreaths did a national dance. It was quite well done. They carried water jugs and pots of incense. The finale featured a girl wearing a dress like an omni flag who held up a picture of the Sultan..

Gifts were presented to retiring officials and teachers. Awards for the best school, best headmaster and best teachers were also given out. I don't know how they arrived at their decisions for these awards.

Lastly came the awards for students. The top student in the region was a boy. The next 20 were all girls. These awards went right down to rather small kids who were in the elementary schools. About 90% went to girls. Something important is taking place with this kind of imbalance.

After the program we went to visit the classrooms that had been set up for exhibition. It was for our benefit only and a one day happening. No parents would see this event. The art room featured wood burning by electric pens. Some were quite good. Painting on glass and other types of craft were on display. My conclusion was that the mediums used did not allow for very creative results nor were they particularly good for secondary school girls. The next room was set up to show science activities. Here I heard some creative apparatus rattling off electronic Christmas tunes. It was time for "Santa Claus is Coming to Town" and "Jingle Bells" but I never did understand what was being exemplified. I was interested in a paramecium model made of an old shoe sole with nails around it. Somebody had done a great job in painting a periodic table on a panel of plastic. There was a color wheel with a motor that actually worked. Then I saw another color wheel. So far I had not seen one hypothesis, experiment or test. I concluded that what I had seen would be pretty good stuff for a grade 4 or 5 class but THIS was a secondary school. Here are some lights showing a digestive system. Jars of pickled critters and scorpions with pins in them are on display on the table. A horrid stuffed rabbit that had seen better days was mounted on a board.

All I could conclude was that their display was better than the boys at the college had done in the media classes for their display day. Here, at least, the pickled frogs were right side up in the jar.

By now I had discovered the girls could speak pretty good English so I started asking a few questions. In the health display room I engaged a girl who stood by a set of student made booklets and asked about their contents. She went on to show me a poster about disease prevention. She said she planned on becoming a doctor.

Another girl explained why it was important to cover food. She wanted to become an engineer. Her science marks were good, she said. I told her to persevere in her goal. A female teacher overheard my comments and was beaming from ear to ear. The displays were not so great but the girls seem to have a determination to get ahead.

I found a poster in English and recognized that the same themes were on other posters. A writing in really poor English clearly stated that girls needed to take their place in society beside boys and that they should plan to be more than mothers and should endeavor to realize their potential. Women's equality is clearly stressed in Oman. Anti smoking messages and environmental and health issues were featured. From these experiences, I learned more about what goes on in the schools and decided that the system was making some progress.

We continued on our tour of the school displays. The clothing room had some decent craft work. The literature room had stories. By now I was more interested in learning about the girls and their aspirations than the contents of the booklets.

We finally departed for lunch. Lunch was with the Nizwa wali and the other walis from the region. We travel across town to a sabla, a large hall, with many carpets on the floor. This place has white plastered walls, fans, air conditioning and not much else.

Kicking off my shoes I walk in with Naggar, the other college dean. One Canadian, one Egyptian and a hundred Omanis, two in military uniform and the rest in regalia, Khanjar , cane, dishdasha and turban, are going to have Shua.

We sit along the wall and rise from time to time as other guests come in. I look about wondering what these guys think about me. I certainly stand out in this crowd. I tell Naggar that never in my life did I expect to find myself in such a situation. The regional walis arrive and sit along the wall just by me. I've been through this before at National Day. I still can't recognize the wali of Nizwa from the rest. The official party shakes everyone's hand in succession before motioning us to sit.

Sheets of plastic arrive and are spread on the carpets. Bowls of sliced cucumbers, tomatoes and carrot strips are placed. Some cut limes and fresh hot peppers are for garnish. Lime juice is quite good on cucumbers. Bottles of water are distributed. Finally huge platters of steaming basmati rice piled with legs and other parts of goat arrive. The goats have been wrapped in palm leaves and cooked on covered coals in pits in the ground for three days. On the whole the goat meat is pretty good. I had to yank chunks off of the thigh bone. By now I can squeeze rice into a wad so it can be eaten with the fingers. It isn't too messy. I plop some of the vegetables on the plastic sheet and nibble on a couple of dates. There are always dates. Seven or eight of us are seated around this platter but nobody talks. Everyone eats quietly with studied silence and contemplation. It is a little odd but seems to be the tradition. Eating is a serious business especially with the fingers and in a suit. The whole thing resembles a picnic. Huge bunches of grapes and bananas arrive and I am quite enjoying the big grapes when suddenly the whole room rises and the wali leaves. We all follow and leave our food unfinished. Nobody is first or last to eat. It is time to go. Nobody says goodbye. We shake hands as usual and return to the college.

Later that day I watch as the boys play soccer in the vacant lot next to my home. They play every day and sometimes in clouds of dust but today a black cloud gathers and the rain falls. The game continues until the wind and rain are ripping satellite dishes off of the rooftops nearby and the ball gets blown away. It takes a lot to stop this game. The motivation to play is really impressive. After the rain some girls come out to splash in the water. They have their skirts hiked up. They stomp and dash happily in the puddles.

.

As I reflected back on the day, I was impressed by the work of the girls in gaining so many awards and in their skill in English. Clearly the girls of Oman are giving the boys a challenge. Clearly the methods in the schools need to change. The boys are not well motivated in the schools and perhaps the girls aren't either. So rigid, so uninspiring and severe a system needs to change. Each day I find out more about the schools and the needs and I wonder if I can ever help make a real difference.

The Embassy Party

A fax arrives inviting Donna and me to the Canadian ambassador's party. He was in Muscat to present his credentials to the Sultan. Being under two hours from the city we decide to go and stay over night at the El Falag Hotel. The reception is at the more plush and expensive Gulf hotel.

We arrive at the appointed hour. Here on the grassy lawns between the tennis courts and the pool one gets a lovely night time city view from the cliff. Over the bay and along the shore line the view is a sea of lights. It is warm and balmy. The palm trees around the lawns are wrapped in strands of twinkling white lights. It is a lovely setting in early October. I have another munchy with my wine.

The reception is in an area offside the pool and by the outdoor bar. The wine and beer are free and we appreciate it even more because we haven't been able to arrange our liquor permit yet.
We give our names and are formally presented to the Ambassador, Daniel Hobson, with whom we have a chat. He lives in Saudi and after only 3 weeks into the job he is invited to present his papers to the Sultan. He has never been an ambassador before and it shows. He is having a good time hosting our gathering. He knows that there are Canadian oil people but is surprised at the education contingent and the role they are playing in developing the country. Nice little snacks are offered by the attentive staff. Hot canapes are waiting beside a huge 6 foot ornamental brass tea pot. Colored lights hang in the nearby bushes. We can take this life style!

There are fifty or so Canucks, mostly petroleum people. The rest are teachers or trade people. A portly English gent grandly allows that he is not a Canadian at all but enjoys the free hospitality. He is a gate crasher for the free beer. We learn that anyone out here for 4 years is a real old timer. We meet a couple from Simcoe, Ontario. We move on to chat to others and pick up details of the social scene in Muscat. News of our living in Nizwa raises eyebrows. "What do you do there for a social life?" Good question. We represent something they don't comprehend. We live with the Omanis not in a Western world enclave.

In Muscat the PDO (oil) people have their own club, beach, golf course and a pool. Muscat has shopping malls, supermarkets that look the part, even an English language radio station. There are cultural events, places to dine and the hotel scene is quite active. Life can be pretty good in Muscat if you have money.

Back at the hotel we watch TV. Indian ladies are singing and dancing. The men follow them through fields of flowers, past lovely mountains, into manicured parks, while they dance and sing the gushiest and seemingly amateurish of performances. Okay let's try CNN, then some channels in Hindi or Arabic. Ah, there are old movies and five year old sitcoms, a wasteland not worth watching. There is a tropical storm near the China mainland. The channel flicking goes on. Omani TV has some English programs. A newscast at 8 p.m. ends with a list of the all night pharmacies open that day. Tonight there is something on Egyptian TV... bands marching about. The monthly showing of Dr. Zhivago is on TNT. I like the music so it stays on.

Well, why not read the newspaper? There are two English ones in Oman. One comes to my desk every day and goes home to

Donna at night. They focus mainly on India news. Gwen Dyer, a Canadian, gets a column in once a week. The Yankees and Orioles are playing for the AL championship. Nothing seems to happen in Oman or Canada. There is an add for immigration to Canada and another about getting a USA green card. Dubai is sending the Indian population back to India, 150 000 of them, 15% of the population. What will that do to the economy? In Oman the Indians run all the stores, sweep the streets and build the houses. They are everywhere and seem to run the economy. The Omanis drive things and sit in offices. The paper does not take long to read. There are many photos of ambassadors and official visitors. A unique feature is the daily listing of the exchange of congratulations and condolences by the Sultan to heads of state. They reply in kind.

The embassy party does not make the news. Yet it was nice to meet some expats. The Brits at the college say their embassy couldn't do such a thing as they would be overwhelmed by the numbers. Probably true. Canada is a special place that can have free parties for Canadians who don't live in Canada.

We look forward to the next embassy party as it is something of an annual event. The notice arrives and I inform the others that I shall be away for the afternoon and next morning to go to Muscat. We now have a kind friend with an extra room. Actually three rooms as it is a 4 bedroom flat. Laurence calls it Canada House as the out of towners often stay there. He is writing the nations new mathematics curriculum by himself, grades 1 to 12. It looks very Canadian.

૨⸻

The HMCS Ottawa is docked at Muscat for Canadian Thanksgiving and it is the embassy event for the year. A glamourous buffet is served on the deck of the Ottawa. The navy eats well. The navy is all spiffy in their best formal gear. We tour the ship and marvel at the technology on the bridge. There are banks of computer screens and the captain's chair is elevated to look above all the screens and out the windows. Our tour detours through the lounges, bars and dining rooms. They are not glamourous but do have some atmosphere. We are taken to the bowels of the ship where the communications room is loaded with computers and more screens. On the way out my eye catches sight of two firemen's axes hanging by the door. I am told that if they are boarded and the enemy gets to the landing outside this room, they are to close and bolt the door and proceed to trash all the electronics with the axes. Across from this room are some quarters for the sailors. There is a table and some sofas around two sides, a tv set and a couple of shelves and a curtain over the area for their bunk beds. There are four. This is a pretty small private space but I was told that due to shift work there was little crowding in these tight quarters. Up on deck there was a helicopter and a series of compact rocket launchers and a single gun was mounted on the deck. This ship was built for pursuit and intercept. The crew are very proud of their ship, now 6 months at sea. Other nations covet the fast, maneuverable, hi tech, interceptor that Canada uses on the high seas to waylay suspicious craft. Our guide for the day is disappointed that he can't accept our invitation to go to Nizwa. He can't be that far from the ship. Their tour of duty is nearly over and they all feel that the navy is the place to be. We take our leave and are escorted away from the base. The ship is bedecked with lights that contrast against the ancient fortifications of the old city. Tomorrow they will sail to guard the Straights of Hormuz. There is a narrow spit of Omani land, Musandam, that pokes at Iran a few miles across the busy oil route where tankers are lined up. The Ottawa will be patrolling there. I will be at my desk having enjoyed the hospitality of my native land at the taxpayers expense once again.

Love and Marriage

Gradually as we got to know people, we learned more about social life and customs. We learned that Mohammed Gamoodi, a secretary in the office who is 25, would like to marry. There are some problems in this day and age that are not entirely unknown in the western world. The young man says there is a teacher of his acquaintance but the problem is money.

Out here in the rural areas it is less costly to marry than in Muscat. The wedding agreement is essentially a business contract between fathers. The marriage on paper takes place without needing the presence of the bride or groom. The tradition calls for the girl's father to make arrangements with the groom's father or the groom depending on his age. Until recently very young girls could be betrothed. Now the law forbids actual marriage until 18 although there still seem to be families who work around this.

In compensation for the loss of his daughter, a cash payment is made. The maximum rate by law in Nizwa is 2000 rials. In Muscat it is, I hear, 5000 rials. The groom's expenses don't end here as the groom is expected to provide some form of personal property wealth to his bride, usually in the form of gold jewelry and again in an amount roughly equivalent to the marriage payment. Finally there is the cost of an elaborate party which is about another 1000 rials. Many young people would like to have their own place to live but most seem to be living at home with the groom's parents.

My friend, a couple of years out of college, is pretty cash strapped and I wonder if he will do as many others do and go to the bank to borrow the money. Banks here make loans for this purpose. When a father is wealthy, the old tradition of the father paying the costs still continues but in these expensive times the sons are usually making the good money or the family is so large the father would be hard pressed to pay. This generation also prides itself on being more self reliant and doesn't want dad to pay. We shall wait and see how our friend's marriage plans work out.

We were invited to a wedding party of one of the Egyptian staff. He went off to the airport to meet his bride. Our inquiries could not confirm if he had even met her although it was widely supposed that he had done so on a couple of prior occasions. What was clear was that this man of thirty something had been betrothed to a woman about whom he knew very little. Again the actual marriage was a civil affair under the Sharia law of Islam. It was also uncertain whether or not the actual signing had taken place in Egypt or after her arrival in Oman. It was supposed it had been in Egypt before her departure to meet her new husband.

The modern Nizwa Motel with its marble entrance lobby was crowded with the college staff and a few folks who had come from Egypt. This was a family affair for all our Egyptian friends and their wives and kids. The Omani staff came without their wives. The bride and groom emerged arm in arm along the main corridor. He in his business suit and she in a full white gown. They looked like any western couple entering the reception. Some women in the crowd began trilling, an arabic custom where the tongue vibrates rapidly making an eerie high pitched sound. The rest applauded as the entourage, on the way to the reception hall, passed the video camera and photographers.

The newly weds were seated on comfortable chairs on a raised platform. The rest of us found places to sit at tables. The Egyptian dean, Donna and myself were given a table in the center of the room. The other women, mostly Arabic, wore a shawl over their head and sat on one side of the room while the men sat on the other.

The evening began with music and folks sitting and visiting. A steady parade of the staff came to speak with we deans and have their picture taken in our presence. I sensed a certain ritual obeisance in this act. The little kids got up on the platform by the newly weds and danced to the music. The young girls particularly tried to do what I took for a bit of lascivious belly dancing. Finally Richard Morse of the English department got up at the back of the room and started dancing with some little kids. Some men got up at the front and began dancing with each other in a style reminiscent of Zorba the Greek with some body shaking added in. Donna and I got up and began dancing with each other but after a few moments we were beset upon and dragged up to the front where at first we danced with each other and then we were dragged apart. I was to dance with the many guys who were dancing and Donna was relegated off to the side.

The Muslim women response to Donna dancing with men was a subject of some interest. They clearly wanted her to dance with the ladies who, of course, were not dancing. Only the girls were up on the floor. The Egyptian guys were having a great time until it was realized the Omani fellows were not dancing. The Egyptians went one by one pulling the Omanis to the front to dance. There was great reticence on the part of these shy Omani men. However, eventually many of them did take part.

We had collected some money to buy a vacuum cleaner. This was acted upon after I made a suggestion that perhaps we should give a gift. I'm not sure if gift giving was an innovation or not.

Finally it was time to present ourselves to the couple and offer best wishes. The reception line activities included kissing the groom on both cheeks. I'm not sure but I think I only shook the brides hand. I was a little unnerved.

We had soft drinks and a snack was brought forth including a bit of the cake which the couple had cut, a definite western influence. There were some remarks that in Egypt there would have been a more lavish feast but out here in Oman we were mostly just casual acquaintances and not family.

The party broke up and everyone left together. The newly weds took a few days off to get to know each other. The bride spent the evening trying to look pleasant although she looked pretty uncomfortable. The groom beamed the whole time. He obviously was happy. From observations on the street we sometimes see a parade of cars beeping horns behind the newlyweds so even this custom has arrived here.

Omanis tell me their weddings these days are similar except that the men and women sit in separate rooms and the groom and perhaps his father or a friend joins the bride only later in the evening in order to have his picture taken with his wife.

Today young Omanis don't marry until after schooling and mostly after their teenage years.

Nasser Kohmyeni, an administrator at the college, tells us that things were different when he was a boy. Now 33 he has a son 15. He is emphatic that the boy is much too young to marry. His reasoning is clearly from experience since he was married at 15. Born and raised in Nizwa he was married to his cousin, his fathers brothers daughter. Later we are told that he came from a wealthy family since the relative costs of a marriage were high then also. His case was not an unusual one since we met other men married at 14 and 15 who are now in their early 30's. They dearly seem to love their kids and want the best for them. They don't want them to marry as they did.

It is legal under Islam to have several wives. Four seems to be the maximum number. In conversation nobody identified anyone with more than 2 or 3. Keeping wives is a very expensive matter. Each one is entitled to equal treatment. However in practice the new wife tends to get favored treatment and resentment develops with the first wife. There is also the problem of them getting along under the same roof.

A new small house is being constructed just down the street from our house. It is for the gentleman's second wife. Each wife wanted their own house. Two wives are rare in the younger generation and 3 even more so. So far I don't personally know of any Omani families where there are even two. Nasser, who spends two days each week at the girls college in Ibri, when asked by Donna, replied in what seemed all seriousness that he was thinking about a second wife. For most of the staff this idea seems more of a joke."I will go to Sweden and find a large blonde woman or I will put an add in the paper." The pros and cons of having a second wife are influenced by many practical matters. Cost and family harmony are to be considered. Ahmed stressed the opinion that for some women who had had five or six children it was a relief to have her husband procreate children with another woman. Nasser said that some women would be resentful for a time but eventually would get over it. It was also clear that strong objection from the existing wife was a matter that had to be taken into consideration. Finally it was pointed out that sometimes there were special circumstances. A wife who was ill or infirm may need help and another woman would be useful. A woman, perhaps a relative, whose life circumstances were such that she needed assistance, would be married to solve the situation. This solution was practical in a society where women had been required to have the shelter of a male guardian. The net result is that on balance, while there was some wishful thinking on the part of the men, it was better to have only one wife at a time.

A wife is not quite the piece of personal property in Islam that one might expect. When she marries, she maintains her own right to property she may have and she keeps her maiden name. What's hers is still hers or her families. This includes the wedding gifts from the groom. It is the male's duty to provide totally for his family. Working couples are something of a novelty and I wondered if the traditional rules would still apply.

Divorce is also a two way street. While a woman may divorce a man, it is most usually the other way around, partly because the woman foregoes her right to any of his property if she does (... and he hers). The traditional "I divorce you" repeated three times brings with it all the material problems that exist in the west. Usually the father has full rights to take the children but of course what new wife wants to raise the husband's six kids. In practice the children stay with the mother until age 7 to 9. The situation appears as messy as in the west but with some different nuances.

Salem Anaabi, of the village of Cullah near El Hamra, lives with his wife and 5 children and his mother and father on a modest garden plot farm of a hectare or so. He is the youngest of his parent's children.

His father is in his 70's, a kindly small man who welcomed us. Later we found him sitting on the steps with his two little granddaughters on his lap. He has had two wives. The first he divorced after having two sons. His second wife had a daughter and a son. These are the children who survived. The ones who died as infants are not counted.

Until recently women regularly lost children so family size was kept down to four or five. Now with better maternity care family size has risen dramatically with ten or twelve children being common. A national program of birth spacing is aimed at reducing not only family size but having healthy babies and mothers. The information program goes into the schools and colleges. The next, better educated generation, speaks of having small affordable families. The Quran is cited as reference for raising healthy children by spacing them apart. The dynamics of change in this society are very great. Within their childbearing years women have gone from expecting to lose babies to not losing them.

When Donna was asked as to how many children she had, her response was "two." This answer generated another question about how many she had lost. The empathetic sense was the poor woman must have lost a number of babies. When Donna told them she had not lost any, the women marveled at the fact.

Salem's two half brothers live in the UAE where they work. His father for a time worked in the oil fields in Bahrain. His sister lives at Misfah on the mountain visible in the distance. She was married at 12 to a man who came to his father and asked for her. The man is now in his 70's and his sister is 35. Salem's arranged marriage was to his cousin whom he knew as a child. She lived but a few yards away. He was 18 and recently chosen to go to Scotland to improve his English. Being the second best student in his college class in Muscat he was offered the chance to study abroad. Later he went to Bristol University in England and still later spent a year earning an MA in Columbus, Ohio. He hopes to gain his doctorate someday. His five children are bright youngsters full of energy. He wishes them all to go to university, including the three girls. He sees a different world than that which he grew up in. However when it came to marriage for his daughters, he thought that he would choose their mate but only with their agreement. (Salem did get his PhD in England and later became Dean of the College at Nizwa.)

We have a glimpse of this world in a visit to his home. We are the first western people to be so invited. His mother sits for a time with us in the majlis, the room for guests. We sit on some fine carpets and lean on pillows. It is only after some persuading that his wife agrees to bring the baby and sit for tea. She appears very, very shy. Donna tries to be friendly but she will not even give her more than a glance. She shakes my hand but looks away. She appears very ill at ease and says but a few words. We are not of her world and she is not of the world her husband has seen. If he gets selected to do a doctorate, he will again be away in the west for several years. Salem is a quiet, reserved, pleasant man. He has grown to know the world yet his comfort base is here with a wife who has just met her first western woman. What thoughts must be in her head?

Being unable to speak much Arabic we have trouble gaining much detail. However through acquaintances who speak arabic Donna has learned that the local women still expect young girls to be "washed" which is a term referred to in the bible and thus indicates that the practice of female circumcision at least in a modified form exists. The women tell Donna that it is just a little snip.

The young girls play in bright dresses with their heads uncovered. They look like they are going to somebody's birthday party as their frocks are so western in nature. They romp and frolic but mothers take care that strenuous activity which may damage the hymen does not take place. Daughters must be virgins to marry and the custom is to take the bloody sheet from the wedding bed and parade it about as evidence. If the sheet isn't bloody, the groom has the right to divorce the woman on the spot for not being a virgin.

Slowly we begin to meet and understand the lives of those around us. New customs and ways to us are counterpointed by the rapid change that is overtaking our neighbors. We meet a family of Canadians and another of Americans who are here as secret missionaries. Their front is a computer training school. I'm not sure just how they go about spreading their religious ideas since the standing joke at the college between the Canadian librarian and I is that we know we are going home when they find a bible in the library. These two western women dress in the Omani style. Donna does not. They raise their children in western ways but with an arabic flavor. The children have toys and sing western children's nursery rhymes. They play with Omani children. We walk along streets where Omani children follow us calling out in English "How are you?" We come from another world that they now watch on television.

An Omani couple we know live with his parents. They have 3 children and are building a house. He works in Muscat and drives home to Nizwa on the weekend. His wife has her own car. They plan the new home together. A pantry with a deep freeze is included plus three bathrooms and lots of nice tile. They are urban, middle class. They come to visit us and seem at home in a western apartment. Life in Muscat is different, almost European. It doesn't take long. It doesn't take long.

Dates

The date is a food staple in Oman. It is ubiquitous in the culture. We lived in an oasis. The vast majority of the trees were date palms. From an elevation the view over Nizwa was a view over a green canopy of palms. The trees are tall with sturdy trunks. The dates hang in huge clusters high in the tree. There are a number of varieties which mature at different times of the year.

Our friend Cedric was a date research specialist. He ran a government research plot outside of Nizwa. His wife Katia and their kids spent several years in Oman before emigrating to Australia. Cedric was born in St. Lucia when it was a British colony. He never obtained a proper passport from the UK and was in a quandary trying to get citizenship from some place. His father had retired in Canada but there was no date research work there!

Dates were dried, baled and stored as a food reserve. The old forts still had cellars with ancient bales of pressed dates.

Dates are a fruit very high in sugar but also have fibre and some other nutrients. They are served at every event and at many meals in Oman. At the college various office staff would bring in a huge bowl of dates, perhaps a few hundred, for the morning cawa break. The cardamon accented coffee was served strong and black in small cups. Unlike most arabs Omanis don't add sugar because the dates provide the sugar. By the end of the morning there would be a pail of pits - a few of them from me.

Dates can be long and thin, fat and short, red or yellow and ripe or green. Discriminating date eaters have their own preferences. A date ripens from one end to the other. A date that is quite edible at one end might be astringent and bitter at the other end. A date at the peak of perfection is not yet shriveled but remains moist and smooth and uniform in color. Outside of a date growing area it is not possible to get a fresh date.

Omanis love their dates. It is a staple part of their diets. The high consumption probably contributes to a major health problem, diabetes. The incidence of the disease is high and along with the high date sugar the practice of marrying close relatives has intensified a genetic tendency to develop the disease.

Dates grow on the female trees. Male trees are not desired except for the fertilizing of the date flowers. At the time the trees need to be fertilized, owners of male trees sell large bunches of golden pollinating fronds. To pollinate the tree someone, usually barefoot, climbs up the tree. The trunks afford a decent foothold. The fronds are brushed over the hanging flowers. Then as the hot days of summer arrive, the dates start to mature and the tree is again scaled and with a machete the clusters are cut down. A good tree can produce up to 700 lbs of dates. The dates will sell anywhere from a couple of rials to several rials a pound depending on the quality. It is a valuable cash crop.

Across the road was an oasis area that we would walk through. Under the palms other crops, mostly vegetables or animal food would be grown. The intricate system of the ancient falag watering canals from the mountains is what maintains the oasis.

The falag Daris began as a series of holes dug at the base of the mountain 2,500 years ago. When water was struck, an underground tunnel would be dug about 60 feet to the next well. As the tunnel moved from the mountain, the water level came closer to the surface until eventually it flowed across the surface in channels about a foot wide. These little canals had diversionary channels that were opened and closed to regulate the use. A person was elected each year to be in charge of the allocating of the water.

If you stand over one of the wells, a cool draft of air blows upwards and the water can be heard gurgling along under the ground. It was this construction miracle that allowed Nizwa to exist. It was this miracle that has allowed dates to grow in Nizwa for thousands of years.

Critters, Creatures and Things in the Night

Our friend Cedric and family lived along a wadi and their location harbored a lot of frogs and scorpions. The frogs at times appeared in great congregations of hopping and croaking. One had to watch where to step when going there for a visit. By the house was a large tree. A scorpion fell out of the tree and stung their 2 year old girl. They rushed the child off to the hospital where they were told to wait out the pain and treat it like a wasp sting. Depending on the type of scorpion the sting can range from a bad wasp sting to fatal. Fortunately the deadly type are not too common.

In the hot weather scorpions came into the house for the cool and I found several in the bedroom at night. When I had to rise in the night I always turned on the light. Before putting on a shoe I would tip it over. Once a scorpion fell off my shoe. Fortunately Donna was away for all of those events or she would have been spooked. We had a large one, perhaps 3 inches long in the kitchen and when it got bug sprayed, it desperately tried to sting anything it could. The stinger in the tail was arched over its back in the venom mode. Another tried to claw its way up a grated drain with its claws thrashing through the holes as if it wanted to attack me. Nasty ugly critters that resembled a crayfish more than it did an insect.

Another impressive creature was the camel spider, a large furry arachnid the size of a golf ball with legs. One of these was sitting by the curb one evening as we entered a restaurant. A large locust, essentially a super size five inch long grasshopper, chanced into its path and the spider with its many eyes spotted it and pounced. As we watched, the locust was drained of its innards and the spider tossed the lifeless shell aside. In less than a minute there was a corpse barely an inch long.

On another occasion we went to visit Florence another Dean who was at Rustaq. She had left the front light on and when we arrived, her entire entrance way was swarming with a grand display of locusts. They clung to the walls in such numbers we could not see the surface. The ground was treacherous to walk on. The road was greasy from their mashed bodies. These critters are giants compared to the grasshoppers of Ontario. Where this huge swarm had come from we never could understand since there was precious little for this hungry host to munch on in our area. We were to encounter this phenomenon a couple of other times during our time in Oman. Now we understood the biblical references to the locusts.

Small insects were not abundant. Flies, gnats and the like were seldom seen. As a consequence there were not a lot of lizards about. We did have one fellow the size of a small squirrel who would dance along the wall displaying his vibrant blue and red colors. He looked ferocious when he reared on his hind legs for a wild dance.

Occasionally a ginkgo with its suction cup feet would wander into the house and hang on the walls. Being harmless bug eaters we left them alone.

There were a variety of snakes and many were poisonous. Most of the poisonous ones had a triangular head. We never saw a poisonous one although the small venomous ader snake had to be watched for when out among rocks. Our Indian house boy was paranoid when a skinny non poisonous milk snake got into the house and had a near fit trying to decapitate it. The snake was not much bigger around than a pencil but was nearly 3 foot long. We moved it outside where it managed to work its body neatly along the bricks zig zagging the line of mortar up the wall. I was impressed that it could flex around the bricks so skillfully but the house boy was in dire fear. Another snake was not so fortunate as he informed Donna "Madam, there is a snake." She was about to step back onto it as he went to smash it dead.

A Trip to Masirah Island

Masirah Island is off the southern coast of Oman. We set out early in the morning of April 17 to rendezvous with Andre, the Canadian Dean at Sur. He met us in Sinaw a village convenient for our meeting. Sinaw was incredibly busy with the Eid Al Adha preparations. The streets were crowded and one could hardly move. Goats and cows for the sacrifice were being bought and friends were greeting friends. We met Andre and as well Patrick from our college who had also been invited. Our mini caravan of two 4x4 headed off down the newly paved road that goes south from Sinaw towards Duqm. After a hundred kilometers the new pavement ended. From here on it was bone shaking washboard. All roads that are not paved fall into this class. They are just passable and at times not suitable for a car. Shaking along we left the modest greenery that had been the aftermath of the recent rains. In places where there were wadis crossing the road, the water had not yet dried away.

Clusters of tarp covered shacks with pickup trucks parked nearby indicated the presence of Beduin camps. A few camels, a mud brick store or tiny Mosque and a few oil barrels as well as a nice blue road sign indicated we had passed a community. After a couple of hours of this monotony, enlivened by playing tag and eating road dust with other four wheeled expats heading to the coast or the sand dunes, we came to a halt at the wadi Halfain. This wadi has it origins in the mountains which we had left in the morning. The rush of rain passes this way and at this point is not far from the sea. From a flat dusty and now arid plain devoid of any vegetation we suddenly find a grassy sea of green before us. Camels in considerable number are grazing. They look like small Brontosaurus from a prehistoric time, some with heads up and others bent grazing. The convoy gently eases across the swamp. The trail is under water. Water sprays out from the tires. No one gets stuck but the water is several inches deep across here. On the return journey we stop and picnic under a tree on the edge of this meadow. We pick a spot without too much camel dung on which to spread our plastic red and white stripped table cloth. (Two years later we had a journey that brought us back to this road. The camels were still in the green meadow but the swampy path was now a modern paved two lane highway elevated above the swamp and we sped past the now inaccessible picnic tree.)

Successfully across we again enter the barren lands. A stop at a building identified as a restaurant is also the intersection we are looking for, the road to Hij. This is not really a restaurant. It isn't much more than a shack and we drink our own pop while we get directions.

Hij appears out of the sand like a series of distant blobs. Eventually we see some modern all white buildings with a flag flying above them. These buildings are for the military or the police or the hospital or the school. Hij is a regional center. The main street is wide, deserted and sand. There is a row of white painted stones on each side of the road. I guess this is part a *beauty thing and part direction to indicate the road area between the buildings. The main area of town has yellow mud brick buildings enlivened by one sign for Sanyo on a building front and the Shell gas sign in front of the petrol station. There are a couple of bus stop shelters with doors. These shelters are a deep maroon color and standout easily. I was sure no one needed instructions as to how to get out of town. At mid day this place was about as dead and sleepy as any remote one camel town can get.*

The main street ended at a wadi, a small stream we had to ford. Farther down the wadi we could see some kids playing in a water hole. Now we were in the industrial section of town. The stores had spare parts, tyre repair, auto repair, steel welding, refrigeration repair. Each small one room shop was to assist the needs of the local people as well as the passer by. Fortunately we needed none of their services. Their presence did indicate the torture that the roads gave to the local vehicles.

When it gets very flat and treeless, the scenery becomes more fascinating. It is flat brown earth and bright blue sky in equal balance. We stop to scan the horizon and also to examine some strange little plants. The leaves are swollen bright green and fleshy. They are gorged with sap. I wondered if the camels found them tasty. I wasn't about to test the theory. The mid day heat kept producing mirages and the land now had a white cast like winter snow. We were entering salt flats, crusty white crystals on the surface of the ground that extended for miles.

The approach to the coast caused some confusion. We couldn't distinguish between mirage and actual water . We pass a sign to

Jennah 3 km. Who could want to live out in this! The intersection has a bus stop. Our travels, according to the map, should soon take us to the ferry. We end up at some fishing huts on the beach. The road ends and before us lie the Wahiba sands, a true sand dune desert. We are lost and the time for reaching the ferry is running out. We are directed back to Jennah which is reached by crossing 3 kilometers of a causeway consisting mostly of mud ruts. At the end of a sand spit is the port of Jennah which is comprised of several metal shacks and oil drums and vehicles and fishing boats. Such is Jennah!

Here also is the rustiest barge I have ever seen. This thing is being packed with trucks of vegetables, insulated fresh fish tanks and four wheel vehicles. To make room for us all some vehicles are pushed sideways. The ramp, which is also the bow of the boat, carries two vehicles, one of which is mine. The front wheels of my Pajero are on the deck. The rear wheels are on the ramp. The ramp is lifted so my Pajero is now at about a 45 degree angle. The ramp is secured up with some decent size chains. This old barge has some pretty hefty engines which roar to life and edge us away from the dock. We are off on our sea cruise.

An hour away is Masirah Island. The passengers are expats from different lands off for a holiday as well as a few truck drivers and a handful of Omanis, mostly women in bright outfits. The fare is 15 rials (60 dollars for a one and a half hour trip). We stand on the upper deck gazing over the vehicles, no cars! The sea breeze is lovely. There are no life jackets, no fire equipment, no clean clothes. This is a rusty, oily, old tub. The most decrepit thing I have ever traveled on. If the engine quits, we are sure to sink.

Masirah looms ahead. There are low jagged hills to the right, a community in the center and numerous huge industrial oil bunkers, radio towers and lots of radar and satellite communication equipment to the left. Masirah does not have a secret RAF base shared with the USAF. This air base is Omani as there is an Omani flag and insignia. We never went into the base and never saw a military person. There is a BBC relay station here. So the secret base is still a secret base. It was a staging area for the first gulf war and the place was full of aircraft and ships as well as men and munitions.

An English couple on the ship are going to a friend's cottage located inside the base and they provide us some details about what's behind the walls. It's a lot different than what we see on the island.

The main street of Masirah town had been oiled at some time, not recently. We lurch over the pot holes. There is a new hotel, so new it is not yet open but we could have furnished rooms. It is conveniently placed next to the electric generator plant and in front of the fish processing plant. The room rate will be 30 rials a night. For that price one gets the sound of the generator pumps thudding at 50 cps and the smell of fish. We pass at being the first customers. A french couple have reservations and they will get to sleep on the new beds as soon as the hotel staff unpack them. Perhaps they too moved on but where?

Before seeking a campsite we tour the island. It isn't large. It isn't very interesting. A black volcanic ridge thrust from the sea with some sand. In 1904 the locals pirated a British navy vessel and killed the crew. In reprisal all permanent dwellings were destroyed by order of the Sultan. The folklore is the locals killed and ate the sailors. The Sultan of the day said if they wanted to act like animals, they could live like them and decreed that nothing could be built with a roof that was higher than an animal hut. This was high enough to sleep under and get out of the sun. Periodically the Sultan would send troops to the island and destroy any effort to build a proper house. It was only in recent years they were allowed to build permanent places again. Outside of the town we didn't see any.

The island has a few small communities, fishing places. The vegetation is very sparse, mostly shrubs. Rocks, salt and sand are not hospitable to many plants.

The villages consist of tin and chunks of wood and perhaps a blue plastic tarp. Small cages for chickens or something else. They are crowded together in a maze and resemble something kids would create out of scraps for a play house. Occasionally there would be a vehicle parked under a section of this stuff. The only place on the island with actual buildings was the main town. At no other place in Oman had I seen what looked like total poverty. Even the Beduin camps seemed to have a better quality of life.

We crossed the island to the south coast and looked for a suitable camp site. We chose a fairly sandy beach at the base of an old volcanic mound. Black rocks, white sand, crashing waves on the rocks and small sandy patches of beach backed by the green blue of the sea made it just the pristine place for us.

We make camp. The Pajero becomes a sleeping room and is actually not that uncomfortable. It proves better than hard ground. There is no one about except us. We can see along the beach for some distance.

As dusk descends we find we don't need a lantern as the moon provides suitable light. We dine by moonlight with the sounds of the surf for music. The only human light is from a distant ship.

While all this sounds very pristine we found ample evidence of previous occupants. Broken bottles, net parts, oil drums, and other junk here and there. There was a dead beached dolphin, hermit crabs and some interesting shells which the crabs occupied. It was a little startling to see a sea shell suddenly rise up and move across the sand. Along the waters edge were specks of glowing phosphorous. Like tiny bits of greenish glitter they washed in and out and then resting on the beach they would slowly fade. Small wavelets glowed as they came to shore.

The star filled heavens I had hoped to see were dimmed by the moon's intenseness overhead and only those who woke early were able to see the full spectacle. The north star is lower on the horizon here.

After breakfast of boiled coffee and peanut butter sandwiches we completed our tour of the island. The rains had etched small gullies across the road and we gave the four wheels a test of their skills crossing these little ravines with their necessary detours. The drive along the south coast is modestly spectacular. Coves and rock slopes, with crashing surf made the trip pleasant until we came back to the northern flat coastal plain. Then it was a race to the ferry. We had no time to examine the secret base and the nice cottages for expats. That would have to wait until we knew someone at the base.

Outbound there were our two vehicles and a fish truck and an old car. The passengers were more interesting. It being Eid an entire family was crossing to the mainland. The oldest fellow, one of the type painters like to use as models, lay down and had a nap right on the deck. Three women had their burkas over their faces. Small girls in bright party dresses grinned and played. The mother of the smallest teased and tickled her at times. This imp had a grape colored dress with silver leaves embroidered on it. Her mother had an abaya over her yellow and navy flowered dress. She carried a Coca Cola duffle bag and tried to make conversation with Donna about her white hair. The boys sat on the end of the ramp/door socializing. All in all there were about 20 in this extended family.

Back on the mainland this group of people all managed to get into one large Toyota Land Cruiser. Greeting their escort the ladies lifted their burkas and rubbed noses with the driver. Everyone now headed off to their mainland destinations. For us there were several hours of shaking and rattling back to the pavement. Sinaw was deserted at 6 p.m. Everyone was celebrating at home. Only the Indian/Pakistani workers were about. All the shops were closed. It was still another hour to Nizwa.

Secret Bases

Oman was never a British colony. In the 19th century the country was a modest navel power which controlled the Indian ocean between India and Africa. For this reason the British courted the Omani Sultan so British influence was strong, not only in Oman but also Zanzibar which was a possession of Oman. In the 1800's the Sultan spent most of his time in Zanzibar and little of it in Oman. Oman itself was basically two places, Muscat and the Oman Interior. Until after the second world war it was known as Muscat and Oman. The Sultan's power in the interior was limited particularly in Nizwa where the local Imam was dominant. When the current Sultan deposed his father in 1970, he did so with the assistance of the British SAS forces. Around 1950 the British helped put down a civil war in the interior. The village of Tanouf near Nizwa was bombed and destroyed by the RAF and the locals in the mountains put up strong resistance to the rule of the Sultan. Later after Quaboos had removed his father, the British provided guidance to build the Oman military and police. As a young man Quaboos attended Sandhurst, the British officer training academy, and was an officer of the British NATO forces in Germany. It was believed he married a German woman and had a daughter. Officially, he like most Omanis, had married a first cousin and they divorced not long afterwards without having a child.

When Quaboos returned to Oman after his military service, his father basically confined him to house arrest. The father was a very reactionary person who did not have a vision for the country which had recently joined the other Arab states as an oil producer. There also were concerns about a communist take over similar to what had happened in Yemen. Quaboos had a clear vision for the future of his desert land and set about to modernize it.

As American influence increased in the middle east, Oman was counted on to be a reliable partner. The USAF built a large base at Thumrait in the desert not far from Salalah in the south of Oman. Like the British base at Masirah Island it had a fortified crenellated medieval fort like entrance with Omani military present and only Omani flags flying.

Some friends of ours were traveling in the desert not far from the base when their car broke down. An American officer in a jeep came upon them and said he was not supposed to be there and could offer no assistance but would arrange for help to come to them. He radioed his base and a message was sent for help to come. Thumrait and Masirah were both staging areas for the Gulf wars. At Muscat nearly all commercial flights came in at night but one person did comment that when they came in during the day there was a lot of military material on the ground around the airport. It was also thought that in the mountains near Izki there was a large weapons storage area. Certainly there were roads going into the mountains with no communities identifiable at the other end. There were also radar and communication towers in the middle of nowhere.

The old Nizwa hospital had a radiology unit that was a gift from the US navy. No explanation was ever given as to why. It is always interesting to see that when information appears in Time or the Economist they mention that there are American bases in Qatar, Bahrain, and the Emirates but there is never any mention of Oman. These are secret bases.

The United States, since FDR met with the Saudi Sheik Ibn Saud in 1944, has maintained a deal with the arabs of the Gulf to guarantee their security. The arabs are largely Sunni but the Ibadis of Oman are a smaller third group neither Sunni or Shia. Iran and parts of Iraq and Syria have the Shia version of Islam. Each version thinks the other has defiled the religion. This division has created all the modern tensions in the region. The Omani Sultan tries hard to play the friend of both sides in the great game. This role sometimes is useful in international politics. Nevertheless, he sleeps under the wings of the US and Britain and their secret bases.

During the few years we were in Oman, it was interesting to read short notes in the paper that ex president Bush Sr. had paid a visit. The secretary of state was in town. His Majesty had an audience with the defense secretary. Hardly a month went by without some very high American or British official stopping by to say hello. Rulers of small countries don't get that kind of attention without good reason.

Musandam

In the 1950's what is now known as the Emirates was called the Trucial States. These were sheikdoms which in 1892 agreed to let the British and Omani navies protect them from pirate raiders. The British undertook to protect these desert sheikhs until 1968 which was about the time oil was found in several of the sheikdoms. The seven remaining sheikdoms federated to become the Emirates. The largest and most endowed with oil was Abu Dhabi, followed by Dubai. The others had less if any oil so they are quite economically different in their standard of living. The United Arab Emirates are Abu Dhabi, Ajman, Dubai, Fujairah, Sharjah, Umm al Quwain and Ras al Khaima. Abu Dhabi in area is about 60% of the total and Dubai about 20% with the rest sharing the last 20% of the Emirate land.

When all this got organized in the 1960's, Musandam along with an enclave called Madha decided it was part of Oman. In the center of Madha is another tiny enclave which is part of Sharjah. Madha in turn is surrounded by Fujairah. It's fun to drive through this boundary maze.

So where is all this going? You will soon learn. Oman is many times larger than the Emirates but not nearly as wealthy. Nearly all the oil is in Dubai and Abu Dhabi. So Fujairah is pretty poor, as is Sharjah. They get handouts from the rich ones.

Musandam is a mountainous peninsula that separates the Persian Gulf from the sea of Oman and Indian Ocean. In order to drive from Oman to Musandam one has to drive across either Sharjah or Fujairah or both. That part of the trip is like crossing any state or province boundary. But you are going out and back into Oman when you go to Madha and Musandam. That means a customs stop and a permit stamp and a fee every few miles. There is not much to see except along the coast north of Madha there are a lot of very large ships clustered off shore well out to sea. This huge flotilla is a combination of oil tankers, containerships and military vessels of several nations. They are all trying to navigate their turn around the tip of Musandam, an area known as the strait of Hormuz.

This 21 mile body of water separates Oman from Iran. Most of it is too shallow for large ships. Only a 6 mile wide strip can be navigated and there is a 2 mile wide strip into the Gulf and a 2 mile strip going out of the Gulf with a 2 mile buffer between. About 3,000 vessels a day make this trip. That is not a misprint. This is one busy waterway. 20% of the world's oil passes through here. We wanted to see Musandam and the strait for ourselves.

We entered from Sharjah along the Persian gulf side after having zig zagged through Madah mostly so we could say we had been there. Our entry was duly stamped. The coast road clung between a cliff and the sea for miles. It was dramatic contrast. The jagged 6000 ft mountains simple drop into the sea. From the road it was like driving along a winding wall with a sea view on the left. At the end of this we came to Khasab the regional center and port. It was a sleepy little town at the end of the peninsula. There were a few Arab dhows and some motor boats. Some of which had just crossed from Iran with a few passengers and goods. These small private craft mostly outboard motor boats ferried back and forth across the strait to Iran ever y day.

Apart from the port office, a school and a few shops there was not much else here. This was the community beside the most important shipping lane in the world and looked the part of a forgotten outpost. The wooden Arab dhows were the most interesting thing to see.

We drove out of town up into the mountains with the objective of taking the road out of Musandam into Fujirah and to the main road back into Oman and Sohar where we would spend the night. We found a lovely vista for our picnic lunch. A small boat was crossing a cove far below us and the sea was partly obscured by an adjacent craggy hill. We could not actually see any of the vessels that traveled the strait. They were farther out to sea than our visibility allowed. Our flat rock on the side of the road was an excellent table and we lingered for the view before heading inland.

The road left the valley and wound its way up to the top of a razor back ridge. The road ran along the crest of the ridge affording the most spectacular view both left and right of other shear mountain ridges. The razor back on which we traveled went on for miles before winding down into an inhabited valley. The inhabitants were few and far between. We worked our way to the border post which was the only occupied place for some miles. It was getting late in the afternoon and we were anxious to get onto some better roads before dark. Such was not to be.

The pleasant Omani customs soldier informed us he could not stamp our book because we had entered from Sharjah and we were going into Fujirah. There was no customs booth in Fujirah so we would have to go back to Sharjah. We sat there for a time pondering our next move. What if we just left and went ahead. It was only a half hour or so ahead and we would be back in Oman. That would not do. He politely said our pass did not allow this and if we got back to the other part of Oman we could not re-enter because we had not officially left. Worse if we did this he would get blamed for allowing us to do this and he might loose his job. His honesty was typically Omani. We left the car to use the toilets and munch on some crackers and stretch. It would be a hasty return trip back along the narrow razor back road at sunset. Hopefully we would get to the well paved coast road before dark. The bonus was the view of the valleys and peaks in the glow of the late day sun behind us. The valleys were in deep blue shadows but the setting sun reddened the crest of the ridges. We reached Khasab at dusk and there was little traffic on the coast road until we got near the Sharjah border post.

I walked up to the border post wicket with my pass and had it duly stamped. There was a small restaurant next door and as usual for this sort of place we had the biriani rice and salad. We also had to find a hotel for the night in the main town farther along the road. Not what we had intended but one does what one has to do!

A Trip to Salalah.

At the other end of the country is Salalah. This is the account of our trip.

At the end of the Ramadan fasting month there is a short Eid holiday. This year it was in early February. We used the occasion to travel to Salalah in the extreme south of Oman. Leaving Nizwa mid afternoon we head down the only paved road across Oman. This journey is away from our usual routing along the mountain ridges and the relatively busy roads connecting the coast to the interior places. Some 60 km from Nizwa we pass the oasis of Adam and rapidly leave behind all habitation. The ragged ridges vanish and we are in a vast gravel plain of reddish brown and grey. In places the sun glistens off of the surface of the earth making it appear polished. Scraggy little acacia trees are sprinkled across the flat earth and in the distance the mirages of water keep receding away. At one point I see sand on the road but it too vanishes. Lakes of the mind! Tricks of nature!

Flat, flat, flat, no trees, no bushes, no rocks, only a black strip of road. The occasional truck passes, loaded to heights that make them top heavy. They are blobs that enlarge and then vanish behind us.

Only an oil tower or a microwave relay breaks the flatness. Then the desert in the late afternoon sun seems green. Green like corn just coming up in the spring. It is early February and there have been a few days of rain in the desert in recent weeks. It is cooler and in the mornings there has been dew.

Around us now are some low sand dunes so we stop for a photo and inspect the land. Here and there inch high grass plants are growing. There are other tiny plants. Look near and the sand is red and gravelly. But look far and there is a green cast. Things are growing.

The roadside markers, triangular shape, have a picture of a camel. Indeed in places we see a few camels grazing on the spare vegetation. Somebody owns them and they live not far away, but where?
 There is no sign of habitation.

The sunset disappoints. It vanishes into a purple haze as we arrive at Haima. This is about the middle of Oman. A police base, gas station, hospital form a definite community. Some miles before the town we pass a cluster of unusual things. There is a park with swings, slides, toilets, picnic tables and lots of sand. After more than a hundred kilometers of absolute nothing this is a surprise. Refueled at Haima we continue into the dusk.

Clearly most of Oman is a large void. Empty. The road runs along the edge of the great Rub Al-Khali, The Empty Quarter. This is desert in the absolute.

Al Ghaftain guesthouse, miles from anywhere, has a mosque, Shell station and a rest house of several rooms. It glows in the dark. There are trees, flowers and a pleasant but dated motel built around a court yard. A 60 ft well, filtration system and diesel generator makes the desert habitable. We have eaten at a sister guesthouse. They are all the same. We have our choice of rooms. There is no one else here.

Peter the manager says this is usual except from June to September when people go to Salalah for the monsoon season. It is cloudy and drizzly there at that season and so quite green. This appeals to the arabs. It is also cooler there than in the interior.

We eat under the trees in the courtyard. It is a pleasant early February night. Several staff, all from India work here. There are 10 in all, 4 Hindus and 4 Christians and 2 Muslims. The owner is the Omani Police force who lease it out. It is for sale. It does not seem to be a profitable enterprise. Our waiter is from Bombay. He came two years ago. He says he likes quiet. He has it. The gas station attendant has been here 16 years since the place opened. There is TV echoing in the night air. We must breakfast in our room as it is still Ramadan.

In the morning we head into even more desolate land. I pull over and walk across reddish sand some distance from the Pajero. I see some camel footprints the size of a big palm.

Another animal, possibly a desert fox, has been here. I see some human foot prints, tire marks and empty pop cans turned grey on one side from the sun. I pick up one and it is full of sand. There are a few well rusted tin cans and plastic water bottles turned black in the sun. I've been a few hundred meters from the road and still the debris of man goes on. This road is less than twenty years old. What will it look like in another twenty?

Further along the earth turns from tan to more red. It is incredibly flat. It is like being on the sea. What great farmland this could be, if only. Then a surprise. A sign says "Quatbeet Farm".

There is a fence and in the distance a well head. It is not clear what is being farmed. Farther along there is an experimental farm which has some trees. It is many more miles before we begin to see a change in land forms. Then there are some gulches. There are trees and dried grass and cows and camels. We begin to descend the escarpment to the coast. In the summer this is all green and even in February it is green with small trees.

Further along the plain beneath the escarpment, the coast becomes visible in a decidedly hazy sky. We arrive at the Holiday Inn, sand, sun , surf, pools.

A few hours on the beach and we learn who is in Oman. An American AID worker informs me it was their money that built the schools around Nizwa. A well burned gent from Philadelphia is here for two months to train people at an airbase how to use runway hooks to slow down aircraft. An aluminum engineer is on holidays. Mike an American professor from Sultan Quaboos University in Muscat fills us in on the good life and big money at the university. We later become good friends. German tourists are here. In fact most of the tourists in the country seem to be German, Swiss or Austrian.

We set off to explore. The frankincense trees are the ancient source of wealth for this area. Salalah has biblical ties. A tomb alleged to be Job's is in the nearby hills. More certain is the palace of the Queen of Sheba and the Frankincense and Myrrh indicates at least two of the three wise men came from the area. Harvesting the gum from the trees began in ancient times and wealth was created in this trade to ancient Egypt and Rome.

The road toward the Yemen border is a remarkable drive. We rise 3000 ft from the sea to a mountain top in under 15 minutes of zig zag climbing. We drive past Joshua trees and look over the sea from this great cliff. Small clouds form from the updraft just out there at eye level. We give some thought about driving as far as the Yemen border. However, some miles before we get there we come upon a road block sentry post and are advised that it is not safe to go further. Yemen is not stable and the general border area is subject to raids and marauders. We turn back.

We drive back up the escarpment and discuss whether we will take a diversion to see the lost city of Ubar which had been discovered by photos taken from the Challenger space shuttle a few years before. Ubar was a fabled place, a desert crossroads where the camel caravans staged to go into Arabia. We were told there was little to see and it was not worth the several hours diversion. So we decide not to go.

On the return journey we choose to stay again at the Ghaftain rest house. Shortly after checking in there is some excitement and a transport arrives with a Mercedes in tow. Three Omanis have lost the electrical system on their car which is not a good thing to happen in a desert night. I have the only vehicle around so I help jump the battery. Like all batteries out here the fluid levels are way down. They take filling every month. Everyone goes into the dining room and I decline an invitation to sit with them as Donna is with me and women aren't usually welcome. Peter recommends we not have the hamburger as the buns are a month old. After the meal I am surprised to learn the Omanis have paid for our supper. Omanis are a very hospitable and appreciative people. They arrange to depart and I find myself called upon to give them another boost. The car had been left in idle and had quit. They decided to go to Haima, over an hour away for a new battery. I suspected that they would not make it. Yet, they never came back. By now it was time for the generators to be changed so we stood outside waiting for the lights to go out and see the stars in the dark night. It was very dark except for the distant glow of an oil well burn off.

Peter the manager seems eager for some conversation. Again we are the only guests for the night. All the food is frozen. The 10 staff play volleyball and go for walks in the desert for recreation. Peter has two children back in India where his wife teaches school. He hadn't expected to be so isolated but the pay is three times what he would make in India. The story is always the same. Money is here, money for a dowery for the *girls even for a Christian fellow. Indian Christians always like to identify themselves to a westerner. Perhaps they think all westerners are Christian.*

In the morning he shows us a tree on the property which he says was planted by the Sultan or/and his father. It is a boundary marker tree of some sort. He shows us his collection of bugs, mostly scorpions which he has collected around the place. They are all neatly presented with a pin through each one holding it to a board. This is one lonely guy.

We invite him to join us for a trip into the empty quarter. I am still searching for a road to take us back into the sand dunes. Peter tells us that the road next to the guest house goes to one of the sites where the Sultan camps while touring the nation. Local leaders and other go there to meet with him. The site is a couple of miles off the road and is identified by the large flagpole. Once there we find large rings fastened into the ground. They are anchors for the tents. The road ends and we head off cross country. On the distant horizon we can see dunes. They could be 6 ft or 600 ft high but we could not tell. After ten minutes without any change in the size of the dunes I decide they are pretty far away. Also there is absolutely no other land mark. If we had a problem here, it would be a long walk back. It is recommended to always take two cars into true off roading. We turn back. A few miles along the pavement we find another road heading towards Saudi. It seems a reasonable one and we bounce along for a few kilometers. A long sand dune 10 to 15 ft high blocks the road. Donna climbs up it and motions me forward. Up and over we go. No problem. Then a few miles farther the road is washed out leaving a gully across it. Past the gully we can see others. The road is no longer passable. It is getting on in the morning and we still have to go to Nizwa so we take Peter back. He had never been out here before.

Near Haima we find another road. This one is on the map and I make yet another try to find a route into the dunes. Again they can be seen in the distance. The road takes us to a gathering station for the oil wells. 6 inch rusty pipes run to this place from all directions. We find a couple of buildings, generators and power lines and no sign of life but there must be someone about. We follow along a pipeline towards an oil well with a burn off chimney. This road will stop at the oil well so we cut across country to the power lines. It is only a mile or so but the tires under us are spinning in the sand. A meager trail follows the power lines. It is better than open country but we could still get stuck so we turn away from the dunes and follow the power line until we can't proceed because of a pipeline. It is about a foot off the ground. We follow the pipeline until it intersects the road. Foiled again. We head for home. There is a spot where there are some dunes 20 ft high or so just by the highway. There is a sign stating, 'Danger, Sand Dunes." They move. A few hundred yards takes us to a good size dune. Across the flat desert there are others scattered about. The desert is tan and grey. The dunes are orange red. In the stiff breeze footprints vanish in seconds. Sand constantly blows across the top of the dune like snow in a blizzard. You can almost see the dunes moving. The warm sand is great on the toes but we must resume our journey.

More mirages, are those trees or towns on the horizon? Lakes so real, sand piled on the road, the eyes play tricks on the mind. There is nothing there but sometimes a camel or an *approaching truck. A sign and a paved exit indicates a road leading 180 km to somewhere. At the end of the paved exit there isn't even a tire track visible. Roads are indistinguishable from the desert! There are a number of these. We approach trees and distant hills. Adam can't be far now. It is a good thing as the gas gauge is getting pretty low. There is not one station between Haima and the several hundred kilometers to Adam.*

Some place out there we picked up an Omani hitchhiker. He actually may have been waiting for the bus. There are three or more a day to Salalah. Big modern coach buses. He had been working at an oil site and was returning to Muscat. He had no luggage or equipment with him which seemed odd. His English was not good and he seemed pretty tired and conversation was hard to make so he sat quietly in the back seat listening to our music tapes.

It had taken all day to do a 4 hour trip but we did see some more of the country. Next time perhaps we will find a road to the empty quarter and its great dunes.

Meetings and Cultural Oddities

I chair a staff meeting of about 50 people. It had a focus... "The role of the staff in student counseling." This was a task they didn't do well last term. I assembled my material and then coached a member of the faculty to say certain things. This was part dress rehearsal and part teaching this professor what to do. I'm sure he added in his own material to that which I gave him.

We head downstairs to the conference room where staff meetings are held. As we enter, those who are already there are greeted with a personal handshake and greeting. Then we take our place at the head of the horseshoe arranged tables. Every person who enters tours the entire room and does the ritual handshaking. The meeting is scheduled for one o'clock. Most are there but I hesitate to commence because I know that when the late arrivals come, they will go around the entire room and shake every one of the 50 or so hands that they have not shaken since before lunch. Even after we commence, they do this even though the meeting has started. The only difference is they speak softly and try to complete the ritual quickly.

My translator for the day did a little keynote in Arabic. I am certain they consider it an honor to speak on my behalf. That was one reason I used different persons when I could. Then I chaired the meeting. I spoke English they spoke Arabic. It takes a certain type of person to do this I decided. It would be similar to being deaf and conducting the orchestra. Anyway it was fun at first but I was pooped after two hours of it.

As we approached two o'clock, a couple of the faculty rise from their seats and place themselves along the wall facing toward Mecca where they assume the prostrate position for prayer. This they do quietly. At first it was disconcerting to see people do this but experience has told me that they had not been able to arrange the mid day prayer and they needed to do that. The first time I went to a faculty office to talk to some staff and I found someone in the midst of praying, I was told to come in and not worry about that person as he was intent and oblivious. I was cautioned not to interrupt. The rest of us then had our discussion. When one has to pray 5 times a day, this has to be fitted into the schedule. Did they all pray this much? The Omani students and office went to a small mosque but not many of the faculty seemed to go there. I suspect there were some who did not manage the five times a day.

The meeting went into overdrive with some grandstanding and I was scrambling to get the gist of the issue. My translator was caught trying to grasp the point and also keep me informed. I had no clue what was happening and would have to wait to learn the gist of this issue when from across the table the speaker was interrupted by another faculty member who did not like the message from the first speaker. This I could understand. Finally my translator is able to turn to me and say " Ismail does not agree with Anwar." That much I knew already. I sensed I was not going to get an explanation right away. I spoke up. "Ismail, Anwar was making a speech, please let him finish." Ismail speaks no or little English. He stops and looks at me but does not comprehend. His neighbor whispers to him. Ismail nods to me and Anwar finishes his harangue. I point to Ismail. Afterwards I read the note from Sadok who has been translating. He has been able to tell me the problem. I present my view about the discussion and give a summary with a compliment to both sides concluding with my view. It is accepted. From two sentences given to me from Sadok I have ended ten to fifteen minutes of Arabic discussion with a statement in English. I never had a clue what was really said but it was my job to manage.

Actually we go through this routine nearly every day at meetings large and small. Someone comes with a problem in pidgin English. I toss in a few arabic words now and then and if I'm lucky we get a solution without going for a third person to translate. In some of the heated group discussions, we sometimes all break down laughing because somebody is looking at me speaking a mile a minute. I haven't a clue what he is saying and somebody else clues in by looking at me and recognizing this and starts laughing. Then we all laugh. When things get boring, I can tell because people start playing with their toes. They don't wear socks and shoes, only sandals. Seeing grown men, many with PhD's fidgeting with their toes puts things into perspective. We are all basically still like little kids. Afterward, on my way back to my office I encounter a group of students who have just emerged from a toilet.

Ablutions

I get a wet handshake. I get a lot of wet handshakes. It means the person has just come from the toilet. They use water but not paper. There are no hand towels. That is why they eat with the right hand since the wet one is always the left. Sometimes when they shake your hand they forget to let go. This is especially true of the Egyptians. I am standing holding a hand shaking and shaking while carrying on a greeting. Egyptians frequently kiss both cheeks when the greeting is after some absence or has greater meaning. Guys' shaves can really be prickly. I observed a couple of Omani students greeting each other by rubbing noses. This is a custom among some of the bedouin tribes.

I do a tour of the college every day. This tour includes checking out the washrooms. The toilets are all simple porcelain slabs in the floor with two raised foot prints astride a 4 inch hole. There are 4 western toilets on the main floor near the office. These are in constant repair. When the resource center opened the second year, I made sure that there was a western toilet with a lockable door. The Canadian librarian and I each had a key and personally kept the room supplied with toilet paper.

The student washrooms are large and there is a circular hand washing station as well as some conventional sinks. It is the custom before prayers to cleanse oneself. Cleanliness is next to godliness. Hands up to the elbow and feet up to the knee are washed. Water is also snuffed up the nose to cleanse the nostrils and water is rinsed in the mouth.

Now and again I would observe someone rubbing their teeth with a twig. The twig was from a certain bush called a toothbrush bush. One was pointed out along a street in Firq. Little bundles of them could be bought in some shops. The end was chewed to create something like a brush and the other end worked like a toothpick. The rubbing may have done something useful but one faculty who was always using the twig also suffered from severe halitosis. I was told the twig bush was mentioned in the Quran. However I think many local people have graduated to the common toothbrush which seems a superior cleaner to me.

The college was designed by some westerner because whoever designed the college did not take into account the ablution needs of the students. I kept finding students trying to wash their feet in the sinks. I wanted to get some foot washing sinks installed but it did not happen during my time there. It was no easier for them to try and wash their feet in the sink than it would be for me. As for the toilet stalls, men with trousers had no place to hang them but around the neck. Perhaps there could be some hooks installed. Fortunately, I had a semi private throne room so getting hooks was not a high priority for the students toilets.

A student had broken his wrist. He was about 19 years of age and in some pain. In trying to determine what happened I learn it happened in the western toilets. He had fallen off the toilet. How, I wondered, had a grown man fallen off the toilet? Gradually I began to understand the cultural gap. Before the resource library toilet was built I used those 4 toilets. The seats were always broken or missing leaving only the bare rim. I realized when cleaning them in order to sit down that I was wiping foot prints off. Why were there footprints on the toilet rims? Were they fooling around trying to look over the tops of the stalls? It now dawned on me that the Omani students were trying to use them as if they were Arabic style by standing on the rim and squatting. This is how the injury had taken place. He had stood on the rim, hoisted his dishdasha and tried to squat. He did this in the belief I suppose that this was how we used a toilet.

I had some empathy for his predicament because a western dressed male who enters an eastern toilet stall has to squat over a hole. This is not easy. The simplest solution is to remove the trousers and underwear and hang them around the neck because there is no place else to put them. There are no hooks. The floors were filthy. So arrange the trousers so the pockets don't empty and wrap them around your neck. If it is well equipped there will be a water can with a spigot. No paper. The water can is used to wash ones rear. It had some merit. An Omani would wear an ablution towel under his dishdasha for the occasion. I had to carry a roll of toilet paper that could not be set on the wet floor. Often there would be a British style pull chain cistern for flushing. Otherwise there was only the cesspool hole to aim into with no flushing. I sought every opportunity to avoid having to use one of these arabic toilets.

Whenever someone new arrived in Oman, we had some specific toilet training instructions to offer them. The first rule was never to leave home without it. It was a roll of toilet paper.

The Hoti Cave

This is an adventure story! Well most things we did in Oman were adventures but this is a more traditional adventure story. This adventure probably wouldn't have been a great one for an intrepid potholer or spelunker. However, at my age it was my first "au natural" time under ground. In the past I have been in Luray, Carlsbad, Mammoth Cave and on some subterranean lake cruise in Yugoslavia. These caves were all commercialized and surrounded by motels, restaurants and souvenir shops and had electricity, staircases and even elevators and guides to show the marvels. Hoti was nothing like that. It was under a barren hillside. This cave, this day, was ours to discover.

A year earlier Donna, Erin, Jonathan and I had attempted to find Hoti and missed it. This year after a number of feature articles in local publications and knowing its proximity to Nizwa, it was decided by a group of us that we should search it out as a Christmas Eve activity. This activity is the sort of thing that seems best on occasions like this in Oman where there is no Christmas but westerners take the day off. This day off does not work for the Coptic Christians from Egypt as they celebrate the holiday 12 days later. They go to work that day.

This time we had a firmer idea of where to go and our three 4x4's headed out of Nizwa toward Al Hamyra which should someday become a real tourist town. They have a full view of Jebel

Shams, old ruins and other adventure activities there. We jostle along a dusty trail until what looks like a cave is seen on the hillside. After parking we have a half hour trip of climbing over rocks to reach the cave. We pass a couple who are returning with a flashlight in hand. They announce that there is no way they are going into that hole. This cave is big but what we are actually under is a large ledge created when the rocks above collapsed into the actual cave. The real cave is someplace below.

We are surrounded by huge boulders and stones. There are, however, four black holes each about twice the size of a toilet bowl. Our flashlights show varying precipitous drops around the boulders into these holes. The guide book is not much use. It is decided that one must be the correct one as the rock there was polished from persons sliding down. We have decided. We shall go down this toilet bowl size entrance.

John and Val Godsmark, Brenna Murray age 13, Rob Fisk, Erin and I are determined to go into this abyss. Elaine who is Rob's wife and Donna maintain that some people should remain outside in case help is needed. I give my car keys to Donna. John Godsmark vanishes. We prepare some nylon rope and secure it to a rock. Brenna, Erin, Val and Rob vanish, all with some difficulty. They simply drop down out of sight into a black hole.

I peer into the hole with my flashlight and determine that it is about 12 feet straight down with a steep sloping ledge that never seems. Dropping in there won't work. I can put one foot on the opposite sloping rock and by clinging desperately to the rope and a rock get a toe hold with one foot on my side. The other foot I have to wrap around the rock because there is a small ledge that I can lower myself onto with some agility and save myself from falling. At this point I can still see out and could call the entire thing off. While contemplating whether or not I was going to go down, the thought occurred that I would presumably want to come out which now seemed a pretty awesome feat as well. However having gotten this far I decided that I might as well keep going.

I step onto the ledge, then move into a crevice and slide along. John, Erin and Brenna I can hear around a bend. The flashlight shows a few bats clinging to the walls. This spot is very tight and from this ledge I can see a drop of another 10 feet onto a fairly flat rock wedged between huge boulders. The problem was the light showed that past that there was a huge drop. Brenna had gone left crawling through a narrow space that if one slipped would have left one wedged in a place of difficult exit. The way forward and to the right was to get one leg into a foot or so wide crevice that had room to crouch in. The problem was getting to that crevice. It meant lurching over a gap that should I miss would send me down to the rocks 12 feet below. This action meant I had to lunge left and grasp a rock tip with a forward motion to get my body in. Erin grabbed my hand as I did so. Having gotten past that we next had to slide down a rock face and target a small round boulder. Missing the boulder meant sliding down without any grip another foot or two. Someone ahead has indicated it was a bit easier. I was definitely wondering how I would ever get back out the way we came in. The reverse of what we had just done seemed awfully tricky.

Now we are in a more open area and can stand. I definitely don't have claustrophobia or fear of heights since the last 20 minutes would have sent such a person into panic. People are passing around a car size boulder and sliding down more rocks then emerging about 15 to 20 feet below us. I attempt a photo at this time and my flashlight which I have tied about me comes loose and ricochets down about a dozen feet but is retrievable, thank goodness. Down we go and now find ourselves in a vast huge cave where walking is now quite easy. It is perhaps 400 or 500 feet across. Big. A huge chamber. Hoti cave is 7 kilometers long and can be entered from either end. About a kilometer in there is a lake with fish.

There is not much in the way of stalactites and stalagmites, a few examples here and there. The cave is very dry, not wet at all. However we can see twigs and debris that have washed through. In a good rain this would be a roaring river. We climb up what in those times would have been an impressive water fall.

At this point I am suffering greatly from thirst and am feeling somewhat shaky so when Rob says he has had enough Val and I agree. John, Erin and Brenna press on for another 15 minutes. We have been 45 minutes under ground and sit and rest in the total darkness. Very total. Now and again we see some distant flashes of light from the other party. They return without finding the lake. The way ahead is much like where we are and the lake still some distance off.

We retrace our steps along a string which an earlier party had placed for guidance. Somebody had left plastic cups and junk which seemed to really be a disgrace. Going this way we see that a boulder whose slope is not too great allows us to move up without too much effort. It is polished and clean indicating that others have gone this way but not that many people have since the cave was discovered in modern times in 1985. I wonder what would posses anyone to even think of crawling into one of those little potholes. I wonder what possessed myself.

Rob instructs me to lean forward. I do pushing the flashlight out of the way. A narrow hole allows me to belly up by pulling myself upward over a boulder into an area where I can get myself a foot hold. It's an obstacle course but a slip here didn't seem as dangerous as most. Another squeeze past some rocks and a few bends gets me to a spot where there is a hole for head and shoulders only. This time I have to pull myself up at armpit length. It's an effort. Val is behind me. It is almost impossible for her to rotate and she has problems getting a grip. Besides, she is shorter and can't get leverage. I maneuver to give her a hand but I am off to the side and she can't make it. Rob angles past me in a crouch as there is no head room and half straddles over her. We both grasp her and pull. The female anatomy makes this a tight squeeze. With this boost she can get her leg up enough to pull through. We hear the other party returning below us but they are emerging up a different chimney. Suddenly we see light and Rob is heard talking to Elaine. He has scaled a fifteen foot incline just off vertical with some places for a foothold albeit they are pretty well polished. There is a few moments delay while the rope is lowered to us. With the rope to help this is a fairly straightforward ascent and there is daylight. However just to give a final touch of excitement there is a rock which had to be passed under on m belly. It was also narrow enough that I could not get but one arm ahead of me. I was glad for the rope since it was now a good fall if I slipped. Once past this rock I had to make a sudden right turn and haul myself still on my belly over a small boulder. Rob gives me a hand and I found I was emerging from the same hole we started down only we went toward the right and not the left side. The exit seemed shorter and less tortuous than the entrance. I had this queer notion that it was like being born out of the earth.

After a few moments the others began to emerge and we took their pictures. It was quite a view, something remarkable, as each one emerged like gophers popping their heads up. Safely too!

We sat around having some welcome water and a few dates. We estimated that we had traveled for over an hour and covered perhaps half a kilometer. I had a feeling of great relief and also some pride in myself. I can completely understand why a lot of people would not do this and why some people could thrive on it. We had wormed our way through some risky places and with no problems but one slip could have altered that.

We scrambled out of the cave and descended to the vehicles some distance away. Here we rested under an acacia that offered some scant shade. We had a picnic before heading home past Al Hamra and some traditional villages with palm trees and gardens and a kid holding a string with the end tied to the tail of a live rat which was squirming to get free.

Later in the day we went to a Christmas Eve service in the home of the new minister. Afterwards some of us went out for a Christmas eve Indian style supper and the photos are passed about of the days caving.

We have a book of caves of Oman. Another cave is the second biggest in the world. I wonder what it is like!

The commercialization of the cave has now taken place.

Here is a quote from a tour guide for Al Hoti cave now known as Al Hoota:

"The guided tour takes visitors along pathways illuminated by a special lighting system during which themed music is played. Stalactites, stalagmites, rimstones and other crystals which garnish the walls, ceiling and cave floor are evidence of the pluvial era. Visitors will also witness the presence of a rare phenomenon, blind transparent fish 'garra bareimiae' which exist in the underground lake and are nourished by organic materials brought by floods inside the cave.

Al-Hoota show-cave is outfitted with a standard of tourist facilities including a visitor center, natural history museum, restaurants, children's area and heritage shops. The cave is accessed by the only train in Oman."

Would we have enjoyed it as much now?

Christmas 1998

There is relatively little interest or even acceptance of Christmas in these parts. However Muscat has a larger expatriate community and we are able to enter another world if we choose when we go there. One such time was a weekend when we decided to do some Christmas shopping. Muscat in December is a lovely place. The main highway is lined with lawn, flower beds, huge decorative items such as urns full of petunias, colorful bushes and lots and lots of bougainvillia with its pink, red, and white flowers. Surely it is the most impressive stretch of road I have ever seen. The Niagara Parkway looks shabby in comparison.
We spend the evening in the shops, some of which are well known, J.C. Penny, Mexx, Hang Ten and then we have supper at Fuddruckers with a big hamburger and fries. Certainly a step up from the Pizza Hut, Burger King and McDonalds but not as up

scale as the Pavo Real Mexican restaurant.

In a department store I see two young Omani men perhaps 18 and I am guessing they are students at some college. They are standing at the Christmas card display attempting to buy a card for someone, perhaps a western teacher. I eavesdrop on their conversation for a few moments and indeed they are interested in a "Merry Christmas Teacher" card. It's ok to do this because Jesus and Mary are part of their religion also.

The next morning we are out to complete our shopping and buy some Christmas cassette tapes which are featured in music stores. This year not many Christmas decorations are out as Ramadan starts just before Christmas but the malls do play some Christmas music. We visit a couple of nice art gallery shops before closure at 1 p.m. for the afternoon.

There is a Christmas craft show at PDO (Petroleum Development of Oman) recreation center. We drive to that area of the city. Here the employees of PDO, mostly British and Dutch, have their company houses. This area is the only place in the country where I have seen normal sloped roofs on the houses. Every garage has a four wheel drive vehicle and a car. Foundation plantings and patios make the homes appealing. We are on a high ridge and many homes have a great sea and also a city view. This could be California. The local FM English radio plays in the background.
 Along the high crest of the ridge we see the golf course. It is all brown and barren except around the tee off and the "green" where there is darker brown soil or sand that is all even and raked. The players take their own chunk of Astro turf with them. It is a grassless course. The astro turf is used when teeing off to reduce dust.

The sea is a wonderful blue out past the oil processing towers. A couple of oil freighters are in the distance. We descend to the beach and past the school and we come to the PDO club area. We wait in the dining area by the pool for the show to open.

The grand opening features Santa and a helper behind a brass Ompah band belting out carols. Santa and the helper are each riding a camel. It sets a nice tone. There is a mixture of booths selling crafts. Some booths are staffed with people with Indian accents, some with Dutch, some with British and some with American.

There are many crafts including newly published works on Oman, special Omani crewel kits, Indian Christmas merchandise, lacquered paper mache balls and brightly colored balls for the tree. There are mince meat pies, short bread cookies and Indian chick pea Chat to snack on. The band plays Christmas tunes and are interrupted with lottery draws. We adjourn for tea and a tart.

Later in the day we go to the church at Gahla, one of two Christian church compounds in the city. This land was donated by the Sultan for Christians. There are a catholic church and a protestant church. There is a new church hall attached to the protestant church which is used by the orthodox and a couple of other denominations. The catholic church has a pipe organ, one of the few in the middle east and also a gift from the Sultan. We came to the new hall to hear the Muscat Singers present their Christmas carol concert. It resembles any western country new church hall.

The crowd is modest and we recognize several folks from Muscat and Nizwa. We also know two of the 35 singers. They are all in white and black clothes accented with Christmas ribbons. The choir is mostly white westerners. There is a mixed white and Indian audience. The carols are as familiar and comfortable as any back home. We feel at home.

An elderly lady rises to do "Christmas 1955." Her reading is politely received and I later learn more of its significance. The lady is Elaine Bosch who came to teach in Muscat with her missionary doctor husband in 1955. Now retired they spend their winters at a home next to the Al Bustan hotel. The home was given to them by the Sultan. This American lady has me in awe. They are THE pioneers in this land and she taught in one of the first three schools in the entire country. They are clearly favorites of the ruler. I am not certain but I think she was his teacher and her husband was the royal family doctor. What I do know is that they are the only western people who have their own cottage given by the Sultan.

After the carols we go into the cooling night air only to discover that next door in the church hall a Pentecostal Indian church service is in progress. I peek in an open window to hear the rhythmic clapping and singing of a pleasant but unfamiliar hymn. Ladies in saris sit on one side on the floor while the men sit on the other. We walk away. Churches in Arab lands are not unheard of but in this case the property was donated by the Arabic ruler specifically for Christians.

The next morning Friday (read Sunday) we head to our favorite shopping mall where the supermarket is open until 11:30 a.m. It is a lovely little mall with a beach side location. Fresh baked bread, raw broccoli, Australian beef, peaches from South Africa and a 15 pound Butterball turkey for 36 dollars can be bought here.

Afterward we go and sit by the beach where we watch some white skinhead males who are racing about on the sea in rented Sea Doos. We wander to the Oasis by the Sea restaurant and enjoy the Friday brunch which we take onto the seaside patio. I can think of no place in Canada or Florida that has quite the same ambience. We are on vacation at an elegant resort.

It is two hours to Nizwa along the base of the mountains. Two hours of dramatic views lay ahead as we leave the city and the pampered life of the urban expat. One can almost dwell oblivious of the culture and remain in their own little world. People remark with some surprise that I actually can speak some Arabic. But then we live in Nizwa where the passing tourists outnumber the expats many times over. And that's just it. Nizwa is Arabic, sounds and feels it. Now after two years it feels like home.

Now we have a plastic Christmas tree not just a string of lights formed like a tree that Erin and Jonathan rigged up our first Christmas here. The tree was decorated extra early so we can enjoy it longer. The tree was bought in Muscat with coupons we collected by shopping at the store. We will have a Christmas social event at our house next week and sing some carols and have a punch bowl. In this little corner of the world we shall celebrate Christmas. Soon Erin will arrive, our daughter unseen for a year while our son remains in Canada. Our first Christmas without all of us together. Under the stars flanked by the great mountain, the frankincense in the air, the goat herd and shepherd passing the door, it will still be Christmas. Christmas in Nizwa.

A View of Indian Culture

Sometimes life out here ricochets from one culture to another. A recent evening serves as an illustration.

About five one afternoon, after messing with an unco-operative shower diverter, I decided to go find a plumber.

I pulled into the front of a shop bearing the significant title " Sanitary and Electrical Supplies". This shop is about as close as one gets to a hardware store around here. The Omani owner welcomed me in English and I trotted out my arabic greetings. The Indian clerk said "Hello." As I was a new customer and as there were dates on the desk, the proprietor urged me to taste his dates and hauled out his plastic thermos of Omani Kawa. The coffee is great after a couple of extra sweet dates. After I take my second cup to observe the correct protocol of the event, I placed my hand over the cup and with a rotating motion state that I have had enough.

Now that we have shared food and drink together, I can be assured that I will be treated as a friend and a new valued customer. The Indian clerk helps me find a couple of parts and I add in some extra things I really didn't need just to demonstrate my pleasure at being able to shop here.

I inquire about the plumber who, I am previously advised, is quite capable. Instructions are provided and I set off to find him. His quarters are across a lane and around the back. Under a large water tank is a passageway entered by a door. Along the passage are several doors made of plywood sheets in a wall partly made of cement blocks and partly 2x4 studs and sheeting. The roof is corrugated fibreglass or some such thing. It is subsistence living at its finest.

I knock on a plywood door outside of which are sandals. A man wrapped in a Indian garment around his waist answers and I state my purpose. He agrees to come and asks me in while he gets ready.

His quarters consist of a room with a partial partition wall past which is a kitchen and washing area. One wall is cinder block, the other 3 are 4 x 8 sheets nailed to 2x4's. It reminds me of a summer camp cabin. There is an electric clock and a couple of calendars in Hindi on the wall. Clothes hang on nails and there is a wall cabinet of wood with a nice brass key lock. There are a couple of small shelves and the bed on which I am sitting. The bed is makeshift plywood covered with, at best, a two inch pad. I think it would be most uncomfortable. There is a ceiling fan and a florescent tube light attached to the cross beams that hold up the exposed roof. I think it could be pretty hot in summer especially as there was no window. A rather dirty carpet is on the grey cement floor. Nothing is painted. A portable radio tuned to BBC Hindi programming plays softly in a corner.

My plumber has apparently just had a shower as his back is wet. He invites me to sit and then turns to face a brown painted box about 18 inches by 18 inches that hangs on the wall. The top has what looks like Hindi writing carved out and this addition to the box forms a peaked roof like a false front. A red curtain on a small rod has been pulled aside to show the interior of the box. There are a number of pictures of faces and two photos. One is in a frame and one is of a small child. They are glued like the pictures of the faces to the front and sides and back and also top of the box in random fashion. There are also 5 small pictures all in a row. A tiny brass bell hangs from the peak of the frame. Also there is a bottle with a candle and a small dish and some other things I didn't get to see. A very dim red electric bulb, one of the decorative flame shaped types, is attached inside the box behind the bell.

Facing this, oblivious of me, he takes the dish and puts in some water and perhaps something else and goes about the room flicking drops of this onto the walls and in the direction of his clothes . He returns to face the box and quickly touches or passes his hands over each of the images and then quickly back to himself several times. Next he takes what appears to be a small bit of cloth and holds it to his face under his nose and then briefly holds it to his forehead and side of his face. I believe he is saying a prayer at this time.

This done he lights the candle and touches all the pictures again including the inside of the box and also touches the bell. He touches or gestures to himself as he does this. Next he lights two incense sticks from the candle and passes them in a circular motion before each picture. He waves the incense ceremonially to each of the walls and over his clothes and also he opens the door and makes a circular motion with the incense in the doorway.

After completing these actions, he returns to stand before the box and again quickly passes his hands over the pictures before snuffing out the candle. The incense stick is left burning inside the box and he again goes through the picture ritual before pulling the curtain closed.

In the next room of the building another fellow is washing up a rather large pot and some utensils in a tiny sink. My plumber hurriedly dresses. The dishwasher looks at my plumber and says "Hindi, Hindi." I inquire about the pictures. Shiva I recognize but the other names are not familiar to me.

We leave his shrine, his radio, his clothes and his very humble quarters so he can fix my plumbing. My place is a palace. He quickly fixes the diverter problem. Afterward we negotiate a price and he declines a ride home as he is off to the cinema. Nizwa has a cinema that shows only Indian films.

My neighbor, Catchetan Fernandes, invites us over as it is the feast day of St. Francis of Goa. They have been decorating and preparing all day. About 9 p.m. we cross to their house. He has been 26 years in Nizwa and is head of public health. Home is Goa, a former Portuguese enclave in India. St. Francis is highly revered amongst Goans and is their patron saint. After several centuries of Portuguese rule many Goans are Catholics.

Eventually about 20 Indians, mostly men, of Goan background arrive including our supposedly Muslim houseboy who comes to clean once each week. We enter a room which has been set up with pictures of the virgin Mary and a crucifix and in a place of honor flanked by candles and plastic flowers is a picture of St. Francis. Frankincense has been wafted about the room and one lady tells Donna that the room is now holy.

We commence a rather lengthy recitation in latin which we read from the sheets provided. My Muslim houseboy joins right in and what is more actually knows all this as he is right in tune. Well, he is from Goa. Another guest recites from memory a number of special verses which the others responsively interject. Finally we have a prayer and Maria, our hostess, kneels in prayer before a picture of the Virgin. We do another song from the paper and adjourn. I've not been to a mass like this one before, or was it?

Beer and drinks are provided. Traditional warm chick peas are served and a spicy fish cake, also traditional, are passed about. After sitting around rather awkwardly and engaging in some chit chat about life in Canada and who is applying to go there and who has an uncle there, some Goan music is played. It sounds very much like polka party time. After a bit some decide to try their hand at singing some Goan folk songs and everyone is getting melancholy for the homeland. Everybody out here gets home leave but for the Indians it can be once every two years and often wives and kids are there, not in Oman.

Finally it is nearly midnight and we all head for the dining room table with its assortment of salads and Indian dishes. The party continues long after we leave. We are the only none Goan folks there. We are just good neighbors and friends.

The nearest white family are New Zealanders a mile down the road. There are nine white women and perhaps a couple of dozen white men surrounded by Indian, Pakistani, other Arab nationals and Omanis. We are the minority in every way possible. After two years it takes a day like this to remind us.

One's Persona

There exists a certain set of standards that define a person out here. Foremost is whether I am known as mister or doctor or whatever. I am not the one to choose the form. It is done for me. So I travel about in spite of my remonstrances to the contrary as Mr. John. Although a few Omani will call me John, since they appear used to the notion of a name without a prefix. Indians and Egyptians however call me doctor or mister even after my disclaimer to both titles. It is absolutely inconceivable to my Egyptian staff that I, their boss, does not have a PhD so I can be called doctor. They believe it is my modesty that I do not wish to be called doctor but they do so anyway.

The arrival at this or that counter where I have to fill in a form or provide details is another jolt to my self identity. A pleasant clerk, usually Indian, will ask " What is your good name?" I am still not sure just what is implied and what gets recorded may be contrary to my expectations. So I receive a form noted to Mr McBride or Mr. John and with luck Mr. Eacott. After my good name we now have to contend with other classifications. "What is your tribal name?" or " What is your father's name." Clearly in Arabic I would become John bin John bin Charles.

Tribal names don't seem to be used a great deal. I think it is because around a given place the vast majority come from the same tribe. Up on Jebal Akhdar for example everyone is Bani Ryami tribe. This name, which is the proper final name, is usually dropped so ones middle name is apt to be the last name in common practice.

Children take their father's name. Wives, however, do not change their names on marriage. Women's names are seemingly more varied and frequently are identified with nature and beauty such as Jasmine or Fatima or names meaning a flower, moon, thunderstorm or gentle rain.

The clerk carefully enters my name to satisfaction. He is unemotional. I am pleased it is right. Progress has been made. Now the next line is address. Oh, Oh!!!

Having now identified myself, the question of where I live becomes a problem. For convenience I give my place of work. I know I live in Al Maddah but that is a small district in Nizwa that only a local person would know. Anyway, who else would care. There are no street names or numbers in Nizwa. Behind the police station, three streets, next to the "poultry" sales and across from ...oh well, look for my car. I get the feeling that if you live here you can be easily found. If you don't, then it is an excuse to talk with a stranger. Recently they gave the streets in Muscat identities and the houses numbers. Someday Nizwa will have "Way 2341 house 29."

An Indian arrives at the door bearing a western toilet. We have not ordered a new toilet. He had been sent here because everyone knew a westerner lived here. The toilet was for the Fisks who lived another half mile along the road. He is directed to the bakery next to the restaurant and go behind there and ask. Are there other bakeries next to restaurants on the road? We don't know. It does not matter as he will find them.

First names, as one does not use the term Christian name for obvious reasons, are more limited in range than in western society. Mohammed is the runaway male front runner followed by Ahmed which seems to me to be the same name. Issac, Joseph, Abraham, Solomon or Abdullah in their Arabic form are also popular. The problem is further complicated with the commonality of family names. Just who is the staff member known as Mohammed Ismail? I get a blank look when I ask to see him.

"Yes, I want to speak with him."

"I don't know him."

"He is in the science department."

"You mean Hamid?"

"I don't know Hamid. I only know the biologist is Dr. Mohammed Ismail."

"Oh no, his name is Dr. Abdel Hamid."

"Isn't he Mohammed Ismail?"

"Yes, same person! Dr.Abdel Hamid Mohammed Ismail."

Name spellings are also a major problem. My self created staff list is phonetic. Arabic is phonetic. Nobody seems to mind if the name is Salim, Salem, Sahlem or Sallum. Whatever suits is usually acceptable. So one just rolls with the situation and when Mohammed Abdula sends a note I have to decide from the context if it is Mohamad Abdullah or not.

Come to think of it, perhaps being asked what "my good name is" is not as crazy as it first sounds.

Camel Races

The sign on the door of the Nizwa Pizza Hut said in two languages:

"Public Invitation...To All Camel Racing Fans, Invitation to all who wish to enjoy a pleasant day with this sport. The organizing committee of the great annual Camel Racing in the Interior Region is pleased to invite you for the racing activities, on Thursday 11th February 1999 at 8:30 a.m. at the Al Bashayir Race Course, Adam."

We saw this notice on our way home from the races after it was all over. It was a nice professionally done sign. Nobody from Nizwa would have known about the races except that we had some previous experience in our group about these things. The Nizwa folks and a few German tourists loaded with fancy cameras seemed to be the only western people at the races that day. The vast majority of the sizeable crowd of a few thousand were either Omani or Emirate Nationals.

The journey south of Nizwa towards Adam is on a modern blacktop road and at a blue and white sign stating "Camel Race Track" a left turn is made onto a gravel road. Across a perfectly flat sand and gravel expanse we follow, for some distance, the dust cloud of arriving vehicles.

The parking is a jumble of pickup trucks, four wheel drive vehicles and a few cars. Camels in small groups are being led majestically and serenely through this jumble to their staging area.

The crowds head toward where ever. Some go to the covered grandstand where the VIP seats are still empty. Under a huge canopy sit women in their black abayas and along the fences are crowds of dishdasha clad men. Many are in full dress with their bamboo canes and fine silver kanjars. A few sport bandoliers complete with 303 shells. Across from the stands are several marquee tents. The pipe band in their white uniforms and green plaid tartans are waiting their turn to play. Teenage girls in bright green and gold native garb are sitting off to one side and are presumably there for dancing but we never actually see them dance.

Several groups of men are engaged in tribal dancing and singing. Some raise their long swords and make them vibrate with a deft wrist flick. I have tried this several times and have not yet mastered the trick. Others have rhinoceros horn shields and a few carry posters of the Sultan. A leader equipped with a megaphone leads the group in their demonstrations. Cameras are all out to capture the moment.

We wander off to the starting area. The first races are 6 km long and start nearby. Later races will start at the 2 or 3 km point way off in the distance. Camels are kneeling in groups with brightly colored blankets and knitted muzzles over their noses. Little boys of three to five years old in satin jockey outfits and protective jockey helmets are waving their spurring whips and want their pictures taken. These little guys face a very risky future. Shortly they will be strapped, hopefully securely, to the backs of these animals and with any luck will complete the ride. There is a reasonable crowd here and a few pickup trucks and 4 wheel drive vehicles are parked on either side of the rails which help to keep the camels on the track. They are waiting to go.

The dances continue and finally the official party arrives. We assume it is the local wali (governor) and perhaps some members of the royal family. The national anthem does little to settle the crowd down. Quran readings and a poem and welcome (Marhaba) speeches are given. The political side completed the crowd prepares for the races.

There are several categories, much like horse racing, according to our racing fan John Murray. Two year old animals will feature in one race. The finish line is marked with chalk and a good crowd mills about here. We head back to the starting area. A good crowd is here also and many more pickup trucks. The back of trucks are loaded with standing men wearing turbans, red and white Arab head dresses and Omani caps. A few men have rifles. Everyone is finding a secure hand hold. A couple of trucks have TV crews and a specially marked vehicle seems to be in the place of honor right beside the track. I take it to be the official race vehicle.

The crowd leans forward over the rails. A long rope holds back some twenty-five camels with tiny riders. Interspersed are a few camels with adult males on them. I take it these are to see that riders and their camels get off to a good start. Each camel has a man in front holding onto restraining ropes. The long green rope falls, the anchor men scramble out of the way and the camels head off down the track. The pickup trucks rev their engines behind us and roar into motion. The camels lope past in a mass swaying and zigging, more or less, up the track. The trucks are off blaring their horns and jockeying for position. The people in the back are yelling and screaming. Guns bark. The little jockeys are whipping their beasts. There is dust, lots of dust. All are off into a huge cloud of dust. The lead vehicles vanish into the fog of dust. The last vehicles fade away. The camels are up there someplace in the middle of all this. The dust clears. The pedestrian crowd wanders off toward the finish area.

At a leisurely pace a red crescent ambulance heads down the track behind the camels as it avoids a returning camel. A camel with a small blue uniformed rider has gotten turned around and is racing back to the starting post. The kid is whipping the animal to no avail. Trainers rush out waving their arms in an effort to get the camel to turn around. The camel comes to a halt, contemplates the situation and then the solitary beast wheels off in a stroll towards the finish line. Camels are not race horses and without noise to prompt them there seemed no rush. Rider and beast slowly diminish in the distance. The race track is a seven kilometer oval.

After this start we walk back to the finish area. The band is playing. The public address is belching announcements. Everyone is standing around keeping an eye on the dust in the distance. There is lots of time to chat.

There is no betting on these races but there are good prizes. Government or private funds sponsor the races. This day the guest of honor is the cousin of the Sultan and the prizes are a car for first (they didn't look like new cars), 100 rials for second and less for third. The objective is to promote better breeding. Winning animals can be sold for handsome prices of up to 20, 000 rials. Many of the attendees are either Omani Bedu here to sell or wealthy Emerati citizens here to buy.

The dust cloud is getting closer. A man on a pacer camel goes past. Sounds in the distance get louder. The noise encourages the camels to run. A running camel takes a good size step but it doesn't look especially fast. It looks more like a semi urgent plod. Still they cover a lot of ground in a race and work up a good froth doing it.

The final approach nears. Several dozen pickup trucks loaded with yelling Arabs are heading twenty abreast right towards us - horns blaring, guns firing, zigging and zagging to avoid collision. A dust pillar hundreds of feet in the air accompanies them. This is a big screen movie event. The desert in motion. Oh, and out on the track there are some camels with little riders who are flogging for all they are worth. Whips tapping one flank and then the other, the camels lope on at 30 km toward the finish. The trucks thankfully all veer away before they get to an earth berm that shelters us. Behind the leaders, a little kid securely strapped on has lost his grip and bounces upside down on his side against the camel's flank. He must be terrorized if not injured. His helmet is still secure. More camels with their riders urging them to the finish appear through the dust. One camel decides to stop and head away from the crowd. A man climbs under the fence and urges the camel to head forward. The animal chases him back under the fence but heads off to the finish line. Winners are declared. One by one the stragglers come in. The trucks have ground to a halt.

Ominously, a riderless camel wanders by. The rider has been lost somewhere along the route. The ambulance comes in last but without any evidence of problems.

The three winning camels are paraded past the small grandstand and led into the grounds inside the track where a vet wielding a giant syringe drains off a bit of blood for a doping test. Camel racing is big business and nobody wants to take chances. When I see the frothing camel being led off, I think the animal has a problem and the syringe I think is an injection of some sort. Only after I speak to the veterinarian do I understand about the doping test.

The dancers come out and continue their demonstrations of folk art. A boy of about fourteen walks past with his face a mask of dust and his turban flapping over his shoulder. He is looking for water to wash his face. He has just come from the back of a pick up bearing Dubai licence plates.

The next race of the six or eight held that day is readied. We watch four of the races, each the same spectacle of men, boys, trucks and camels engaged in the most participatory demonstration of reckless fan encouragement I have ever seen. The sight of these trucks racing along the track toward us is truly a spectacle. It has the feel and sound and look of an invasion approaching.

A student of the college, who I only know as Mohammed, a Bedu from Mudhaibi, tells me with some pride his camel came in 2nd in the 7th race, a three kilometer event with a prize of 100 rials. On this day three firsts went to Mudhaibi camels, two from another village, 1 from Adam and 1 from the Emirates.

Camel races are held around the country and are an important part of the life of the Bedu who raise them. The animals are a curious sight whether browsing, running or as we often saw, riding around in the back of a pick up truck. Seeing camels sitting with their knees under them in the back of a pickup truck while they contentedly chew their cuds and enjoy the ride was a fairly common sight. The races are an Arab tradition and our presence in the cultural blend was minute. Tourists would love this but we were glad there were few of us. We learned that in the Emirates non citizens until recently were not allowed to attend the races. The sun was getting hotter and as there was no food, no drinks and no toilets, we decided we had enough. After a couple of hours of sun and dust we were ready for lunch at the Pizza Hut in Nizwa .

Gardening

Parts of Oman are suitable for agriculture. The coastal areas have limited farming. There are some dairy cows and crops. In the interior there are dates, goats and small market gardens.

The vegetable souk in Nizwa is a large airy building with entrances all over it. The fish souk is next door and beyond that the meat souk. Counters are laden with fresh produce and much of it is local. There are clumps of cilantro and bins of carrots and tomatoes. The tomatoes tend to be small and tough skinned. They usually had a white film on them. Perhaps this film is a salt residue from the watering. Onion, garlic and most other common fruits and vegetables were for sale.

A couple of blocks from our house I discovered two plastic greenhouses. I was under the impression that greenhouses were built to keep out frost. That was not the case here. These two green houses had been set up by a young Omani fellow who was growing arabic cucumbers. These cucumbers are short and smooth and not very big around. They are the Amira variety sometimes grown in my garden.

He explained that the humidity was too low for the plants to set good fruit. The green houses had a huge fan at one end and curtains of wet fabric at the other end. The fans drew the air through the wet fabric and sucked it out the fan end. The evaporating water helped raise the humidity and lower the temperature. The exact opposite of growing plants in a greenhouse in Canada. He had strands of great looking cucumbers hanging in racks. I bought a bag full.

Most of the gardening was not so high tech. The local folks had plots of vegetables which were grown in square sections about ten feet by ten feet. A small berm went around each of these little squares. The idea was to flood the plot with water from time to time and the berm held the water long enough for it to soak in.

Sometimes, where there was a falag, water from the little canal was diverted to flood the berm. Out in the open country water came from wells or was trucked.

Up in the mountains there were some marvelous tiers of irrigated land. Row after row of carefully created paddies, some only a couple of feet wide, clung to cliff sides. Everything from roses to garlic grew in these irrigated slopes. Rounding a corner and seeing these ancient earthworks, lush and green against the barren rocks descending from the village on the high ground above, is a stunning sight. The water from the mountain rains and gravity from a stream arising yet higher in the mountain maintains these marvels of tenacious agriculture where only goats would be able to scramble over barren rocks had men not crafted these tiers.

As for my own garden it was a strip just inside the walls. We planted a couple of trees outside the gate. The petunias, bougainvillia and other plants thrived. Tomatoes and beans did okay but sweet corn just could not make it. The soil had very little if any humus and was likely quite alkaline which made some plants happy but others not.

Over many centuries these patches of garden land have kept these folks alive in an otherwise harsh and inhospitable land.

Our Social Group

When we arrived in Nizwa, it took Donna several months to meet another western women in the town. Dorothy Young was the British wife of the head of the English department at the Technical College. They had come from Papua New where the living was much more hazardous. They told the story of coming home one night to find their houseboy's decapitated body in the pool. At one time we had considered taking a post there ourselves and were advised one should not take a teenage daughter to such a place.

Gradually over the three years other couples came to live in Nizwa and we formed a congenial social group. This in no way discounted from the social contacts we had with the other ECS people in Oman or the Indian and Omani friends we made or the faculty community based on the college.

The social group flexed in size and composition and represented British, New Zealanders, Irish, Americans, Canadians and others.

Robert Fisk came to the college to teach English. He replaced Major Richard Morse who had returned to England but later came back partly at my request. Rob and Elaine had a home down the road from us. It was two story and featured a barren gravel courtyard. In one corner of the courtyard a tiny sprout emerged over a drain of some sort. Soon it was 3 feet tall. Watching it grow was amazing. Some days it grew 6 to 8 inches. In six months it was towering over us affording decent shade.

We sat sharing supper on the roof of the house one night. The surrounding hills and mountains were visible in the light of a rising full moon. Someone noted that there seemed to be a cloud near the moon. Normally there were no clouds. This cloud drew our attention even more when it was noted that it had a distinct funnel shape. One that I identified as a tornado. This whirling apparition hung suspended in space for some time as it worked its silent way across the sky.

We resumed our meal which was one we had picked up at the take out restaurant. First though we had gone to the bakery where the bread was made by tossing the dough as if to make a pizza and then the dough was thrown through the oven door onto the dome of the oven where it stuck. The oven was a large clay mud affair with a bed of coals that heated the dome. Several throws of dough were stuck to the ceiling where it took only a few minutes for the bread to cook. When it was ready, it started to fall away and a large paddle was shoved in to catch the freshly made arabic pita.

Next door the restaurant had a rotisserie of chickens turning on spits beside the front door. They were all buttered, glistening and glowing golden, ready to wrap and take home. Inside the kitchen had large pots of various items steaming like stews on a stove. Rice was waiting in huge pans and a mixed salad was scooped from a large bowl. We selected what we wanted after making inquiries as to the contents of the pots. Dinner was wrapped in cardboard boxes and aluminum foil. The fresh baked bread served as our scoop for the Indian curries that accompanied the roast chicken.

❧

Our group put on some elegant parties. We dressed in costume for a medieval theme supper held on a rooftop decorated for the event. The lords and ladies had tarot card readings and we brought our literary compositions for the maids and knights present.

The Phantom of the Opera dinner was a formal dress event Everyone wore jackets, ties and gowns. The white table cloth had a candelabra and copies of a formal program were laid beside our formal seating name tag. The sound of the full opera was played between courses of the meal.

We dressed Omani style for the Arabian nights party. In the courtyard there was a tent with carpets and here a skit based on a story from the "Thousand and One Nights" was presented to us to act out. This was a totally made up slapstick event and the only time I drove around town dressed in an Omani outfit.

It was believed that dressing as an Omani was frowned upon. When an Omani guy arrived at the airport from abroad, he wore jeans and shirts. The girls also arrived in western clothes. The only other time an Omani wore anything but national clothing or uniforms was when they were playing sports. My Omani secretaries always wore a turban at work. Outside of work they wore an embroidered cap. When I saw some playing at a soccer game, I did not recognize any of them without their headgear.

Our group had parties and dinners for all sorts of other special events. A British Christmas party complete with ham and a Harrod's plum pudding included a singsong of British music hall songs.

As a diverse group of expatriates from the English speaking world, we had a lot of great camaraderie and fun teasing each other about the specialty words that kept sneaking into conversations. Hydro from Canada for electricity, spanner for wrench with the Brits but what really set us off were the different meanings in our cultures. Donna and I were curled up laughing when we were told that our friends would come round and "knock us up".

At most we were 7 couples. The ladies would go to the Falag Daris Hotel for a swim, go on sightseeing expeditions or meet at a home to watch a movie. This was a huge change for Donna who spent our first few months thinking she was the only western woman in Nizwa. We felt so isolated that when one day we met a British couple from Muscat shopping at the Al Reef store, we invited them home for supper. Complete strangers they were but they were white westerners. Somebody like us. Neither of us thought it odd to bring a passing shopper home for dinner.

Our best friends from those days were Mike and Rosette. Mike from the USA was teaching economics at SQU (Sultan Quaboos University) in Muscat. We met on the beach at Salalah and became good friends. SQU was a far different type of school than Nizwa College of Education. The faculty was heavily English speaking and classes were in English. The selection system for students in Oman was done by the state. If a student spoke good English and had top grades, then they got to go to SQU. To maintain half girls and half boys the girls grades had to be far higher than the boys else there would be few males. The students at my college were the rejects from SQU. They could become teachers or not go to school. Another group was sent to technical schools. There was not much choice there either although some sort of aptitude test was given to help sort them into their assigned future. Thus a student who was to become an X ray technician was assigned that career based on an aptitude test and not particularly because he had an interest in the career.

The working conditions at SQU were far better than what our college and the technical college staff had. On the other hand they lived a far more normal life than what we had in Nizwa. In Nizwa we learned to make our own fun and we were using our free time to endlessly explore our environment. Sometimes it was a local trip hiking up one of the magnificent canyons to picnic and swim in a secluded pool or it was the exploration of the ruins of a nearby town it was or heading out for a weekend of off roading.

Robert has been looking at a road shown on a map west of town. It is visible from the highway as it twists incredibly back and forth up the side of the jebel rock face. We each have a four wheel so we can back each other up if there is a problem. A few minutes driving gets us in to some high level views over the countryside. The trail crosses mostly barren rock with virtually no vegetation. We climb higher and soon take a bend that obscures the highway miles below. I spot an object and stop to examine it. It is a ball of woven plant material like binder twine with a stem. It is a light tan and has almost no weight yet is a good handful. It's identity is a mystery. When I took it back to the college, no one could identify it. My assumption was it was intended to be an incendiary device. Soaked in fuel, the stem ignited and thrown, it would be effective. Since there had been no conflict in the area since the 1950 wars, I wondered if it had survived on this dry barren mountain side for all this time.

We continued on with no idea where the road was going. We came to a solitary home and animal coral. The owner was sitting on a decent size pile of goat pellet dung. He had some burlap bags and was shoveling the pellets into the bag by hand. We thought it would be great fertilizer for our gardens. He was bagging the dung for just such a purpose. It would be taken to market and sold. We each bought a bag. Robert had parked closer than I had and said he would put the dung into his vehicle. Goat dung is very pungent. The smell lingers and lingers.

The goat farmer had a pen for his animals. They returned there after a day of wandering the mountainside. Just what they found to eat was a mystery. You could walk hundreds of feet across solid rock to find a six inch twig in a tiny crevice.

His children stood behind their colorfully dressed mother. Not many customers came this way, especially foreign strangers. The rock home had a tin roof, an open doorway and a window. There could not have been any well in this location. He must have had his water hauled to his hovel. This was one tough solitary existence. However the views were spectacular.

We parted with our treasures and stopped at a gas bar at the highway for some drinks. Robert and Elaine were perfumed with goat. When they opened their doors, the smell caused other customers to look oddly towards them. It took some time to rid the vehicle of the smell of goat.

Almost across from the college was the entrance to a large canyon. A fine gravel road led off the highway and the wadi bed was flat and sandy with a few boulders here and there. After a time hiking there with our friends Val and John, we passed a small village with a well and some garden plots. A little further along the canyon narrowed and the ruins of an abandoned community clung to the bottom of the cliff. Now the canyon walls were rising vertically for hundreds of feet on either side of us. We found a place to park and note that it is 110f. It was pleasant as the canyon created a steady breeze to keep us cool. We carried our water and lunch and headed up from the valley floor. While it was to difficult to drive, it was easy walking. We came to a small stream which was ending near where we parked the cars. The water trickled into the gravel. The stream came down the hill and simply vanished at our feet like it was entering a sewer only it was just gravelly ground. It seemed mysterious. We now followed the stream which oddly kept getting larger as we went upstream. In such terrain it is necessary to be watchful for vipers and scorpions. The heat probably had driven them well away from these hot rocks. There was the odd large bird soaring above but otherwise there was just us wandering between spectacular soaring canyon walls, polished rocks and the odd scrubby bush.

We found a nice ledge for our lunch and not long after discovered a lovely pool of water sheltered under some huge boulders. It was wading depth and big enough so we could float on our backs and gaze up at the huge boulder wedged above to form our roof. We did all of this fully clothed because once we got out, the wet clothes would cool us. We ascended the ravine a little more to a higher point but the rock debris became too difficult to clamber over so we headed back down for another swim as our clothes had completely dried in the interim. It was odd going down since the lovely stream which flowed so abundantly above the pool gradually became a trickle and again vanished at our feet. By that time we again were all dried out and ready for the short ride home.

From rocky slopes affording vistas of distant scapes to skyscraper canyons, our world was a many faceted place happily shared with interesting adventurous friends.

Omanization

Oman has a small but rapidly growing population. With the discovery of oil the country began to modernize. The native population had none of the skills needed to carry out the development. The first literate generation was just coming of age. There was abundant work but no young Omani people were trained sufficiently. Now there were a lot of unemployed young people. It was decided that various segments of the economy would be manned by Omanis and not by foreign nationals, mostly Indian. One of these projects was the Omanization of the propane delivery. When it was announced, the sales of propane cylinders jumped dramatically. People were buying a spare. Since nearly everyone cooked with propane stoves, the business of propane delivery was important. It was customary to call the distributor when the old tank ran dry. A replacement tank would be promptly delivered. With Omanization it was feared that a reliable service would not take place.

Apparently the water delivery system had recently been Omanized as well. Everyone had a galvanized roof top tank that held a supply expected to last some days, typically a week. The water might be scheduled for your house every Tuesday. The tanker came and pumped water to fill the galvanized cistern tank on the roof. Every homeowner with a cistern had to learn how to ration their water use. Water trucks were blue. Septic tank clean out trucks were green. If you ran out of water before Tuesday you might get a truck to deliver off schedule or not. But if your Tuesday driver stayed home, you simply had no water until somebody got around to filling your tank. Every so often someone would tell us they had washed too many clothes or taken an extra shower and now had an empty tank. It was important also to verify the truck delivering water was blue and not green. Fortunately, although we had a cistern, we were part of the minority who were also on city mains. The city water went to the cistern and from there we had gravity fed water for the house like everyone else.

The gas station attendants were next to be Omanized. I pulled into the station and filled my tank. The newly hired Omani came to collect the money. I had a 32 rial fill and handed the attendant a 20 and two 10 rial notes. He had roll of money and began fumbling with the roll. It became obvious he did not know how to make change. An Indian attendant stood of to the side and finally came over knowingly and took the roll of money from him and handed him the correct change. The shy Omani handed me 1 five rial and 3 one rial notes.

Modification to the program was soon announced. Indians would continue working the stations on weekends, nights and holidays. It seemed that it was not convenient for Omanis to work at those times.

The announcement that farm equipment machinery drivers would be Omanized resulted in back pedaling as well. It seemed Omanis could drive cars, trucks and tractors but they did not know how to use a plow or a front end loader.

School bus driver Omanization filled the newspapers with letters commenting on some simple facts. Children had to be picked up at the same time each day and delivered safely to the school on time. It was decided that every bus would continue to keep the former Indian driver for emergencies and in the meantime the Indian would be on the bus to help the children get off and on at the right places.

The general effect was there was no decline in the number of Asian expats in these industries even though they had been Omanized. This was officially noticed by the powers that be who wondered just how well the Omanization programs were working. It had been expected that a country where the expat population was larger than the native population that the expat population would begin to decline as Omanis took over the workforce. This was not happening. Many of the jobs in the country had no appeal to the young Omanis. Besides many Omanis were sponsors of Indian workers and got a kickback from the lowly salaries paid.

A factory opened in Muscat to make blue jeans for the international market. It was designed to employ women who would do the sewing. As near as I could tell it was a success and one of the few industries where manual work was done by Omanis.

At a pleasant upscale store a young Omani woman had been hired as a clerk. When I approached her, she became nervous and shy. After explaining my needs the Indian clerk in his pressed white shirt and tie, who had stood in the background , stepped forward. The young woman wordlessly stepped aside and for the rest of the transaction she simply observed. This was very common. The Omani was there as a figurehead employee to stand around. The Indians were in no hurry to train Omanis to replace them.

When I discussed the employment problem, I was told that a young Omani would not work for the wages paid to laboring Asian expats because they could not buy houses and cars on such low salaries. The problem meant that menial work would remain in the hands of the expats who were happy to have any job while the host country youth were left unemployed.

Such is the conundrum of a society run by indentured servants whose masters skim off money from their wages to enrich themselves. Replacing the expats with Omanis meant giving up the sweet skimming deal. Omanization looked more like an ideal than a take over of the country by its citizens.

A Camping Trip to Madrakah

Expeditions into the interior are usually best taken with several vehicles. Three 4x4's loaded with our camping gear and lots of water headed off for the heartland of the country. The recommendations of the tour book suggested taking extra everything, including tires. They were serious.

We revved up our engines and made for Haima, an outpost famous for being just about the center of Oman and half way to Salalah. After several hours on this now familiar road we knew we were approaching Haima when we saw the first sign of man made structures other than microwave and oil towers. It was a kids playground, swings, slides, picnic tables under a shelter and all the sand you could ever want to play with. Then came Haima which then boasted two gas stations, a police station, a hospital, a school, a few shops and not much else.

Seeking shade, we sat on the steps of a newly constructed set of shops. Someone suggested it might be a department store! Here we ate our lunch and watched a large helicopter come in to land at the police station. Some other travelers, French we learned, sat on the steps of the next building also eating their lunches. We peered off down the road we were to take. From the center of the community it was easy to do this. A line of power poles and a dusty road through a very sparsely vegetated plain lay ahead.

The poles soon ended as we passed the TV relay tower. For the next fifty kilometers the road headed in a straight line through the Jiddat Al Harasis, an area of scrub desert. This desert is the home of the Arabian Oryx, a white animal with a large pair of antlers that could almost pass as a unicorn. It was made extinct until they were introduced from herds in captivity. They live out here but we didn't see any. We did manage to see quite a few gazelles who also roam freely in this broad area.

For the entire fifty kilometers there was virtually no sign of human existence. Then gradually we could discern a large grey building looming in the distance. Around it were some construction shacks and we learned that it was an uncompleted school. The only sign of human existence out here was this school. After passing it, I began to search for other evidence of human life. Occasionally off in the distance I could get the glint of sunlight off of something. Probably it was the glass in a pickup truck parked by some lowly bedouin dwelling ... nothing certain but schools are not built unless there are some kids about.

Out in these barren areas one tends to search for things on the horizon. Any thing! It really is an area of impressively extreme monotony. I catch a glimpse of something white and pull over to the edge of the road to see what it is, perhaps an oryx. No such luck. Our convoy of three is spaced out so we wait to regroup before setting off again.

Thump, rumble, thump! I've not gone a hundred meters when I know something is wrong. My right rear tire is in shreds. A 3 inch metal object impaled itself into the tire when I pulled over. How does an object like that come to be out here? I am now without a spare and continue the journey with some apprehension. However, it is determined that the spare on another vehicle could be used on my car if needed.

A hundred kilometers along the same monotonous road we go through a complete rerun of the school under construction routine. Incredible! We have not seen one evidence of any sort of human habitation and yet here is a second big new school half completed. This time there are a couple of shops being constructed and there are some plywood and tin shacks advertising tailoring, car repair, and food stuffs presumably for the workers and any travelers. It certainly wasn't a place to look for a new tire or anything else for that matter. The map indicated that this was Hab Hab.

After Hab Hab we began to dispense with small scrubby trees and the land settled down to being just a broad gravel plain without any vegetation of any sort, none, not a bush, shrub or thumb size bit of green. The dust rolled and we continued on toward Duqm although it was our intent not to actually go there just yet. It was indicated on the map that gasoline could be bought there and we presumed a tire could be arranged there as well if necessary.

Just past the large welcome to Duqm sign we came to a roundabout and took the right turn to Madrakah. We intended to camp on the splendid beaches that we had read about. About this time two of us got ahead of the rear member of the party. The road dust made it particularly hard to see if any one was following us. Unfortunately, the reason for being ahead was the fact that the poor fellow had stored some of his gear on the roof rack and the roughness of the journey had dislodged some of his stuff. He lost his sleeping bags. Discovering his disappearance we went in search of him and then tried to find the missing bags. We backtracked some distance but we never did find them.

We continued on through barren land, reddish and rock strewn.

There was cluster of shacks and another school. This one was completed and bore a flag pole, beige paint, and neat signs. It was as nice a school as one could want. The rest of the community was composed of tin and plywood shacks which surrounded the school. Some of the shacks bore advertising. Gasoline is available from some oil drums complete with a hand crank pump. We don't need any. Tire repairing is available; mine is past that. There are some old trucks parked about and there is a barber shop. We don't need that right now either. Some Indian laborers and shop keepers are standing about. A couple of Omanis are talking. Everyone is observing us pass by. This unnamed place exists because of the school. The school is generating a crossroads community.

The next place at a fork in the road bears a sign directing us to Madrakah 27 km. Here at the fork there are two tiny mosques, a shack, a wrecked truck, a water tank but no people. Bleak! Really bleak!

The road to Madrakah begins to take us into a rather unusual rock formation area. Everything here is rock - no earth - not a single plant grows. We didn't expect any. The unusual kinds of rock structures are fascinating but not pleasing to the eye. We crest a hill and the sea is visible in the distance. So is Madrakah, huddled up against a modest mountain. We approach this community which has yet to be visited by electrification. What power there is, is generator created. The resources of greater Oman have been brought to this remote headland in the middle of the country. The flag flies proudly over the clean and tidy school. There is a desalinization plant for water and an ice making factory so the fish catch can be packed in ice. Clinging to higher ground right against the mountain are some brown beige government subsidized housing units.

The rest of Madrakah is a conglomeration of shacks made of collected debris. There are fenced compounds and huts all scattered in disarray back from the beach. What shops exist are determined by awkwardly painted signs and some goods piled outside their tin and plywood walls. The local vehicles are mostly rusting old trucks. This village of a few hundred souls huddled between the rocks and sea is the poorest most depressing place I had yet seen on mainland Oman. Only Masirah Island was worse. It appeared that most of the people were too poor to even afford subsidized housing.

We drove off to find the beach and managed to drive a mile or so from the village before being forced to stop. The beach was miles long and fairly broad. Unfortunately it was quite steep and unsuited for walking. In addition the surf had a bad undertow. Worse the high water marks were covered in quantities of tar that gave the sea air a distinct oil smell. What could have been a lovely beach was also covered in debris, bits of lumber, plastic Styrofoam chunks, plastic bottles, a construction hat, rags, all tossed here by the sea which was all to eager to rid itself of this junk.

We camped near the sea behind a dune that afforded the sound of crashing surf. After dark we were able to burn some of the junk to make a decent campfire. The dew that night was so heavy that everything was dripping wet. In the morning we could pour it off the canvas shade awning over our dining spot.

After breaking camp we passed through the town. Everyone

waved at us including the garbage collectors. Clearly they welcomed tourists or for that matter anybody who made the effort to visit. We are off to visit another beach noted for its black rocks and white sand. It was the same cove where the local fishing boats went to sea. It was a clean beach and various sea creatures were attached to the rocks, one of which looked like a modern version of the ancient trilobites I have seen as fossils.

Returning to our vehicles, John Godsmark finds it is necessary to change a tire from a nail we picked up in town. Now there are no spare tires on two vehicles. John decides the only option is to wait until we get to Duqm to have it repaired as the "Tire Puncher Repair" shop in Madrakah didn't appeal to us.

We retrace our steps and head off toward Duqm an apparent town a good two hours away. Here we hope to get refreshed and have the cars attended to. Perhaps I can use the bank machine and get a tire for my car and we may do some shopping and have lunch.

At the roundabout which we had passed yesterday with its big welcome to Duqm sign we turn toward Duqm proper some eighteen kilometers farther on. A sign indicates the Shell station is one kilometer. We are about to arrive in Duqm which the map indicates in large print accompanied by a red star indicating that there is a gas station. It isn't hard to find. Duqm consists of one decent small mosque, a school, a coffee shop and some sort of grocery shop both nicely housed. The other shops are shacks, all closed except the tire repair but then we don't need car repair, hair cut or tailoring. People live here. We can see away from the road some dwellings or reasonable facsimiles thereof. Duqm also has electric poles along the road and the shops have had at least one coat of paint. Clearly we are a notch above Madrakah but not near the level of Haima. There is no bank machine.

We have tea in the restaurant which can seat just 6 in a cramped fashion. There are curtains in the window in national colors. There is no glass. The Indians are able to serve pita sandwiches with a fried egg accompanied by tomatoes and onion all rolled up. Donna and I pass. The cooking area is divided from the seating area by some shelving that holds bottles of hot sauce and ketchup. The display of sauces is on both sides of the serving window. The entire tiny restaurant measures about ten feet square. A road grader operator, his head enshrouded with a tarpaulin contraption save for a hole for his face, leaves clutching a black plastic bag containing his lunch.

Some curious Bedu teenagers come in for a soda and to stare at us.

Meanwhile John is having an inner tube placed in his tire. The tire repair man does not know how to repair a tubeless tire. There are clearly no tires I'd want to buy from his pile. The locals prefer tube tires without steel belting. Better on these roads they claim. Refreshed and clearly wondering why an effort is being made to bring the paved road several hundred kilometers from Sinaw to Duqm, we head northward again. Duqm did not live up to our expectations as there was not much there, but what there was, was clean and tidy and there was no problem with parking.

Over our lunch we comment that it is unusual that there are "tyre" repair shops in every tiny place. We suspect that nails are distributed outside the towns on the roads to promote business.

While crossing mud flats near the coast we see an unusual feature off in the sea. A large white mesa like object rising out of the water is the first of some unusual land forms in this part of Oman. We travel now through some rugged landscapes. Ancient sedimentary rocks have been eroded and pushed about. Their colors range from dark red violets, through ochre, oranges, yellows, browns and even green. Flat top hills and black cliffs are crumbled and eroded in random fashion. Here in these rocks fossils and dinosaur bones have been found. This terrain is totally different from any other part of Oman. It resembles the badlands of North America. The road is terrible but the views are fascinating.

Our destination for the night is Khaluf and we approach it through an area of white drifting sand. It looks exactly like drifted snow among the sandstone rocks, even where it piles up along the roadside it looks like snow.

We are approaching the sea and the road winds into the village of Khaluf. Wooden Arab dhows are anchored off shore. The village is partly shacks and partly grass or palm frond huts. There is no evidence of electricity or any government services except the school. The schools dominate these communities. It is impressive to see the pattern. This is a subsistence fishing community just as poor as can be but it won't stay like this much longer. The paved road to Duqm has just been completed to the turn off for Khaluf . We drive through the village to discover a beautiful white sand beach. Many miles of it stretch off into the distance - clean white sand to drive along. We are not alone. A handful of other campers are here but so few we have our choice of private areas. This is prime beach. If it were America, it would be lined with development. We set up camp and head for the sea - no shells, no debris and wonderful breakers to enjoy.

There is no driftwood tonight for a fire but we sit watching the sea. Actually we keep checking the high tide since we are only a few feet from the water on a pretty flat beach. By nine in the evening we have decided that we are safe from the high tide and prepare to spend the night with gentle breezes and the soothing roar of the surf.

In the morning Donna and I take a long inviting walk reminiscent of our walks on Florida beaches but this beach is virtually deserted. We return from our walk to find a Bedu family busily engaging our fellow campers. Mom and Dad and the 9 kids have piled out of an incredibly rusty truck. They live inland and visit the beach to sell the grass craft bowls and pots which the Bedu women make. Jennifer and Valerie have each bought one and Donna is eager to see what is available. We negotiate for several with the burka covered woman. She demonstrates her skill on a partially finished bowl. Using a brass awl she deftly creates a master piece. Dad sits by beaming. The little girls have henna designs on their hands probably because it is Eid. On of the boys speaks some English and we mix languages. He is in 7th grade which means he has had two years of English and goes to a school at Mahout which is inland some distance. The family has come to the beach hoping to find some buyers of the mother's crafts. Her quality is good and Donna buys her remaining stock. We also get some photos of this fine family. We pass out some snacks and the older boys are curious to inspect the inside of the cars. One boy tries to lay claim to one of our chairs but I decline to give it to him. His mother wants an empty orange juice jug. That we gladly give her. They pile into their truck, kids standing in the back and drive back up the beach. I have a sense that we are seeing the end of an era approaching. This backwater now has a paved road nearby and soon there will be many more 4x4s coming to the beach.

We were out on a holiday week for this journey and so the expatriate community was out exploring. We passed and sometimes spoke with them, French, Dutch, German, English. The off roaders will be coming here more frequently now that it is within a six hour drive from Muscat.

After our surfing and sun burns we pack up and head homeward. Our decision whether to try some more back roads is tempered by the fact that the trip has rendered Walt and Jennifer's air conditioning useless and John Godsmark has yet another flat tire. We are again two vehicles with no spare tires so we decided to take the new road back to Sinaw.

A few miles along we pass a sign indicating the turn for Masirah Island. Donna and I have been here before. Two years ago this same Eid we came this way. The contrast was amazing. When we passed through the wadi Halfayn area then, there was a great meadow, a sea of grass and many camels grazing. We picnicked under a tree and maneuvered the vehicle through barely passable swampy tracks. I wrote up that experience then. Now the tree is still there but it is beside a paved road elevated up above the flood plain. The grass is all gone. It is just a huge flat dry area void of green. There are no camels. It is absolutely barren. This season has been drier, more normal than what we had two years ago. The new highway sped us through a different place. The road to Duqm from Khaluf did not exist on my ten year old map. Now it is gravel and soon will be paved. Two years ago we rode the washboard road to Sinaw and we arrived worn out. Now we whiz along easily at twice the speed. The miles of beaches along the coast are now easily accessible and will soon be different places. The isolation has come to an end. Oman is changing right before my eyes.

Easter 1999

Today is 18 Dhu'l-Hijja in the year 1419. Sunny and nearing 40c. It is a normal working Sunday in which virtually no one wishes me a Happy Easter. During the afternoon I stop and chat with a couple of first year students from Jebel Akhdar. They are polite and friendly and Easter is not part of the conversation. This is the Muslim world.

Apart from work my greatest concern is replacing a bad tire and after 5 days I had some hope that the new tire had been sent from Muscat. Only it was the wrong tire again. After three years, I have learned to shrug my shoulders and drive away still missing a spare tire. That's just the way it is here.

The TV is full of news about Kosovo refugees. Western propaganda from BBC and CNN tells of bewildered Serbs wondering why they are being bombed. The Christian century is ending much as it began without much evidence that the message is any more understood.

In the evening we go to Marty and Emily's. The Reverend Marty is one of the few ministers in Oman. His home is also a place where Christians gather. Marty lives in a home loaned by a major in the Omani army. He is here to provide religious service for Christians working for oil companies in the interior. He had been a pastor in New England and the US Virgin Islands. Emily was a chain smoking raconteur who added some verve to any gathering. Marty would go into the interior for days at a time. I found it unusual that he never held any church services in Nizwa. I also found it unusual that the US secretary of defense William Cohen was an ex parishioner of his. Cohen seemed a very Jewish name. At a Robbie Burns party at their home I had a lengthy interesting discussion with a very knowledgeable gentleman. We roved over the issues of the day in the Arab and larger world in remarkable detail. Afterward, Marty took me aside to inform me that I had been chatting with the head of US military intelligence for the middle east. Other American guests in the room had also come from Muscat. Marty had a lot of high level friends. My guess was Marty had a job as eyes and ears for the CIA in the interior of Oman. But that's another story. It was Easter.

Here in an almost clandestine way we gather barefoot in Marty's living room. A multi-cultural mix is crowded into this large room. There are tall black Sudanese, Indians in saris in saffron, greens, golds and reds, western women in flowered dresses and kids of every hue. The air fills with "Christ the Lord is Risen Today." It's easy to forget being a Christian when Easter passes unmarked, unnoticed. An effort must be made and sixty or so folks from the region have gathered to share. We sing, we pray and finally with some women singing in the background we take communion. Red and yellow, black and white we are gathered in his sight.

We stand around socializing, I am introduced to John from Sudan and John from Sri Lanka and John from India. I know the other John from Canada. Five Johns all gathered from around the world on a warm Oman desert night as we commemorate Easter and wait for supper.

Then it's time for a pot luck supper like no other. It is an eclectic meal of biriani, pizza, samozas and potato salad, spaghetti and coconut pita bread, many kinds of rice and a macaroni salad. Everyone has produced a dish from their ethnic background for this meal. It is a meal as varied as the collection of people who have gathered here from around the globe, New Zealand, Philippines, Indian subcontinent, Europe and North America.

We are full of joy, people of peace sharing a Christian Easter in a land where we are the minority in every way.

We leave and I put a tape of Smokey Mountain banjo and fiddle hymns into the Pajero's tape deck and we cruise down the back street of Nizwa belting out "What a Friend We have in Jesus." Hallelujah!

Ancient Times

Along the line of honey shale, the ridges rise beneath the higher crests. Here on the higher ground the ancients chose to rest their dead. What once seemed cluttered and random in nature now leaps out as sites of human habitation. Wherever we see these characteristic hills and their slopes laden with natural building stones, we scan the summits to search for the tell tale humps of ancient burial sites. Beehive shaped tombs are all around. Their origins are consistent with ancient Mesopotamia and the rise of civilization. It just takes a little skill to recognize them.

Using the abundance of conveniently sized and shaped shale blocks these people built rings of stones and by piling them up carefully were able to close in a cone shaped top. These hives were small, big enough for a body or two, big enough to stand or crouch in behind an arched doorway. The there was time, lots of it. While many of these structures have collapsed, there are some marvellous ones which remain intact as their builders intended when they built them four and five and six thousand years ago. Just to stand in the doorway and look out across the mountains and valley and contemplate those who had built these shelters so long ago charged my imagination.

Until we visited and saw for ourselves these tombs we were unaware that we drove past many sites all over the interior which had been occupied by these people. It is easy to ignore bumps on distant hills.

Now we know that these ancient places are there and their abundance is impressive. Sadly their existence is vulnerable to anyone who would knowingly or not destroy them. Only in the last decade have roads come to these places exposing them to the whims of the, as yet, few tourists.

The greatest collection of the Magan culture ruins exist in an area known as Bat which is between Ibri town and the mountain Jebel Shams. The most spectacular site is a collection of about two dozen tombs well up a narrowing valley virtually in the shade of the massive Jebel Misft, a rock which could serve as the model for the Prudential Life Insurance company logo. Misft is a shear angular rock hundreds of feet high and away from the general line of the mountain. Near this unmistakable view is a ridge of honey shale that provides a rewarding view and the opportunity to wander around these tombs. They are unlike the mud and stone ruins we see elsewhere. Some of the stones have darkened with age and appear as if they have been burned by the sun. They clatter with a metallic ring as we clamber over them going from one stone hut to another. The dead are long gone from these burial huts but the site carries a lot of mystique. The Magan people lived here 5000 years ago and mined copper from these mountains.

In the same general vicinity, a few kilometers away, is a much larger site. Here at Bat the tombs are more random and more extensive. There must have been a fairly sizeable community here and I suspect that some of the mounds are not tombs at all. We stop along the roadside to inspect a completely different sort of structure. This one is made of smooth boulders and is in a star shape. What once were small rectangular rooms are easily identifiable as part of the remains of walls. This site is not on a hill and some of the stones would require the work of several persons to be moved. The burial mound stones on the other hand are small, angular and flat and could be picked up easily with one hand. Next door some kids watch us climbing around and I wonder if they have any idea that this site is thousands of years old. Perhaps, probably, built by their ancestors.

Once the stark mountains of the Jebel Akhdar (green mountain) were green with trees of economic merit, tall timber pines. The more abundant rainfall made the valleys green and the local folks made a fair trade in mining copper for ancient Sumeria. We are on the edges of the birthplace of civilizations and second and third millennium BC communities thrived in what is now an undeveloped and mostly unexplored bronze age UNESCO site, the most complete collection of settlement and necropolises from the 3rd millennium in the world.

The story and legends of antiquity abound in Oman. The marks back in time are extensive. Glacial scours from when this land was at the south pole, before it moved to crash into Asia, can be found. Meteorites are scattered about the barren ground. Somehow in our travels we missed finding the dinosaur bones found along the road we often travelled in the vicinity of al Khoud. Oman is one of the few places in this part of the world where dinosaur bones are found.

While we were travelling the coast near Sur, we watched an Italian team excavating an 8000 year old habitation site. Layers of shells found under the surface of a high ridge located between an ancient swamp bed and the sea gave indication of human activity. These ancient people had been digging clams and making knives and scrapers and arrow heads out of the shells. The evidence that the clams were used for a food staple is clear. The place is a treasure trove of the remains of the early inhabitants.

The excavation team was pleased to show us their efforts. We inspected their sifting screens, their digging sites which were carefully marked out and their campsite which was just off from the work area. We were shown how it was possible to know how a shell was used by those long ago residents. The fact that the site was a few feet from a high cliff which drooped off into the water made it even more impressive.

A land so stark, so dry and harsh hardly seems the ideal place to build great civilizations but human activity is traceable here for a very long time. Traceable to a time when it was a wetter and greener place.

Yet in every instance it seemed the habitations were placed so as to be able to gaze out over the land or the sea, to peer into far away places, to gaze into clear starry nights. I ponder a world I could not know while I stand kicking at rocks once held in a human hand. It is rubble of their time, rubble of which I can only know but a trace.

How much of their skill transcended to the mud bricks and plaster of yet crumbling villages and streets that hide behind the cement block and painted shops of today? My eyes move from "Poltry for Sale" and other signs in a foreign language to crumbling towers defending palms and then upward to neatly lined piles of shale from earth to the heavens and backward in a glance over so vast a span of time. All is evident here, all around, all part of the enchantment of Oman.

Picnics

Omanis have a great affection for picnics. They have elevated picnicking to a high status in their society. Of course they may not always consider their manner of dining a picnic but to my mind they are the world's most dedicated picnic people.

At times we have even taken to emulating their habits and find them quite satisfying. The picnic is not unknown to most other cultures but in Oman it has a special exuberance and spontaneity.

Where else, for example, would one find six or eight good friends sitting about on the stony ground under a roadside street lamp sharing an evening picnic. A red checkerboard plastic sheet and a small portable grill sizzling with meat set beside a cooler of Mountain Dew and Pepsi completes the picture.

In fact at most any time of day one can find a group, usually of only one sex, sitting along the road or under or beside a bush having a picnic. The picnickers seem to choose locations at random. Suddenly one or two vehicles will pull off the road and everyone emerges to spread a mat or red and white checkered plastic sheet over the rocks. A sturdy little metal BBQ cooker is retrieved from the back of the car. Most cars seem to have these two items there so as always to be ready for the opportune moment.

The BBQ cooker or grill is locally made of solid sheet steel. I had one in the early days of our time here. It is great for grilling meat on sticks. They are very sturdy and quite portable and consist of a rectangular box with handles and a rack with slotted bars. The whole thing is about the size of a shoe box. The same design, but in large models, is used at the outdoor restaurants.

There are picnickers on small rocks in the wadis and on top of large boulders. In the popular places there is usually the smell of mouth watering roasting kebabs. Often at these places we find groups of young people and the ever present portable radios boom out the latest in Arabic hits. In other places young Omani families have stopped for a family picnic in the great out of doors.

Oman abounds in little parks often with carefully watered real grass. Here in small enclosures there may be covered tables and lawn space to spread the mats. Some come with flowering bushes and some have recreation equipment for small children. These are popular places to visit and Nizwa has a number of them.

The picnic is not just a day time event. At night for a special event a group may drive off into the desert and prepare a goat to roast over a fire or take meat to cook on the grills. There will be lots of cola and fruit and rice to eat. Any restaurant will prepare a take out feast and this even applies to the local Pizza Hut where we sometimes saw a huge stack of those cardboard boxes being carried to a waiting car.

I am invited to join a group of students and faculty at a picnic at the Tanuf dam, a popular spot. The customary dishdasha has been replaced with sweatshirts and shorts or a sarong. Heads normally seen under a kumar or a mussar are bare. A drum is produced and several fellows dance about and frequently burst into song. This is a happy event and we dine on fresh roasted goat pieces from the spit. A salad has been bought and we have bags of chips, oranges, apples, grapes and lots of cold pop from a cooler. We are perched either on the boulders or the plastic mats.

The cameras come out and we all pose for pictures. Before the meal is complete several curious and hungry goats appear. They get chased off but keep coming back. A bag of chips gets pinched and the goat eats bag and all. They are not choosy. I toss a tough bit of goat meat away and it gets quickly cannibalized. Goats eat anything including their roasted brothers.

We also have picnics inside. Any family event, whether a promotion, a new child, car or house is reason enough to have a lunch sent in for the office staff and administrators. The venue could be a hall, one of the old office areas or the cafeteria. To a casual observer it might seem odd to enter the cafeteria and find the chairs and tables pushed away and a red checkered plastic sheet spread on the floor. We would all be seated cross legged sitting around a large platter of roast chicken and fish sitting on a huge pile of fried rice mixed with diced veggies. We would have salads of sliced cucumbers, and tomatoes, some lettuce and a bowl of lime halves. The lime is the preferred salad dressing as it is squeezed over the salad. Other than the soda pop it is a pretty nutritious, healthy meal. The food is eaten with the fingers and I have mastered the art of doing this without messing up my shirt or tie. We would all be seated so as to prove that when we eat we are all equal. No one is higher than any other person in the eyes of god. After the meal the huge platter, still laden with an abundance of food, is removed and the plastic sheet is picked up with the scraps on it and tossed into the garbage. We all go back to work in a better frame of mind. We were all equals during the meal and that helps keep things in perspective.

In Muscat in a shopping mall we wander past a restaurant which has tables set outside the door. There are four Omani men in their mid 20's seated at a table and the Indian waiter arrives with a large plate of carrot sticks for them to munch on. They are sipping a drink made of fruit juices. I am contemplating when if ever I had seen anyone order a large plate of carrot sticks to share with friends. In my minds eye I can imagine the conversation. "Well guys how about we get a plate of carrot sticks and some fruit punch.?" " Great idea!." On the other side of the world it would be "Lets get a beer and some wings." I wander over to the magazine stand and notice that there are pages missing in the

Time magazine. Mine arrives in the mail with the added pictures. Scantily dressed photos of women had been left in mine but not on the news stand issue. The censor had been at work. Islam is a very conservative religion.

We expats picnic ourselves.

A meteor shower was expected. It was to be an exceptional night display especially after midnight. An expedition is organized to go into the desert in the evening to picnic and star gaze. We are well away from the city and its lights. I play my harmonica, we snack and drink and arrange ourselves on blankets and chairs to get a good view of the sky. The heavens are dense with pricks of light. We pick out a satellite and a few aircraft. It is well past midnight when we decide to go home. We had seen a total of two rather frail meteor streaks. The event was from a viewing perspective a bust but we all had enjoyed ourselves beneath the heavens.

Wanderings in the Heat

The major, Richard Morse, an English teacher at the college, had spent several years in Sudan with the British Army. He had decided to come out to Oman. His wife was in England and Donna had gone back to Canada for the summer. It was mid June and the days were pushing 50C or 125f. My annual leave took place in July. Richard had been studying about the 1958-59 uprising in the interior of Oman. The Sultan had called in the British to help put down the rebellion. Richard's commanding officer in the Sudan Lt.Col. Peter de la Billiere was a young SAS officer in Oman in 1958-9 and found and led the troops up wadi

Kamah. He was first to reach the top and was awarded the MC for his effort. Later this same man was the lead British officer in the first Gulf war. Richard wanted to explore the venue of the 1958 action.

The old town of Tanouf had been bombed by the British and the rebels had been attacking near there from bases in the mountains. Even when we were in Oman, travelers required a military pass to go into the high mountain villages. The loyalty of those people was still in question. Richard had suggested we go into the wadi canyon called Wadi Kamah where he thought the rebels might have had some defensive positions during the fighting. His interest came from the fact that he had served under an officer who had fought there and had received the military cross. He wanted to see what might still be there. His call at 5 p.m. gave me time to assemble a hasty picnic and we headed off to explore the ravine area a few miles away. The thermometer by the house read 115F.

We parked near the mouth of the gorge and after we hiked past some date palms, we were able to witness an Omani youth scramble up a sizeable tree to hack off a large date bundle that was matured. I had not seen this done before. The trunks are pretty rough and in his bare feet it seemed no more difficult that walking up some stairs. We continued on past the grove and the homes into the rock strewn wadi bed. After a time we were clearly into the ravine with its towering rock cliffs on either side. The hot breeze kept us comfortable. Richard was able to identify two locations that he said looked like rock fortifications well up the side of the cliff. These would be ideal places for machine guns and although they were too high up for us, we concluded that indeed these were man made. We selected a large boulder on which to sit and eat our picnic supper. The sun was large and red as it was getting quite low in the sky and we realized that we could not spend too long sitting on the rock. I put my hand down on the rock to steady myself as I sat and instinctively pulled it away. The rock was too hot to touch. We could not sit anywhere near this spot. Supper was enjoyed standing up. I missed the opportunity to have taken a rest but as it was drawing near dusk it would not have been a long rest. Our investigation established we had found at least one possible artifact but there was no time to discover more. In retrospect we did not think it odd to go hiking in such extreme heat because it was that hot every day. We just made sure we had lots of water.

One a similar day I was walking from one part of the campus to another about noon hour and it was quite windy. The wind was very hot coming off the desert. I observed that my scalp actually felt cool and when I stuck my tongue out, it too felt cool from the intense evaporation. A few yards further along I realized I was walking with my fingers clenched in my palms, just like I might do on a very cold day. Only this time I was protecting them from the intense heat. When I located a thermometer, it was reading 54C (129) in the shade. Later in the afternoon the wind picked up and a sandstorm drove sand, bits of paper and debris around so dramatically it obscured the sun in an orange haze and going outdoors would not have been pleasant for those fifteen minutes that it blew past.

Sometimes in the evening, after the street lights were installed, I would go for a walk to the pharmacy or one of the shops not too far from us. I soon learned that almost every evening about 8:30 to 9:00 a strong wind would come down from the mountain and blow out into the desert. I suspect it was a shift in the radiation cooling that caused this ritual. After fighting my way home in one of these mini dust storms and finding grit in my hair, on my face and in my clothes, I made closer note as to when one of these events was coming. It was not a pleasant experience getting sand blasted.

A trip to the pharmacy was interesting. The shop had a room behind where I supposed the pharmacist lived. If you had a prescription, that was fine but it didn't matter. If you knew what pills you wanted, he would sell them without question. In this way I kept up to date with all my medications without ever going to the doctor for refills. The tiny shop was filled to the rafters with goods for sale. The counter was small and the conversations with the pharmacist indicated that he knew his stuff. He was open from whenever he got up until he went to bed. I always thought pharmacists lived a life in a little confined area, counting out pills. This fellow did this virtually every day all day long. I think I would have gone stir crazy spending my life like that.

The Barbershop was next door. My barber was an Urdu from Pakistan. He wore traditional Pakistani trousers and a tunic bowed at the bottom. There were a couple of barbers working there depending on how busy it was. Omanis frequented the place to get their beards trimmed or have a shave. These activities more frequent than getting a haircut. The shop was pretty typical with a row of 3chairs along one wall and a ledge with tools behind which was a panel of mirrors. A TV set blared from a shelf near the front window. The set was angled so everyone in the room could see it. I got the impression that tipping was not a custom or my tip was considered a lot because the barber was delighted to see me and would change the TV channel to the BBC when I came in. I actually thought the Pakistan TV was interesting even if I could not understand a word of it. The barber would co-operatively fill me in as to what was being said. He seemed pleased I did not want the BBC.

On one occasion two black abayah clad Omani women were there with a little boy about 3 or 4 to get him his first haircut. He was remarkably good although there were some small whimpers at first. Mom and grandmother stood right beside the barber offering instructions as to what to do. It was such a universal experience seeing a small child getting the first trim.

My barber and I were able to discuss the events of the day. He lived over the shop and had been in Oman for some years. He sent his wages home to his family in Pakistan like nearly everyone else.

I had observed an interesting activity where the barber took two stands of thread and twirled them around. The spinning thread was pulled taught and grazed over the ears and other face parts where there were small hairs. Most of the Omani when in the chair would submit themselves to this routine. I thought I might try it and then found out that these hairs were being yanked out in a decidedly uncomfortable manner. I sat there desperate for it to be over. Having hairs plucked this way might be efficient but it sure smarts a lot.

At the corner just past the barbershop were flats occupied by some Moroccan teachers. At night under the street lamp they would clear out a patch of dirt and play Bocce ball between the apartment and the road. It was the first time I had ever seen the game. For these fellows it proved to be a popular opportunity to be outside on the warm evenings. These teachers worked at some of the schools in the area and were very bored. Only the money kept them out here. Bocce ball was the only game other than soccer I saw played in Oman.

Soccer was everywhere. Every vacant building lot turned into a soccer field after school. The boys, never the girls, appeared no matter the weather and would continue playing in a spirited manner until the call to prayers was broadcast. Then the games would end abruptly as it was the signal to go in. No mother ever had to call her kids to come inside as the muezzin's call to prayer was enough.

Near the flat was a remnant of an old fort. It had greatly decomposed into a mound about 25 to 30 feet high. The sides had crumbled away so it was possible to scramble up to the top. During some rains the side of the fort was quite slippery. Some boys had figured out that by dumping more water onto a narrow strip they could grease the mud so they could slide down the side either on a cardboard, an old prayer mat or just their rear ends. This was great fun and a girl of about 7 appeared and stood near the top watching the boys take turns sliding. Finally, she seized the opportunity and stood at the top, crouched down and skidded to the bottom. Then she was racing back up the side to get in line again. The group of around a dozen kids were having a great time but their mothers would have something to say when they got home as they were mud from one end to the other.

A Visit to the Empty Quarter

The border area of Oman and the UAE with Saudi Arabia is within the Rub Al Khali, the Empty Quarter that is the largest sand desert in the world. This area of Arabia is the stuff of imagination, vast seas of sand. Oman has two areas of sand. The Wahiba Sand area, a couple of hours from Nizwa, is a popular place to visit and camp. However, these dunes are more like rolling ridges than the classic moon shaped barchan dunes we think about as sand dunes. Such dunes are found in the south of Oman along the Saudi border and while the edges are visible from the main highway, entry into the areas of high dunes is difficult. The road that leads into them is a 900 km round trip back to the nearest gas station. Extra gas must be taken along with camping supplies. The area with the biggest dunes farther south has no roads. These dunes are 140 to 170 meters high. Only inside Saudi Arabia do dunes go higher.

After examining some maps, I found that a northeastward extension of the dunes along the UAE and Oman border had some access roads and some of these were partly paved. Donna and I decided first to go to the Emirates and take a circle tour into the Liwa Oasis. However, on a hunch we decided that it was not even necessary to travel so far to gain a feel for the Empty Quarter. A paved road from Al Ain just inside the UAE - Oman borderenters a significant dune field where dunes averaging 40 to 70 meters exist.

We set out from the Al Ain Intercon hotel and drove past the 1300 meter high rock of Jebal Haffit from where we had been able to view dunes in the distance the previous day. A few kilometers outside the city the landscape changes from gravel plain to low yellow sand dunes. The height of the dunes increased as we headed farther south. First they are 8 meter knolls, then 20 meter and finally 40 plus meters. The color changes to a coppery red orange which is very pleasant to see. As far as the eye can see are sand dunes curving, dipping, meandering in random patterns. The sky is blue. The contrast is marvellous.

All of these dunes merging onto each other are splendid but are not the only thing of interest. As soon as we get into the sand, the sides of the road for a few hundred feet back are vibrant green with crops of market garden produce. Plots of five to ten acres are surrounded with fences braided with palm fronds to keep out the sand and the camels. In the fence line of each plot is a low building with an air conditioner and windows. These homes are for the workers . Overhead on both sides of the road are huge high tension power lines. The road is busy with trucks. Some of the gardens have rows of plastic tunnels over the plants. Tomatoes, potatoes, corn, alfalfa, strawberries, and greens of all sorts are grown. This farming is intensive. Here and there teams of big yellow bulldozers are pushing down sand dunes to level the sand to make even more space for gardens. They simply tear down the dunes and make terraces. Where the water comes from is a mystery but there is a lot of it being pumped onto this land. In essence since the soil is pure sand, the crops must grow with intense fertilization. It's almost a hydroponic style of farming. The agricultural strip extends for a hundred kilometers along the sides of the road.

We continue on impressed at the contrast. Beyond the gardens there isn't anything growing at all, absolutely nothing, just sand, piles of golden, red orange sand.

Here and there in the gardens, trees, mostly palms, have been planted. Then we come into a large low valley that extends the green for a couple of kilometers back from the road. The sign says "Al Ageer Forest." A hand planted forest of good size trees are on one side of the road and a bare flat plain, void of any vegetation, is on the other side. A few miles along we come to the Al Zalaha forest. Dense wide expanses of trees are each drip watered from below. Here in the UAE the oil money is used to provide water.

Sheik Rashid Al Maktoum said when he was informed oil had been discovered in the 1960's replied that he wished it had been water. These irrigation plots are testimony to his way of converting his oil money into water.

At the large oasis of Liwa the gardening has taken on the desert in an even larger area than this one. The sand that drifts about in arid wasteland hides an underground aquifer that lies just a few feet below the surface. It provides the water to irrigate these places. Farther along we see a tractor bailing the January hay. A twenty acre hay field, perfectly square and flat, is surrounded by sand. The contrast of what water can do is startling.

With all the roadside activity there must surely be a town some place along the road. We come to Wagan. Government buildings, a big new Abu Dhabi Commercial bank, a jumble of one storey coffee shops and agricultural supply shops with their entrances piled high with bags of fertilizer line both sides of the road. The parking areas in front are full of pickup trucks and trucks with high iron racks. In the middle of them we are surprised to see a portable, prefabricated mosque painted green and white complete with a tiny minaret and an amplifier horn - a park and pray facility. Farther on there are more agricultural shops and a red and white sign over one stating "Honey and Medicinal Oil Sales" and then we drive back into the sand and the ribbon of garden land along the road.

Coming toward us on the side of the road is something unusual. We make out that it is a rider on a camel leading two other camels each with brightly coloured camel blankets and bundles of goods on their backs. The last time we saw a group of camels being led was when the camel halter ropes were held by a guy driving a pickup. The camels have to trot right along when the lead is a truck. Behind this group was another group of five camels and a single rider. This sight was what one expects to find in the desert. Traditional Bedu are taking their goods with them on their camels. Only now it is a rare sight to see someone actually riding a camel. The camel caravan still exists.

The road ahead is blocked. Pickups have stopped in the middle of the road. A group of men, with robes flowing in the breeze and red and white head gear fluttering, have gathered for a social chat. No problem, we drive off the road and go around them.

At Al Qua'a we see rows of white and green houses that are two stories high with lots of windows and attractive green arches. A satellite dish is on every roof and a white fence is around the outside. The sign says it is low cost housing under construction. The occupants have not yet moved in. They will move in soon. The gardening ends here.

We drive onward past the town to find the road has vanished under drifting sand. We are at the Oman border and the map indicates that the road continues into Oman. We did not want to take a road that might or might not exist, so we decided to backtrack a little and take another road which is newly paved. On our left on high ground we can clearly see the new housing site again. We approach on our right an unusual collection of corrugated metal dwellings, acres of them assembled into walls, roofs, court yards, and car ports. This sea of grey metal 4 x 8 sheets is unusual to see. The flat metal roof tops, interrupted by water tanks on stilts, extend regularly over several acres. Cars and trucks are parked all about. Electric service runs from abode to abode. Power poles poke up all over. There is a space with a few camels and then another tin shack village. In spite of its primitive nature the area appears rather neat and clean. These are probably seasonal Bedu dwellings, places to stay when they emerge from the sands. The pavement ends and a gravel road begins.

Here and there by the side of the road is an isolated shack, a 10 ft by 10 ft prefabricated box with a door, a green vine growing up to the roof, a water tank on stilts, a hut of palm fronds with a door and a beat up pick up truck. Another place has a small coral for a couple of camels. No goats or chickens are here...... nothing at all to eat. This is living on the edge. There does not seem to be anything quite like this in Oman although we are virtually on the border.

We drive through hills, big, little, all sand. Sand blows off the crests like snow off a snow drift. A road and steel power towers wander through this maze of sand dunes. Now and again a flat plain interrupts the ridges of dunes. This area shows clearly that the dunes are piled onto a flat plain. We drive on and as it is getting lunch time we select a vantage point to picnic and survey the vastness of this sand. Part way up a dune we stop for a picnic. I climb up to a higher crest near the top. This large dune is approaching 300 hundred feet in height. The map indicates that the average dune size in this ridge area is 70 meters which is about half that of the highest dune areas of Oman. It is, however, an impressive pile of sand to me. I survey the awesome splendour. Donna is a speck waiting below. A matchbox car moves along the distant road. The electric towers wind off into the distance. There is not a building, bush or tree in a 360 degree scan of the horizon. I slide in soft sand and my shoes fill up. What a ski slope this would be. As we picnic, we admire the view, a very unique spot.

Driving out of sight of this powerline across country one would soon get lost. The dunes can be driven on with 4x4's but being a lone driver, it would not be a wise risk. When the plan is to drive on sand, a couple of eight inch boards six feet long and a couple of shovels are needed. It is a lot like driving on snow. Blowing sand crossing the road looks like yellow snow.

The road below has a surprising number of vehicles. The last road sign indicated that the next place was 120 km south. From there at about the point where the three countries meet, a track leads to the Liwa oasis (perhaps another 100 KM) and from there a highway is accessible to the coast. We could go on but the scenery will change only by the varying sizes of the dunes and the addition of numerous small salt basins caused by the inability of water to drain anywhere. We are in the only easily accessible area of the Rub Al Khali. We are not very far into it but far enough to be impressed. Southward there is only sand and oil fields for a journey of many days. The tune of Lawrence of Arabia keeps running in my head as we head back the hundred and forty km to the oasis city of Al Ain. We have seen the sea of sand.

Al Ain is an unusual town. Half is in Oman and half is in Abu Dhabi the largest of the Emirates. The Omani side is called Buraimi. The border runs down the middle of some streets. The city has a modern university and a medical center and is an ancient oasis town. It is the second largest city in Abu Dhabi. The expressway to Abu Dhabi is 160 km of modern highway fully floodlighted at night for the entire distance. Along the highway are groves of trees each with a black drip irrigation tube beside the tree. Water tanks are located here and there. On the Oman side is a decent two lane road but no trees.

Al Ain has an elegant Intercon Hotel with all the facilities one could want. We lodged there and at the bar in the evening I spoke with a pilot from the Emirates airlines who was staying over. He informed me he was a Papuan New Guinea person and the first of his countrymen to become a commercial pilot. Most of his family were still running around in loin clothes as hunter gatherers. He however was schooled by missionaries and got an education. The next morning we were sitting in the plush leather chairs in the lobby when a woman passing by turned and said questioningly, "Donna?" It is a small world. Here was a woman from Woodstock who was also a member of the Woodstock University Women's club to which Donna belonged. She was teaching at the local university. During our conversation I became aware that the large screen TV behind us was playing the movie "Canadian Bacon" with John Candy. Al Ain may be a desert oasis but it's part of a modern world now.

The Fernandez and Lily, Little India

Cajetan and Maria arrived in Nizwa as a young couple from Goa, India. He was a public health worker and in due course was placed in charge of the Nizwa region. When they arrived, Nizwa was reached by a dirt road and the electric generator ceased at frequent intervals and indeed until just before we arrived, this problem was an ongoing one. The regional service power plant was modern and reliable. When the Fernandez arrived, they had no air conditioning and soon after she arrived she had her first child.

The house they lived in next to us was their first home in twenty years that was not an apartment. They owned a decent car and had worked hard to save for their kids' education and their retirement. There were three boys and a girl "Princess."

Shawn was about nineteen when we met him. He was born in Oman but when he became twenty one he had to leave. He had not gone on to University in India as his brothers had and this distressed his father greatly. Shawn spoke flawless English, Arabic and Hindi. He dressed in jeans and was up on the latest western music. He would have been at home in Toronto's youth scene. But he was living on borrowed time in Oman. When he turned 21, he had to go back to India or get his own Omani sponsor. Shawn was how we knew him but that was his assumed western name.

Princess turned ten and we went to her birthday party. She had her party dress, balloons, a cake with candles and we all sang "Happy birthday." It was totally familiar.

In fact when we saw a group of Omani kids at another birthday party, we were surprised when the cake came out and they too sang "Happy Birthday" in English. Talk about a ubiquitous song and cross culture learning! How little Arabic kids with little to no English came to have a cake, ice cream and presents along with simple games remains a mystery to me. It could not have been part of their culture a decade ago out here in Nizwa.

The Fernandez were in their fifties and doing quite well or so I thought until totally crushed he came to see me . His job was to be Omanized. There was no one trained to replace him but he would be replaced. He had been in Nizwa for decades and knew everyone. He was a proud man who now felt humiliated. He went hat in hand to speak to anyone who could get him more time at his job. His ace was the fact there was no replacement being considered. He got a two year extension.

He had been saving and investing back in his native Goa on the west coast of India. He had put 28 000 rials into a shrimp farm at Goa. It seemed like a good investment to secure his future. However, the government closed the operation down. His future was a mess. He acquired a certificate to practice Ayurvedic traditional Indian medicine. When he went back to Goa, he tried to keep up appearances with large donations to restore the ancient Portuguese catholic church in his town. He was in no financial position to do that.

We attended several events at their Nizwa home and they in turn kept a close watch over us. Cajetan also seemed to take great pride in having us as friends. Indians in Oman in general seemed to value having western friends. The reasoning behind this was unclear. We were happy to share that friendship.

Shawn went to work in Muscat selling and installing home theater systems before returning to India to marry and set up his own company to provide sound and light for entertainment productions. His university educated brothers eventually became his employees.

While we lived in the apartment, Donna became friendly with Lily who lived in the downstairs apartment. Lily worked at the hospital as head of physiotherapy. The Physio center was the gift of the US Navy. Just how that came about I never understood since this desert town was nowhere near any water and had no other connection than it was a gift.

Lily came from Madras and her husband was a policeman who was on disability. She had young girls at home and was trying to direct him on raising them while she worked in Oman. They had a two room house in India with electricity but no running water. Lily would go home once or twice a year and would be laden with everything from a tv set to school clothes. She had her own apartment in which she sub let bedrooms to some nurses. Lily was a Christian and so we invited her to Christmas dinner.

She accepted and then refused. It took some persuading and understanding to grasp the nature of her problem. Lily had never used a knife and fork at a meal. Understanding that, we assured her we really wanted her to come. She arrived resplendent in a gorgeous sari. She was a stunning looking person. We learned that she had married her husband against her parents' wishes. It was a true love marriage but her parents were no longer supportive of her. Dinner consisted of turkey and ham and mashed potatoes and the like. Lily confessed it was very bland. Her dish was a much more lively contribution.

Lily was getting more and more distressed over affairs at home. The girls were teenagers and Dad was not able to cope. Finally Lily made a decision to give up her well paid job and go home. She had been able to buy a modest house and provide schooling and furniture but there was little for the dowry for the girls. There would be a huge income drop once she went back. In order to prepare to leave she began sleeping on the floor instead of the bed. She said she had to do that now although it made her bones stiff. She had to prepare for life back in India.

Although we had no real need for hired help, we decided to get a house boy to clean the floors and windows. Cajetan sent a cleaner from the hospital who needed some extra work. We paid him for a couple of hours each week after he finished his day job. He could spend more time cleaning a single window than anyone I ever met. It didn't matter because we were hiring him to help him out more than for the work he did. After a couple of months I noticed that a bottle of booze that I had left out had disappeared. The only explanation was he had stolen it. I told Cajetan this suspicion and the little guy never came back. The booze was likely worth about what we owed him in back wages. Since we no longer trusted him, there was no point in his coming back.

The next house boy was a polite young man who had been brought out ostensibly to be a truck driver but his sponsor stuck him into the hospital to be a cleaner. He cleaned the windows in record time. In fact we had a problem finding enough work for him. We had some good discussions and found he had a great fear of snakes. He did not want to continue on with the day job and was looking for better employment and more money. When he got a lead on a job, we were able to give him a good reference and he finally got a decent truck driving job in Muscat.

Religion

Religion is a daily part of every Muslim's life. Prayers are expected five times a day. The call to prayer is made five times a day from every mosque large or small. The muezzin or caller is paid. He climbs up the minaret tower and calls out over the sound system. However, the call before dawn is not done over the sound system. The caller just uses his natural voice. In this way unless you live next door, you usually don't hear the call. Since we were not very close to any one mosque, the morning call usually never woke us up. The little mosque in the college had no caller and no minaret.

The most prominent call was the one just before the sun began to set. It was like an echo with the same call being heard from all directions over a ten minute period. There was no consistency and sometimes several minutes after the calls had died away a lone voice would begin. The caller was late getting to the microphone. The exception was the call at sunset during Ramadan when everyone had been fasting all day and wanted to eat. It was like a well rehearsed chorus. The calls were totally in unison.

During Ramadan the food stalls would be stacked high with samosas and other deep fried snacks. As soon as the sunset prayer was over, business would be brisk for hungry shoppers. We walked through the market area and the Indian sellers would be waiting with platters of these snacks. There would be no one around. The Muslims were doing their prayers. It was not unusual just before sunset to see cars pull off the road and the occupants unroll their prayer mats. Then suddenly the street was full of people.

The Sultanate maintains a special department of government to deal with the sharia law as distinct from the national secular laws. I also learned that the Imam in each mosque was on the Sultan's payroll. Any Imam not preaching in accordance to the Sultan's wishes could be fired. Imams hold great authority.

On one occasion while Donna and I were walking in an unfamiliar neighborhood not far from our home, some boys started pelting us with pebbles. This pelting is not a prank. Pelting infidels is a mark of disapproval. Donna as usual had not covered her head and her arms were bare. This could be haram, (forbidden) for some Muslim but not expected of others. Jews and Christians are people of the book and thus have a higher status than Hindus but are still not equal to a Muslim. The stone throwing was observed by a young girl sitting on a step and she was clearly upset at what the boys had done. We walked over to some Omanis who were working on a car and we explained what had happened. One of them was distressed and said that the boys should not have done that and he would go to the local Imam and tell what had happened. We were not to go to the police. He then insisted he walk with us through the same area and take us to a view spot at the falag. The young girl came up to the man and told him what she had seen. We could see the young boys spying on us as we walked through. The man was showing that we were his friends. The Imam would, we presume, speak to the parents in that area. This event did not frighten us because they were a few small pebbles. It was a symbolic event nevertheless.

During Ramadan, restaurants are closed all day. Travelers can get meals in hotels. Anyone who is away from home or who is frail or ill may eat during Ramadan. A good Muslim would substitute other days to do the fasting for the time missed. A Canadian woman who worked at SQU university had a wry sense of humor and joked that during Ramadan she would fry bacon, drink beer and blow a fan out of her window to waft the smells onto the street.

Previously, I mentioned my ham sandwich which I ate in my office. No pork was sold in Nizwa. Pork products could only be bought in a few supermarkets in Muscat. There were 50,000 westerners working in Oman. Most were in Muscat. So ham could be bought. Pork room prices were steep. Whenever we had visitors coming from Canada, we would ask that they pack a nice Schneider's Black Forest ham. Muslims were not supposed to go into the pork rooms or into the liquor stores either.

There were several places in Muscat where one could enter a door with a small sign that said "retail store" . Inside was a complete tax free supply of beer, wine and hard stuff. I took a fancy to a cheap Indian dark rum that sold for about 4 dollars for 750ml. I enjoyed it until I poured out a chunk of pickled cheese cloth. South African beer, Molson's, Labatt's, Scotch and fine wines were all available. In order to purchase any booze I had to obtain a permit from the police. My little blue book paged back to front had entries for my total purchase price. I was allotted 70 rials a month for my own personal use. That translated into about 25 to 30 jugs of hard alcohol. The volume allowed increased with the status of the job. Mine was pretty hefty. The only month I actually spent my limit was before Christmas when it was coinciding with Ramadan. The retail stores were closed that month. I went into the bootleg business. My Indian neighbor had no permit. "Could I get him..." and an Egyptian professor on staff who had expensive taste indicated he would like some Johnny Walker Black label and so I was the courier.

The Johnny Walker got hand delivered. I knocked on the door of an upstairs flat. A two bedroom apartment held a lovely large new fridge which was being shipped back to Egypt when he went on leave. A table and two plastic chairs and a bedroom with a chair, bed, dresser, night table and TV completed his furnishings. The rest of the flat was empty. His family was in Egypt and all his money went there. The booze was a simple luxury for him. He had a PhD and a TV. Almost all the Arab faculty had this quality of life in Oman. I found it disheartening to see them live like this just to save up some money.

Anwar was an exception. His wife and girls were with him. Their flat was well furnished and comfortable. It was also on the second floor but directly across the street from a mosque. We were having supper with them when the call to prayer blasted me from behind with the force of a truck horn. I made a mental note never to look for accommodations near a mosque.

During Ramadan the Indian workers were forced to continue building homes, sweep the streets and perform their normal day duties but without any food or water. They had to fast. The college went into slow motion mode. Classes ended at 1 p.m. and I was home by 2. Usually I got home at 5:30. Driving with starving motorists who had neither food nor drink and who had been up celebrating most of the night made late afternoon driving a real hazard. The Omanis tended to share a meal with family and then go visiting. The Egyptians held huge feasts, gorging themselves and partying big time. The more modest Omanis though them vulgar.

At certain times of the year there would be religious broadcasts in English. One of these looked at the value of a human life. A parable or story was told about a woman whose husband had been killed by another man. She asked what she should receive in return and in the final outcome it appeared that the life of 1 man was worth 100 camels. These instructive stories gave extensive background to elements of Islam and the application of the sharia law as interpreted from the Quran and the Hadith sayings that go with it. Islam is a highly structured religion where the codes to live by are fixed. In a case of wrong doing to another person justice is served not by going to jail but by compensation to the aggrieved person.

However it was explained to me that sometimes what looks to be religion was in fact just a custom. The Quran basically says that women and men should dress modestly. These desert people take this a step further and I was told perhaps in jest that in the old days tribes would raid each other and steal the women. If a woman's face was covered, raiders would be discouraged because the raiders were unable to size up the beauty of the woman. Another reason given was the desert sun caused faces to age prematurely. Relatively few women covered their faces. The burqa covers the entire face and the niqab leaves space for the eyes to be seen. Most of those who used the niqab or burqa were Bedu nomads. The Quran does not say modesty includes covering the face or hands. Around Nizwa most women simply covered their heads. Some wore them so no hair would show and some wore only a light shawl or scarf. One day while walking down a busy street, I observed a fully veiled woman who was trying to dodge across the traffic. Finally she saw an opening and pulled the veil from off her face and looked both ways, marched across and promptly replaced her face covering. Another time I watched a burqa veiled woman being assisted up some stairs as she could not see through the veil where to step.

My rather worldly director might show up with a light scarf or just a nice perm or have her head fully scarfed with no hair showing. A woman professor we knew at the university had a reputation for wearing fine suits and dresses. We met her and her two kids in a Muscat Burger King. She had on designer jeans which showed under her hooded black abaya. We got the opinion that this was a hasty trip out and she had tossed on the abaya just to cover up her messy hair, lack of make up and old clothes. It was a convenience. We often recognized women wearing some pretty nice clothes and makeup under the abaya (cloak) and hijab (head scarf). Women from Tunisia and Jordan came from cultures where head covering was not common. In Oman they felt pressured to conform to the local norms. Western and Indian women as a rule never did cover their hair.

Omani men who worked in government were required to wear a turban (mussar). Otherwise most men wore a small embroidered cap (kimma). Head covering is a part of the Oman culture. The mustache and or beard also has religious significance for men. In the Islamic tradition, God commanded Abraham to keep his beard, shorten his mustache, clip his nails, shave the hair around his genitals and shave his armpit hair. Just how this was done a thousand years before the modern razor is a mystery. Other rules regarding the beard go from not cutting a single hair to keeping it trimmed to a certain length to being clean shaven save for a trimmed mustache. In Oman the police and military were forbidden to wear beards. This was something of a litmus test to sort radical Islamists from other Muslims as a fundamentalist would not go beardless.

We were approaching the time of the Eid Al Adha and when I walked over to the faculty building, there was considerable commotion. Several of the professors had been allowed to go on their Hajj, a pilgrimage to Mecca which was considered one of the seven duties of a pious Muslim. They were being prepared by some of the other faculty. They had all their body hair shaved off including their heads. They had been dressed in simple white robes much resembling bed sheets. The journey would take a couple of weeks and no one had bothered to tell me that they were departing. I assumed that they had been allowed to go by the Ministry and was later told that the Ministry could not deny a Muslim who made the request as it was a holy duty. The students would understand why their classes were cancelled.

The entourage of college pilgrims set off in a couple of cars with much waving and shouts of encouragement. Some of the Omanis who departed had told me that they had been on a Hajj before and this time were going in place of someone who could not go. This was acceptable to do on behalf of a person who had never gone but was unable to do so. While they did not go, they might have helped with the expenses or in some other way. In this way their obligation is met.

Unlike a Christian who gets to go to heaven by repentance a Muslim gets there by following the rules. These rules are all pervasive and go from forbidden things (haram) to discouraged things to simply frowned upon things and vary from sect to sect and interpreted opinion. It is also the duty of a Muslim to see to it other Muslims toe the line. This duty can get to be a big problem. Islam however can be accommodating because almost every obligation or rule has a loophole, necessity. If necessity demands it, then it's okay. Observing the belief systems of others close up, raises some interesting questions.

The Omani neighbor who appears not to have a regular job and who I seldom see or speak with has bought a goat. The goat is tied to a stake outside the house and his kids are delighted to feed and pet it. For over a week the goat is the center of attention. After school it is the object of much petting and playing and feeding Then it is Eid. The goat's throat is slit in a ceremony witnessed by the kids and others. It is skinned and roasted. I'm not sure what the kids thought but it is the custom each year. It represents the offering of Issac to God. A lot of the old testament gets reinterpreted in Islam.

Slaughtering animals in the front or back yard posses public health issues. The government has provided a public abattoir and supervised assistance at a site just out of town. At least this guy and others did not take up the offer. The evidence was in the dumpster near our house when I went to toss in my plastic bag of garbage. The entrails and skin of the goat were tossed in and were starting to stink. I noticed other dumpsters had animal parts hanging out of them.

The goat, sheep or calf is the usual creature chosen. A boatload of Australian sheep had arrived and animals were for sale. Signs were posted so buyers could go get their animal. A slaughtered goat is wrapped in banana and other leaves and buried in a pit of coals for three days. The meat is tender, a little smoked and pulled from the bones with your fingers. It is quite tasty.

We are invited to our landlord's father's home for the Eid breakfast. It is a fast broken by the meal. We are welcomed into the home. We remove our shoes and Donna disappears to sit with the women. I am given a bowl of some sort of thick porridge that has no particular flavor. I scoop it up with my fingers. Saud's father is a basket weaver. He is an older man who has very liberal views. His two daughters have been educated and have professional careers. They are in their early 20's and have little desire to marry in the near future. Marriage would mean leaving their careers to be full time wife and then mother. One was a graduated nurse and the other was still in training. Both were eager to have a career and enjoyed helping the family at home. The traditional life did not appeal to them.

We had met Saud's aunt earlier. She had spotted us on the street and insisted we go into her house for coffee. We did not at first know who she was and when we accepted the impromptu invitation, we had no idea what we were getting into. However it was not uncommon for us to be a guest for tea with a stranger. Once she had us seated she told us how happy she was we lived in Saud's house and what a nice guy he was. She was pleased that we had come and she began telling us all about the family. Two teenage girls came to speak with us as we were departing. They were also relatives. They did not want to spend their lives looking after their parents and a husband and kids. They wanted more in their lives. They also were fearful about being forced to marry someone much older. This was something they were quite hostile about. This confiding with Donna about their situation was quite revealing as it showed their aspiration to have something for themselves in their lives. They spoke with her several times and apparently drew some comfort from an association with a western woman.

There were some customs involving children at Eid. At the end of the Big Eid the children engage in a custom where relatives and friends give them small amounts of cash. The kids went door to door amongst the family. Gifts for children vaguely reminded me of Halloween or perhaps Christmas.

The same Omani neighbors who slaughtered the goat had, I think, very few kind thoughts about his infidel neighbor. One day we came home to find a funny woven hex and some odd items arranged before the outer gate. Not long after that he opened the outer gate and kicked in the front door. He never entered the house because that was forbidden in the Quran. Kicking in the door caused our Indian neighbor to call the police. When we got home, the police were there as well as the landlord. I was told that likely nothing would have been stolen and nothing was. The landlord had a door to get fixed and the police left. The landlord asked that we leave the settling of the matter to him. I was happy to agree.

The Omani family on the other side of us had a death in the family. For three days they left their front door open and all the lights on. Usually the door was never open. We took that as an open invitation to drop by. Our visit was brief and we were invited to sit and have dates and coffee. It was no different than we might have done at home with a neighbor.

෴

Since we lived next to a cemetery, funerals were a common event. The body would be carried over head in a simple wood box wrapped in funeral green cloth. The Quran would be recited during the procession. The mourners would all follow the deceased and the reader, I assumed, would be an Imam. The body would be placed in a shallow grave and covered. An unmarked stone went at the head and feet. A woman would have three stones.

A Jordanian teacher had died. I had been out for supper with several Jordanians and they decided to visit the family. The deceased was in a casket on a dias in the middle of a green painted room lit by some bare light bulbs. We filed past the family members, men only, shaking hands and offering condolences. I was a little awkward as I had never met the man who had been teaching at one of the local schools. However the fact I was there to show respect was recognized by several in the room whom I did know. We shook hands with everyone in the room and lined up along the wall facing the deceased. After a time, with not much happening except making small talk, refreshments were brought in and passed around. The wake then became a more social event and after an appropriate time we departed. The ritual was similar to the ritual at Gamoodi's engagement announcement party.

The wedding would be some years off but the deal had been arranged between families. At that event I was ushered into a much more lively crowd. The young office clerk was in his finest regalia, sword and all. Many of the guests also were in their Omani finest as well. Instead of a body there was a huge feast tray of fruits in the center of the room. After the greeting of handshakes with everyone in the room, we lined up along the wall facing the food. There were a few welcoming remarks and then it was time to socialize and eat. The bride did not appear but the bride's father and male family members were there.

The Omani Student

Our students were to dress in dishdashas and turbans at all times while at the college unless there was a sports activity. We established a sports day and the first one was rained out. The only rainy day in months and we had a muddy field.

Their skin tones were varied. Some were ebony black while most were simply darker skinned than myself. The only game they seemed to play was soccer. I took a couple of frisbees which created a sensation for a couple of days. Some of them were married and a few had children. While their age range was 18 to 20's, some seemed older. They organized a few day events among themselves but nothing at night. The only night activity might be a picnic under a street lamp.

The most popular event among the students was the poetry readings. Poetry is very popular and they recite their compositions at presentations. A group of students will sit together on the ground while they take turns reciting poems. There are popular poetry competitions that students enter in hope of some recognition. The notion of young men seriously engaged in reading poetry seemed quaint and yet very civilized to me.

They were also fond of presenting skits on the stage. These skits often had moral or behavioral themes. One which I found particularly interesting was a short play in which a sick person went to a traditional shaman for his illness before going to see a proper doctor. Having nearly died under the shaman's treatment, he was saved by the doctor in a white coat.

Another skit was framed around a recent campaign to have birth spacing between babies. The state was urging a three year birth spacing program for the health of the mother and child. Other skits were straight out of boy scout campfires. I went to several of these at the college and came across other such events in the schools. One involved a teacher who used a cane to discipline the children. Caning, while not popular, did seem to still exist in a few places.

Some historical displays and science exhibits or fairs were put on. These would have met stiff competition from the average grade five class in Canada. Still they were proud to have me see what they could do.

Once in a while I would go to the cafeteria to have lunch with the students. All spoke some English as it was required in the training. They were welcoming of me but always reluctant to openly express any concerns they might have. I think the idea that the Dean would voluntarily consult them was decidedly strange. They were generally not inclined to complain about anything. Perhaps they suspected a trap. The cafeteria at the college served biriani and curry dishes, yoghurt drinks, salads, bags of chips and soda pop. These young men did not use alcohol or smoke. Smoking was forbidden at the college and I seldom saw evidence of much smoking around Nizwa.

However in a mall in Muscat I came across hip young Indians who were offering free samples of cigarettes and had prize draws for various items sponsored by the cigarette companies. It was a real effort to promote their products. I engaged one young sales person about the evil they were promoting and got a very sheepish knowing response. The impression I got from Omanis passing by was one of bewilderment at the promotional hype. In Salalah there were hookah pipes in shops but they were not permitted in Muscat. A different standard was applied in the Salalah area on a number of different issues. It was a slightly different culture in that part of Oman.

When we were at a fishing village north of Salalah, the curious teen age girls were quick to poke their uncovered heads into our car windows. Such forward behavior would not have happened elsewhere in the Arab world.

There never seemed to be much spirit among the students. Omani young men are very polite and reserved and only on the soccer field do they get excited. In general they were not too committed to their studies and keeping them in classes on Wednesday afternoon before the weekend was impossible. They were on their way home to the mountains, desert or Muscat by lunch time.

Some lived in fine city houses with satellite dishes and they drove their own cars. Others lived in mud walled homes in towns across the Sultanate and some lived in tents in the desert in the company of camels and goats.

When I posted some supposedly amusing wordless cartoon jokes on a board outside my office door, I was asked what they meant. Their sense of humor was entirely different. Things which would make a westerner laugh was not understood and was puzzled over for meaning. On the other hand they had sayings sometimes similar to ones we know well such as "birds of a feather stick together" but others I learned were quite different. One was "the son of a duck is a floater". When I used the term "tempest in a teapot", I got quizzed as to the meaning and it seemed to delight them. Omanis have a fondness for using proverbs and a new one was always appealing.

Another curious fact was the total absence of vernacular expletives. I never ever heard the equivalent of a curse word. Perhaps my ear just could not adjust. However I often heard "god is great" and "god willing." My sense of the matter is language is held in religious esteem and cursing and blaspheming are shunned. There are curses and comments of derision that are more than the expletives of the English language. These are well chosen and pointed but never blasphemous.

My students were sent to be teachers and it was up to us to motivate them to that end. It was not their choice and they sometimes expressed it. One sore point was the student stipend at the college. This stipend was to cover their living expenses while away from home. It was less than what was given at SQU. Unfortunately it cost more than they were getting to live in Nizwa and go back and forth home. I landed into this mess early on at the college. The students wanted to launch a demonstration for the visit of the Director General. Some of the organizers politely came to discuss the intended event. These were clearly not western students. Fortunately, having been given a heads up about the intended protest, we were able to meet with all the student leaders and convince them there was a better way to make their case. Other colleges had some serious demonstrations but ours did not. As a result the DG was impressed and willing to sit with our students and hear their complaints. They got a stipend increase based on some pretty sound reasoning.

One of the student leaders who I came to know as a result of this event later came to see me for some advice. He was a bedouin from a tribe in the desert near Adam. His family still lived in tents and herded animals. When he came to me, it was to tell me that his father had died and he was uncertain about whether he could stay in school. From our discussions it was learned that he had an uncle he could trust to care for the camels and goats so that he could continue with his studies. But when it came to discussing whether he should kill a camel in honor of his father for a funeral feast, I was of no help. I suggested he consult with his uncle and others who would better know the protocols.

As the first schools had only opened in the 1970's some twenty years earlier, these students were among the first to have had a complete education. Many had come from families where they were the first generation to be literate. Some were bedouins, some the children of former slaves, some were the children of Zanzibar Omanis who had answered the call to be repatriated and some were from tribes from all over the country. One important aspect of their education was to become first and foremost loyal Omanis. Unfortunately few of their teachers past elementary school were Omani.

The West and Islam

We lived in two worlds simultaneously. The locals were emerging from the middle ages into the technology and culture of the western world. I could sense bewilderment, confusion, anxiety, but little hate or resentment. I suspected that there was some resentment but the authority of the Sultan was used to manage it all . There was some discussion from time to time around the college. When I put up clocks, I could find none in Arabic and no one complained. Somewhere it had been discussed that we westerners had obtained the numerals and 0 from the Arabs. Their history books dwelt on the Arab world and there was always some concern as to why the Arab world had fallen so far behind the West when 700 years ago they were ahead scientifically and technologically. It was about that time that simply written books became discouraged in Islam and replaced with the ornate writing of all texts in calligraphy. Poetry was acceptable but reason and innovation were not. For hundreds of years learning was discouraged except for the study of the Quran and other religious books. Rote memorization was acceptable and required.

I never entered into a discussion on this topic with the Arabs because inevitably it would come down to the fact that Islam had ceased to be an open vibrant religion and had become rigid and conforming. Blaming Islam for anything was not open for discussion.

One of the students came from a well to do family in Muscat. The young man came to the college with his own car and used his video camera at any opportunity. He was into arabic music and my take was that he was very influenced by the west. His music taste was Arab pop and he brought me some tapes so I could hear what was currently in vogue. His English was quite good and he displayed a lot of interest in many subjects including the modern methods of education that I was there to encourage. He took part in some seminars I ran.

I was surprised when he came complaining about his marks. They were not good and he was in danger of failing his grades. I attributed these grades to the fact that he did not like to commit and regurgitate. The current system was not good for one like him. I took the trouble to do some background checking and basically found there was little I could do. This answer didn't satisfy him at all and suddenly I found myself being threatened because he was using his influence with his family to get his marks altered. Now this was a boy who did not get admitted to the University and was sent to Nizwa as the alternative. Now he was not doing well here. Rather than see him forced into taking a year over I spoke with the other Dean who usually dealt with student issues. It was agreed that his exams would be remarked. Naggar had also had some pressure brought to bear on him from the Minister. After he got bailed out, the young man became his pleasant friendly self but I was wary of his other nature when he was not so pleasant and prepared to use threats.

After I returned home from Oman, he began sending me emails in which he complained of the situation in Oman, of the Sultan and of the United States. I entered into a correspondence with him in which he increasingly seemed to be influenced by strong anti western views. I found myself engaged in defending the Western world to an increasingly disaffected young man.
Knowing that the Omani authorities would be monitoring emails in the country, I suggested that he be more careful in expressing his angry views so openly about the Sultan and the state of affairs in Oman. My explanations about the intentions of the USA seemed to be falling on increasingly more deaf ears. His increasingly worrying hostility to America caused me to tell him that America would not bother Oman and the Arab world unless something was done to infuriate them and then they would use their power. America I explained was not interested in dominating the Arab world. Here was a youth who seemed to have turned from pro Western to anti Western. That was the last I heard from him. Less than a year later the 9/11 attacks took place. I heard that some students at the college had stood and cheered when they heard the news. I was glad I was not there.

Yet friends still there said many Omanis had expressed sorrow personally to them.

The crusaders of the middle ages may have been long forgotten as important in Western culture but they are still fresh in the minds of the Arabs. The thinking goes like this: Why are the Arab lands so backward? Why don't we lead anymore? Why is it always done the American or British way? God is great so why aren't the Arabs? America and the west defile the moral standards required in Islam and this should stop.

Oman was never a colony of anyone but even well educated Omanis thought that they had been owned by the British. In fact until the advent of steam ships the Omani navy was force to be reckoned with in the Indian Ocean and Oman had colonies in India and east Africa most notably Zanzibar. That imperial coastal power meant nothing to the interior tribes. Until 1970 life in most of the country was exactly the same as it had been for a thousand years. Now Oman was a managed oil rich nation building a modern state. We arrived just as the cell phone and the internet arrived. Long before I owned a cell phone, nearly every student in the college seemed to have acquired one. Yet along with all this technological advancement comes cultural change. Having your culture altered so drastically right before your eyes must invoke all sorts of emotions. Men who recall seeing their first white man, automobile, light bulb and telephone and who went from herding goats to learning to use computers must surely have havoc played with their sense of self.

 When I attended my last staff meeting, I decided to emphasize in my remarks the fact that the world was rapidly becoming one global community and that it was up to we educators to help the next generation come to terms with this fact. The challenges of globalization making the world smaller and more interrelated is of great importance to educators so that we may all learn to live harmoniously in the future. The applause was polite and I sensed a few grumbles as the translator expressed my words. My view of reality was not appealing to all present for I suspect it represented to them a world run under western terms.

Two Cultures in a Day

After a morning about the house we went for a swim at the hotel. I checked out the Pajero and found the rad fluid down a little. There must be a tiny leak. We had to go back to the house to fill the rad and get some extra water and so we were a little late leaving for Muscat for the weekend. About halfway to the city we saw that the big trucks were pulled off the road. Guessing a routine inspection we proceeded on to discover that the 50 KM length of recently erected flag poles, one every 1/10 of a KM now had flags. As we approached Samail there were more flags and posters and a growing number of people along the road. We passed a huge decorated gateway over the road . Off to the left in the distance we could see a tent camp and a newly paved road going through yet another archway. It reminded me of a boy scout jamboree. We now were traveling amid a lot of people. Groups of singers and tribal dancers, school groups and ladies groups were milling about or rehearsing. At the main turn off for Samail we were stopped by the police and diverted down a side road.

Such a gathering as this could only mean that the Sultan was coming. We parked and had a good view spot right at the main corner. There was tribal singing and sword waving and drum beating to entertain us. I took a couple of pictures and a police officer came and politely told me to put the camera away ...no pictures of the Sultan. We were told the Sultan was coming to celebrate the upcoming Eid with the people of Samail. After an hour of standing and no prospect of a photo opportunity we decided we had to get to Muscat so we took the detour route. This route led us into Samail and along a Wadi. I had never been along this road so it was interesting. This road also was flag lined and there was evidence that the Sultan would probably be visiting some places along this road while he was at his mobile camp.

As we left Samail, we thought we saw the complex that was his personal camp as the tents were a little taller and lighter in color and a flag pole was in front of the tent.

We came out at the Sur road and doubled back to meet the expressway. Here and there along the expressway were a few persons waiting so it was clear that we would have waited another half hour or more just to see him drive through town to take up residence at his camp. He does these camp outings several times a year in different parts of the country. They are kind of a meet the people thing.

A few kilometers along the road we see an approaching helicopter and then a lot of car lights indicating an approaching motorcade. Our side of the highway is open and the other side closed. At a good speed we are approached by a police car, a pair of vehicles with gun crews manning antitank guns, and a couple of trucks full of gun toting guys standing up in the back. I have my camera in my hand but decide to forget the photo. Donna says she saw a guy in a land rover with a white beard and 3 others in the car. The Sultan drives his own vehicle so it was probably him. I missed that. There were more soldiers in trucks then another pair of antitank guns facing backwards. Everyone was dressed in army green. Finally there were 50 or 60 big Mercedes carrying the ministers and other entourage potentates. Usually there was only one person to a car. Then at the end there was a lone police car followed by normal traffic. In two minutes the entire entourage had whizzed by. That was as close as I ever came to meeting the Sultan.

When the Sultan toured past our house a year or so earlier the entourage had been much larger. It came in sections. The camp travels with mobile kitchens, fuel trucks, portable washing places and who knows what else. It is self contained and represents a totally portable government. The Sultan's tent is air conditioned and I was told the ministers tents are not. They are expected to sweat it out in more ways than one.

When we saw this parade from our roof top, the Omanis who were visiting us had rather negative comments about the waste involved with such ostentatious behavior. Those remarks came as the endless stream of black Mercedes passed us. It was one of the few times I ever heard an Omani being even mildly critical of the Sultan and his behavior.

We continued on into Muscat to enjoy our own special event, the Calgary Stampede! Several years ago the rather modest Canadian contingent at the Petroleum Development company, PDO threw a party that has now become the expatriate event of the year in Muscat. It was our first opportunity to actually go.

The PDO recreation club forecourt was transformed into a very Canadian environment. It had the atmosphere of a fair. We had chili, roast beef on a bun, beans, chicken fingers, popcorn, Nanaimo bars, rice crispy squares and a bar with Mexican beer and margaritas. They didn't want to push the Canada part too much!

Our Educational Consulting Services group had our own table. We wore red bandanas around our necks which were given to us at the gate. Little Canada flags were handed out to wave and there were signs with "EH!" added after the other words.

About 500 turned up. Many were American, British, Australian and Dutch wannabees. So when the Canadian national anthem was played, the response was a little thin. We were badly outnumbered. We were told that this is THE event to go to for expats. Canadians get the first dibs on the tickets and then it's open for anyone.

There was a chuck wagon to sit on for photos and corny photo models to stand behind with your face in the hole. There was a shooting gallery, bales of hay, people with big buckled belts and wide brim hats, jeans, jeans and more jeans. There was line dancing before a stage with mountains and real teepees and huge plaster bucking bronco. Lots of impressive work had been done to create the atmosphere. The DJ was imported from a Calgary radio station and had the latest Calgary weather news. The grand prize of the evening was a trip to the Calgary Stampede from Muscat for two. We had a great time and whooped it up like real Albertans. There were a handful of Omanis present who must have wondered about us especially when they saw 300 people trying to line dance.

We had a double dose of celebrations in the Omani world and the expatriate world all within a few hours. That was the exciting reality of our life almost on a daily basis.

Wadi Bani Khalid and the Wahiba Sands

In the extreme eastern end of the high mountains before reaching Sur and in the same area as the northern end of the Wahiba sands, there is a valley between two high ridges known as Wadi Bani Khalid. Until recent years this valley must have been a pretty isolated place. Now a fine paved road winds itself up and over the mountain and down into the valley.

Here there are several villages along the stream. The pavement ends and the road snakes along the wadi floor and up over another small ridge back to the wadi bed. It is not much of a road and although the area is interesting, we wonder why we have heard so much about this place. The trail up the wadi comes to an end and our party decides to take lunch under some shade. There seems to be a lot of traffic including western tourists. Cars are parked all over the place. Many must have come some distance as the area has a small population.

After lunch Rashid appears and offers to escort us further up the wadi. He is 10 years old and is taking great pride in assisting us. As we go, the sound of music from boom boxes and the smell of roasting meat surrounds us. This is obviously a popular picnic spot. Then we see the reason for our journey. The wadi has been transformed into a series of pools of crystal clear water. The pools are natural and a good size. We carry on climbing up rocks to get a better view. The place is quite tranquil but the rocks around us bear the marks of having seen a lot of water buffing them smooth. We are 40 or 50 ft above the water and heading upstream to a small canyon.

Here in the canyon we discover a rare item in Oman, an ever flowing water fall. It is not large but certainly attractive. The rushing water comes from the mountains above. These mountains look as stark and bare as all the others around but for some reason Wadi Bani Khalid has a flowing stream. A stream in Oman is a very rare thing and so on a weekend lots of people come to see the waterfalls.

After the water falls and the trip back down the valley, we head back over the mountain. From the heights we can see the orange red of the Wahiba Sands. We have decided to camp in the sands again. Camping is a favorite weekend activity for expats especially those from Muscat.

We decide on this trip to enter at Minitrib an oasis village right at the very edge of the sands. The Wahiba are both ancient and active sand dunes. Long parallel ridges of dunes with scattered vegetation make them a disappointment for those who want to see the classic Barchan style dunes. These are however real dunes of real sand. The town is small and after passing the old fort we leave behind the usual cement block houses and pass into an area of makeshift dwellings. There are tents and palm leaf shelters and animal corals of the Bedu who live here. The Bedu shift from dwelling to dwelling as needed and are not inclined to make permanent homes. These are nomadic people by choice and life style.

The road becomes a sand track or more accurately a series of sand tracks weaving across the bottom of the valley. This countryside is great for four wheel drives and we slither about in our convoy of 4 vehicles. Each one produces its own cloud of sandy dust so we spaced our vehicles some distance apart.

Now about half an hour into the sands we begin to look for suitable sites to camp. Our first venture up a dune results in disaster and two vehicles are down to their axles in sand. We dig them out and return to the main trail. Farther along I determine that we should be able to get about half way up along an old track.
 I shove my foot on the gas and gear right down. We slowly manage to reach a level parking spot. I am up. The next vehicle tries several times and quits a few yards from the crest. The others decide to camp at the bottom.

For me this accomplishment is a point of satisfaction because last year I was the one who couldn't get up the dune. Now Donna and I were about half way from the highest level of this section and had a splendid view.

After dark it began to cool rapidly and by 9:30 we were all chilled and tired and abandoned the campfire which was composed of our imported wood since there was none to be had out here in the sand. Our sleeping places were diverse. In our case it was inside the Pajero whose fold down seats make a reasonably comfortable bed.

The stars were brilliant in the desert sky and several times we were treated to shootings stars that were bright lime green and appeared as large as pencil erasers as they cast a strange light.

We awoke to see some of the others of our group wandering about on the high crest of the dunes in the rising sunlight. Donna and I dressed and went to explore for ourselves. After a bit Donna went back down the hill to search for some breakfast while I got interested in looking at the various marks that were left in the sand overnight. I followed the trail of what appeared to be a house cat. There was a Bedu home off in the distance. Then I found some tracks that looked like beach crabs had been here. The most interesting were tracks of a small creature probably smaller than a squirrel but a creature that hops like a rabbit. I followed them along and the hops were very small and then the sand was scuffled with the carved arc mark of what I assumed was a wing tip. The hopping tracks ended there.

I walked further along the ridge looking for other signs of life when I noticed that a pickup truck was carefully following my tracks along the crest of the dune. A beat up old white Toyota with a galvanized water tank on the back pulled up and I met Saleem Al Wahibi, father of 4 boys and 5 girls, who in addition to the truck came equipped with a GSM cell telephone and a pair of binoculars. He was the modern nomad.

It was his farm in the distance and he kept 5 camels and about 40 goats as his main livelihood. He had a gas generator and electricity and TV, yet his home was a tent with plastic mats on the sand, an animal coral and a dried palm leaf shelter.

He kicked off his sandals and dashed 50 ft up a steep sandy slope. I did the same and there with a grand view. We squatted in the sand and examined each others driver's licences and shared some general information as best we could in my limited arabic and his equally limited English. He spoke about how much he liked the sand as it was soft and pleasant. He asked if I had skiied on the sand yet. I hadn't. He pulled out the tiniest little pipe resembling a cigarette holder more than anything else and put in a pinch of tobacco. We spoke of his world. I asked about the tracks and we went off to examine some. The crab marks were scorpions and we flushed one out of a tiny shrub. The hopping creature was a hopping mouse and we found a burrow. The cat tracks were his "Meow." He was a man clearly content with his world. He had spent 5 years in the army in Muscat and had been to Salalah but these sand dunes were his home. He liked it here. So did I.

Beckoning me to come I climbed into his truck and we set off along the crest of the dunes picking our way carefully around the sand. How he could drive this truck so readily here was amazing. I doubted that any of us could have driven so adroitly in these small soft ridges of drifting sand. We climb up and for a moment I am looking at the sky and then suddenly I am looking straight down a steep 20 ft slope. Gently we go. Remember, this is soft sand. We travel along the ridge then turn and go up again to a crest. This time we are aimed down the main lee side of the high dune. Earlier we had decided not to drive up here concluding it was too steep. Now I was going down it. Straight down.....I have my arm braced on the dash to keep from falling out of my seat. I can see everyone sitting about eating breakfast. Nobody is looking up at this vehicle dropping down on top of them. We come down to the level of my car and keep right on going straight down at a leisurely pace. Perhaps we are sliding more than driving. A couple glance up as we approach the camp. Nobody had seen me crest over and down the steep slope. Only two great streaks of slithered sand was evidence that we had done driven down.

Donna, unaware of my adventure, looked up in surprise as I emerged from the truck. Saleem stayed for some tea and ate an orange and part of an apple. He left a part of the apple to show that our generosity had provided him with more than his needs.

He drove off and shortly reappeared with 3 boys, his older sons and then left again. The boys sat politely and accepted some fruit. Then after a few minutes Saleem reappeared accompanied by his wife. His truck's water tank was now full of water. She offered to sell us some woven key chains and I bought one to use as a Christmas tree decoration in memory of the time I spent squatting on the peak of the dune chatting with Saleem about his world.

The sun was now rising high in the sky. Our guests departed and we packed up readying our convoy to churn our way back out of the golden sands. We would return to the Wahiba area several times. Our daughter and son accompanied us on one of these excursions. They would come from Canada for the Christmas college break.

On another adventure in these same sand dunes, we left the last village and followed a trail along a depression. We headed some distance into the sand dunes. The trail left behind all habitation and vegetation of which there had been precious little of either. On the return journey we came across a pickup truck that had a water tank on the back. The truck had broken down on its way to deliver a load of water to a camel station. Two men waved us down. They need to go back to the village on the edge of the dunes from which we had just come. Erin was driving at the time and one of the men sat up front to give directions. The rest of us sat in the back. Both men were deeply impressed that Erin was doing the driving. There were comments and smiles and indications that they thought it was great she could drive so well.

As we neared the village, they pointed off to the left and the Pajero lurched over a ditch and veered off toward a building that was our destination. The men got out and went inside only to emerge in moments urging us to come in. There was much arm waving and smiling and we were ushered into the living room. Kawa was brought out and tea with camel milk was also provided. Grapes, oranges and apples were served along with dates. We were all seated on the carpet when one of the men got up and brought his wife and mother and children in to join us. Much conversation went on and the women were looking and smiling at Erin . The older woman raised her thumb and kept commenting "zain" which meant "good" and moving her hands as if on the steering wheel. Driving in sand is a lot like driving in snow and having an automatic gear shift made the task simpler. Nonetheless driving in soft sand takes some skill and the locals were duly impressed. We took it that everyone approved of the idea that women should learn to drive. The men would arrange to get a tow truck and warmly thanked us for the ride. They wanted us to spend the night but I explained that I had to be at work the next day. We left some juice in our glass and food on our plates, thanked our hosts and resumed our journey.

Sea Turtles

Where the Gulf of Oman and the Indian Ocean meet is a point of land known as Ras Al Hadd. Near it is the village of Sur, most notable for the making of traditional arab dhows. This industry of making wooden sailing ships just as they did for hundreds of years is one of the reasons we wanted to visit Sur which was a seaport for the Oman traders who roamed these seas. Dhows in various stages of manufacture are easily seen. The sense of the process is easy to figure out but the actual manufacture of these vessels in a land with no trees adds to the fascination. We made several trips to Sur but always with a secondary goal in mind.

Along the coast is a nature reserve at Ras Al Jinz, a nesting site for the green sea turtle. It had just become a reserve and paid access was required to enter the park. We arrived with all our camping gear and staked out a spot near the newly constructed toilet and washing facilities. Our camping gear was pretty basic since we slept in the Pajero. It was tempting to camp out on the ground under the stars as it seemed safe enough. Along with our friends we sat about the camp fire waiting for night. The sea turtles come to the shore during the night.

The turtles had hatched here years ago and have traveled the ocean for thousands of miles from Zanzibar to Malaysia. Now they were returning to lay their eggs. This particular spot of sandy beach is one of the densest egg laying sites on the Indian Ocean.

It is long after dark and we are dozing off when the guide comes to announce that the ladies are arriving from the sea. We take our flashlights but are told to dim them. We don't want to disturb nature at work. The beach looks like it has been under attack. There are craters everywhere. The pits are up to six feet deep. A giant turtle has created these by flipping and digging the sand. We can see one of the ladies from the sea crawling into a pit. Another turtle is just emerging from the sea and it is the first time in 2 years she has been on land. Her shell is easily 4 ft across and she will be hauling 400 lbs of herself by her flippers.

We see tracks that resemble those a tank might make across the sand. The tracks are everywhere but go only from the water to the beach and back to the water. How she decides upon the right spot to make her nest, I don't know. But I do know she was born on this beach and has been back every two years.

Our small group follows our guide to watch a turtle digging her rear flippers to complete her nest. She takes her time a few strokes at a time. Finally she is ready and begins to lay her eggs. Only now does the guide turn on his muted flashlight to show us the white ping pong size eggs. There seem to be a lot of eggs. She is laying them one after another, periodically shifting and covering them with sand. We are told she will lay from 70 to 200 eggs during the night. After everyone has witnessed the egg laying, we are led along the beach to a location where eggs are hatching.

We see these little guys flailing their flippers and climbing out of their pit and heading to the sea. We pick up one and it fits easily in the palm of the hand. His flippers are going full blast so we set him down pointed to the water. He can see the water and the moonlight on it. That's one reason we have no lights to distract him from his race to the sea.

We stop to observe another lady on her way back to the sea. She is climbing out of the crater. It takes some effort. It's steep and she has to haul her full weight up the sand with her flippers. As she nears the top and after a particularly mighty effort, she lets out a deep sigh. It's hard work. It was the only sound we heard from them. Finally she crested the crater and paused a few moments to take in the view before making her distinctive track back to the sea. We watch her pass another turtle emerging from the sea and as she meets the surf, she pauses from a few moments before taking the final push into the water.

We follow the guide back to our campsite.

At dawn some of us are back on the beach. There are egg shells all over the sand. The predators have been out dining on fresh turtle eggs that they have dug loose. A few little ones have not made it to the sea before daybreak and the seabirds are still circling looking for breakfast. One lone sea turtle remains on the beach perhaps to let us take her picture. She must have arrived late and now needs to get back in the water before the sun gets too high in the sky. We stand aside as she uses her flippers to drag herself back to the sea. She vanishes in an instant without a ripple once she is able to float.

Our day now begun we organize breakfast and plan our trip down the coast road. Last year there were poles lying along the road waiting to be erected for the power lines. There was no electricity in these fishing villages. At best there might be a generator or two. In fact there was a pole lamp with a generator beside it in one village. The signs on the shops along the dirt road were the usual. One decent looking building bore a painted sign that said "Car Parts for Sale." This year the road was paved and the electric poles were all along the road complete with lines. The village pole lamp was there minus the generator. The car parts shop had gone and an illuminated plastic sign said "Computers for Sale." Electricity had come to Ad Daffa and the other coastal villages.

While the traditional small fishing boats still plied the sea as they had for a thousand or more years, their owners had moved into a new and exciting electrified world. Turtle hunting had ceased but new ways of making a living awaited them.

The Wadi's Coming!!!

The term wadi has more than one meaning. It can be a rocky river bed but also it can be the river that went over the bed. When the wadi was coming, it was a warning that a flash flood was on its way. People would speak anxiously about the wadi coming. "The wadi's coming. The wadi's coming!" It was as if some horrible calamity like a tornado was about to occur.

Oman is a country that sees very little rain although in our first spring season we had a considerable number of cool rainy days. The wet weather started about the time the bathroom window fell out. I went to close it and the entire casement, made of iron bars, glass panel and frame, fell all in one piece into the room. We now had a cement hole in the wall for a window. I pushed it back in place and tried to get the owner to fasten it back in permanently. That took some time. In the apartment which we lived during that year, the rain water simply flowed in around all the air conditioners and window frames. Drapes would get soaked and puddles would lay on the cement floors. During that time the nights were chilly and we huddled under the sheets and comforter. Outside the locals riding their bicycles had huge scarves around their necks and over their heads. Nobody had a decent coat.

I learned that rain in Oman was the equivalent of a snow storm in Ontario. The threat of rain was enough for students to go home and for faculty to ask to leave early. Rain meant the wadis would be running. Rain meant the roads would be closed.

The roads did not have culverts or bridges. When it rained in the mountains, the water rushed down the wadis and across the roads, sometimes several feet deep. Large stones and boulders created an impasse as they would roll onto the road and stop. The water might takes several hours to clear from the wadi during which time no one could cross it. Afterwards two problems existed. The first was driving around the debris left on the road. The second problem was the one that really stopped all movement.

We joked that Arabs would never win a war because they had no sense of order. The first car to arrive at a closed wadi crossing would stop. The next couple of cars would also stop behind the first. Sooner or later cars would pull out and occupy the passing lane. Later cars would zoom up the shoulder on one side and then the other. If there was room for other cars to form even more lanes on the shoulder they would do so. Meanwhile, five hundred feet across the wadi, the exact same scenario was taking place. When the water subsided, there would be 8 to 18 cars lined up abreast facing each other across the wadi bed and waiting for the signal, "Gentlemen start your engines." At that point gridlock was inevitable. With luck a police officer might arrive and start figuring out how best to get things moving. This crossing could and did take hours. Reports of 12 hour traffic jams were common.

My worst was four hours and I was near the front in my proper lane. The police officers usually instructed those who had done the right thing to go first. On that night we had picked up a couple and their infant who was hungry. The father rather adroitly announced our car was too crowded and left his howling child and wife in the back of our car. I was not happy he had done that!

Going home from work I spotted a crowd gathered by a dry stream bed. I parked and went to see what was happening. I was told the wadi was coming. The sun was shining in Nizwa and there had been no rain but there were clouds over the mountain.

I heard a cannon shot. It was a warning to get out of the wadi. We stood milling about when an even louder cannon blast indicated the water was coming. I saw a trickle coming through the rocky bed and a few seconds later a brown boiling wall about 4 feet high was pushing everything moveable along with it. With a roar the wadi, wearing cardboard boxes, plastic bottles, garbage cans and a mis-parked car bobbing sideways, came surging past us. A wadi clearly was to be respected, even a small one like I had just seen. After about five minutes the water settled down to become a gentle stream. Within an hour it would be a memory.

The next day we read in the paper that a wadi west of the town had carried two children and an adult to their death in this same storm.

The wadi in front of the souk in Nizwa was a large paved parking lot that on Friday morning featured a giant flea market. During the rest of the week it served as a free parking lot. When we had the serious rains in the spring, the parking lot became a roaring muddy river hundreds of feet wide. I saw several rolled over cars thrown up on the shore downstream from the parking lot. One story went around that an Omani went into the post office and left his wife in the car. When he came back, she and the car were gone. She had to be rescued from the wreckage downstream. During the same event two police officers drowned in their vehicle. It was one of the acts of nature that one has to see to be believed. For nearly a week the river ran and then it simply dried up. The street sweepers were out and cleaned up the parking lot/river bed and the Friday market was back in business. It took a while before all the trashed vehicles were removed.

At the college we had a view of some steep hills over which waterfalls cascaded when it rained. Month on end these were just rugged hills but in a rain they were even more impressive as water falls were everywhere. The Omani staff would go and stand on the roof and just stare at this scene. It was so unusual that most said they had never seen anything like it before.

As for me, I had never seen a flash flood and took to heart the caution implied when I was told the wadi was coming.

Banking and Finance

Usually I used my bank card at the ATM machine to obtain cash. This now ubiquitous process was no different than in any other place in the world. Oman seemed to have a pretty modern banking system that worked efficiently. There were several different banks from which to choose. I chose the National Bank of Oman for my daily banking but invested some GIC's at a better interest rate in another bank. A trip to the teller, who stood behind a glass counter, usually meant standing in line for the Indian or sometimes a western person to wait on me. The Omani in the line in front of me would present his pension check, show his ID card and press his thumb onto a stamp pad and then onto the check. This thumb print was his verifiable signature since like most older Omanis he could not read or write. From my observations most of the transactions in the bank took place in English.

One day I was impressed by the signs put up to advertise the latest banking option, a share the wealth lottery. Instead of taking interest on your money deposits, you could opt for the lottery. What would have been interest became a chance to win. I could not imagine why a bank was in the lottery business with their clients money until I understood that those who followed strict sharia law would not use the bank because it paid interest which is considered haram (forbidden). The solution was to offer a share the wealth lottery which was okay. On the other hand, I understood that gambling as at the camel races was also haram. The distinction between a lottery and gambling was something I never did grasp.

An Omani who bought a car or had a mortgage also created issues with the interest owing. I understood that instead of a mortgage or loan one contracted to a rent to purchase scheme. At the end when the loan was paid off, the car or house was yours. There is always an angle! As for my investments, I was happy to accept the interest rates for short term loans as they were significantly higher than I could get outside of Oman. While Omanis used the banks, it seemed to me a disproportionate amount of the business was with expats. The banks also had a lot of western people working behind the counters.

There was a small stock exchange in Muscat and I started following the course of some of the stocks they listed. The exchange was not a decade old and there were not that many stocks. I had some thoughts about buying into a couple of local companies so I went to a local Nizwa broker's office to investigate purchasing some stocks. The sign over the door was in English and Arabic and inside were several office desks and a couple of clerks, one of whom was female and Omani. All the staff was Omani which was unusual. They could not explain how I could go about making a purchase and conducting a trade. The person who could do that was not in. By the sound of his name I suspected he was Indian. My information gathering session led me to conclude that I would be a lot happier putting my money elsewhere. With large risk comes large gain or loss and here the risk did not look like much gain. However every day I followed several of the stocks on the Muscat exchange and on paper I was doing fine had I actually invested.

Bills were not generally paid at the bank. The monthly telephone bill had to be paid at the telephone office. I would stand in line and wait to advance to the wicket that resembled an old fashioned bank wicket. The clerk had a large ledger to duly record the transactions. The customers were a mix of Omani and off shore workers. I usually had to go at noon because the place closed early. One day a large Omani woman dressed in very bright colors stormed into the office. Everyone of the Indian staff went obsequious. The few women who came to pay a bill were automatically taken to the front of the line. If Donna came with me, we got moved to the front. This lady didn't wait to be asked. She demanded to see the manager. Fear washed over the entire staff. I don't know who she was or what was wrong but the workers were in fear of their lives. Any illusions I had about the demur decorum of Omani ladies vanished. This gal was a "battle axe" and in charge. Nobody was going to give her the run around.

The College Changes

Salem was the first college librarian. Elsewhere I have written about him. We became friends over his dilemma with running the library. He was standing in the middle of a huge pile of boxed books and was clearly unhappy. These textbooks and reference books he had and had not ordered. Whatever order he made bore little relationship to what came. At this point we had plans under way to create a library learning resource center. This edifice at the time was still only on paper. Crates of texts had arrived with no place to go. Most of these books were destined to be handed to students for a semester and then placed back into storage. At this time I was not clear who had ordered the books, Salem or the faculty, but he was responsible. We stood discussing the logistics as to how to handle the situation. This dilemma did not fully account for all of Salem's agitation. I began examining the books which were all printed in Arabic and mostly imported from Egypt.

A "Modern History of The United States" was handed to me out of a case of like copies. It was printed in arabic right to left and back to front. Totally the reverse of an English book. It occurred to me that it was perfect for a left handed person like myself. If I wrote like that, I'd never smudge the ink. The modern history ended in the 1930's. I discovered this information from examining the fly leaf. I went on to check the vintage of other texts. Not many people are engaged in translating books from English or any other language into Arabic. It is a slow process rendered more difficult because Arabic is a phonetic language which means the spelling and word meanings change depending on who is doing the reading. It is a language meant to be read aloud and thus dialects alter the words greatly. Furthermore, recent texts often can't be copied until copyright runs out or royalties are paid. Since most Arab lands are poor, royalties pose a problem. Thus the modern history of the United States was sixty years out of date. We had several cases when a couple of copies would have done. Why this was so, was not clear. Every student did not need a copy since to the best of my knowledge there was no course on American history.

The same story was equally true of science books which also were decades out of current science knowledge. This is a fundamental problem in a world where English is the cutting edge language of nearly every field of learning. Getting timely translations of material is a huge problem. Being forced to be decades behind means you never have a chance to take part in developing anything new. The use of English becomes essential. The material available to teach with was anything but cutting edge. I suddenly had a new understanding as to why English is the universal second language.

We were getting huge numbers of copies of a few books. The Librarian was relegated to being custodian of a student text warehouse and the library was nearly bereft of any diversity. This issue continued throughout the entire time I was there.

We built a fine library, modern in every way, with a computer resource lab. A Canadian, John Murray, was hired to manage the library. He inherited the mess while Salem went abroad to further his education. The library was designed with the intent that it be stocked with diverse publications, journals and books. Getting suggestions was a problem. Unlike a western school the college faculty had little input into the text selection. Most of the professors did not seem to have any idea that they could specify texts. No one ever requested a journal be purchased.

We had map cases but no maps. I approached the geography people about this predicament but they had no experience with maps. I found that maps could be purchased from the oil company PDO so I requisitioned sets of Oman topographical maps. Maps are useful for people who are planning military activities. Oman was not in the habit of passing topographic maps around. The Ministry of Higher Education wanted to know why we needed maps. Why did I think students needed to study maps of Oman? PDO would not send the maps unless approval was given. It was concluded by someone that our reasons were valid and that the students were not about to stage a rebellion to depose the Sultan. The maps finally arrived. The geography teachers were amazed and admired the maps. That was about all they could do. I realized they didn't have a clue what to do with them. They had Doctoral degrees in Geography and they probably couldn't read the maps.

I ordered some English magazines about education and arranged them so I could tell if anyone had visited them. Few ever touched them. Some couldn't read well enough and some thought they were unclean as they were from the west but most found that the useful pictures bewildered them. Using a library as a resource was a skill they had not yet acquired. Students and faculty only knew how to use a textbook. We had lots of those.

Gradually we built up what should have been a useful library of content designed for such a college. Still it was the view of someone that when one book was ordered, an entire class set would be sent. There was no provision for the new library to be the warehouse for thousands of texts to be used by the students. The library was expected to dole out and collect these books and store them. The librarian, John Murray, stoutly maintained it was neither his job to deal with this nor his responsibility. Nevertheless, he was stuck with the issue. To make matters worse, the other dean took it upon himself to intervene and refuse to provide any storage space for all these books. They did not belong in the library as it defeated the purpose of the place and John was given no alternative storage. So I sided with my quirky Canadian compatriot. This silliness made no sense since the problem had to be resolved. I finally found a couple of rooms not being used for any discernable purpose which we could use to keep the student loaners under lock and key.

Now all this sounds silly but it illustrates the mind set both in the college and the upper levels of the Ministry. Money was not the issue. Control was. It does not matter what you order it's what I want to send you that's important. The only time the pattern would get changed was when I could intervene and spell it out.

The Canadian imported to set up the library was self directed and determined to be fully in control of his domain. I had no problem with that, librarians being what they are. Unfortunately he was part of a system and did not see how to fit into it. He was also employed by a different agency than I was and it became apparent that his company wanted more of the action in supplying people to the colleges. He was their employee and saw it that way. This made little sense to me as there were other agencies placing staff in the college and it was a none issue with the others who like myself saw us as all being in the same pot.

John was in some ways typical of all westerners who came to Oman. They have distinctive personalities. John had a daughter Brenna about twelve years old and a spouse in Canada who expressed an interest in being in Oman with him. The problem was they lived common law and had done so happily for many years. In order to come to Oman they had to get married. And so they did! The local Indian academy school in Nizwa was conducted in English so Brenna went there for her 7th and 8th grade. She learned the Indian national anthem and being the only western child in the school had the task of carrying the flag for western culture. She topped her class.

The library had a western toilet with a lockable door. John and I had the only keys to that room which became our place of refuge, stocked with our own toilet paper.

Nevertheless by the time we left we had a functioning library. John had established it as it ought to be but had made an enemy of Dean Naggar who choose to report him as unco-operative. The college also now had a fine computer lab that was operating well and getting lots of enthusiastic attention by the students. While the library was very much under used, the computer lab was always bursting with enthusiastic students.

The computer department was staffed by Jordanians and Maghreb natives from North Africa whose computer skills were mostly based on programming languages. The early lab in existence when I arrived was pretty sad. When they discovered that I was computer aware and prepared to deal with their problems, we had excellent rapport. I most impressed them when a new printer arrived for the main office. No one could get it to work. For a couple of days various members of the department tried. I went at the end of the day when everyone had gone home to see what I could do. In about five minutes I found that the machine needed version 6 of the software and they were attempting to use version 5. I located the version six drivers and downloaded them. Presto, the printer was working. I left a note saying I had it running. I never explained how I did it. It helps to have practical problem solving skills. Unfortunately that was not a strong part of their training.

A western educated science teacher wondered if we might be able to get a video projector. I had it there in a week. The problem was usually the reverse of expectations known in the west. The faculty had few wants so when they wanted something, the money was there to provide for their request.

During the first year there were six to eight faculty in an office with desks jammed together. I arranged for an old unused student dormitory, left over from when the college had been a residential school, to be renovated so two faculty could share an office. It was a needed and popular move. I was determined to raise the moral of the faculty.

When I went requesting computers for the faculty, I was able to acquire some. Not for all but enough to set up some faculty centers. This caused a stir. First of all I don't think the majority of the faculty believed that I could deliver on my promise. When they arrived, every department head wanted a computer at their desk not in another room where all had to share time. Their argument went nowhere. I had the Director General completely in agreement with where the machines were to go. There were not a lot of computer users in the faculty and the rooms we had set up proved adequate. I had better luck with the telephone system because along with a shared office for two faculty members, we were able to provide a telephone. There was great fear that lengthy calls to Egypt would bankrupt the system but we installed a block on long distance calls so they could only make local calls. Best of all I could pick up the phone and call the building that housed the faculty and find out who was about. The rules required attendance from 8 to 5 for faculty. That seemed unreasonable to me and outside the academic tradition and besides the faculty simply vanished when not in class. Instead I insisted that heads cover their departments so that at least somebody was there during college hours. Sometimes I called to find out.

Bringing the college into the modern technical world was easier than re-educating the faculty into the methods of modern education. These methods were being laid out in the Ministry of Education by other Canadians for the new elementary and secondary schools being built. There was blunt refusal by most faculty and dean Naggar to engage in mastering these changes. The college was way behind the methods being introduced in the schools. These methods were supposed to be used to train the new teachers; however, most faculty were almost totally ignorant of these methods and were afraid to examine them. To all intents and purposes we were running a post graduate secondary school not a training college. We had an outdated faculty with no commitment other than to preserve their jobs so they would not be sent back to Egypt. That was the great impasse that had to be surmounted. We got the framework up but did not have the contents.

Even worse the practical teaching portion was a worthless waste of time. We would send ten students to a classroom to do practice teaching. The supervising teacher would not let more than one teach a class in the morning or the afternoon. All sat there observing. Each student teacher had a chance to teach one class in a week and had nine chances to talk about a lesson by the others. There was no opportunity to do real work with the students or engage in other ways. When I had time, I would go and suggest that the class teacher assign one on one tasks, akin to tutoring. I wanted them to do anything to add some value to a very bad system. There were far too many students and far too few placement opportunities.

One fine afternoon not long after the resource facilities were completed, someone produced a CD version of the movie "Titanic" and a small group of us sat around the library watching the latest great hit. A year earlier we could not have done that. Sometimes I felt like the college was the Titanic.

High over the main entrance was a flag pole bearing the national flag. Apparently the Sultan had passed the college and noticed the flag pole. It was too short. What the correct length was supposed to be I did not know. Nassar, the Omani college business administrator, was in charge of this problem. It was a matter of the highest importance and that pole had to be made regulation height as soon as possible. The Sultan was camped somewhere in the desert not to far away. He would set up these camps and the local Bedu and others would come there to see him. The government in fact would be run from the tents. The entourage was always enormous for these full scale military like events.

The Minster of Higher Education arrived at the college in his white dishdasha, tribal turban and a holster and pistol harnessed around him. My meeting with him was perfunctory as he was there to speak with his Omanis. A brief tour was in order and while he spoke excellent English, most of the conversation was in Arabic. I might have been the dean but Nassar, the Omani business manager, was far more senior than a western infidel contract employee. The Sultan had either sent the minister here or the minister just happened to be in the neighborhood. I could not decide. Whatever, he was not in his usual formal attire of black, gold trimmed robes over a white dishdasha but he was ready for a desert shoot out. I was glad he wanted to deal with the business administrator and not me.

Who's your Boss?

ECS or Educational Consulting Services was the continuing name for several owners of the company during my time in Oman. Initially it was privately held and then sold to Stantec another Canadian concern which soon decided to sell it off to other private entrepreneurs who had worked for ECS. So I had three owners in as many years. The members of the English department were hired by a British firm and the Canadian librarian by yet another small company which wanted to expand their operations in the country. Australian universities were active in soliciting contracts as were some American schools. The British Council provided all sorts of services and competed along with British universities for contracts. Canadian universities were nowhere to be seen which I thought odd since the country was buying into educating their kids on a Canadian model.

Every placement agency got a contract with someone in Oman. If it was a government Ministry, then the contract was awarded by the state. The agency was responsible for finding suitable candidates, providing them accommodations, a return ticket home and salary. In our case there was also a bonus if you completed the contract. After that the person was at the disposal of whomever they were placed. So in my case I reported to the Director General of the Ministry of Higher Education and did what she required. The English faculty members reported to me but worked for one of several placement groups. We were more or less indentured servants. The same rules applied to the thousands of Indians, Philippinos, and Pakistanis working in the country.

ECS dealt directly with the Ministry of Higher Education with whom they had a contract. ECS provided our accommodations and paid us. Over our three years we had several liaison contact persons who were sent out from Canada. Since the company's primary interest was in planning and constructing campuses and other facilities, having a half dozen administrators was an alien concept to them. The result was we were pretty much on our own. The Ministry of Higher Education had a grand scheme to have teacher education produce teachers to teach in their newly designed elementary and secondary school systems. Canadians were hired by ECS to produce large parts of the curriculum for the Ministry of Education based on methodologies we were advocating in Canada.

The problem was a huge disconnect between the two Ministries. The colleges were manned by faculty that had no idea about what was being introduced in the school system. While the objective was to produce teachers, the average faculty member lectured in his subject based on what he knew which was usually rote learning from Egypt. Only the education department had an interest in methodologies of instruction but our student population was so large we could not begin to find enough placements for student teaching.

Making matters even more complicated was the inability to connect with the Director General who had many irons in her fire and the result was we seldom had concerted focus on any topic nor the opportunity to discuss them.

By the time we had some cohesive co-ordination with ECS to push some strategies including a 53 point list of essential changes, the contract had ended. I had largely created the 53 points because I was the only Dean there who had actually taught in a teacher training college and who had been in Oman long enough to understand the situation. Along with one other Dean we were the only ones to have survived 3 years in the colleges.

There were six colleges - four male, one female and one mixed. During the span of my contract a total of sixteen Deans had come and gone. Florence at the girls college and I completed the project. One of the new arrivals we never ever got to meet. He went to his College, looked at the accommodations and left the next day. We heard he had been a superintendent on Baffin Island or some such arctic place. I guess he didn't like the desert. Others had mighty rows with the other Dean and quit, a couple had health problems, some stuck it out for a year and moved on. It was not an environment in which to assemble an effective team. One of the greatest frustrations was that highly organized and demanding people came expecting to change the world and found themselves trying to cope with an enormous level of frustration.

For some reason I understood that before I arrived. I also came with a desire to learn and a realization that I had been here before. When Ontario began implementing the new curriculum back in the 1960's, I was one of the first to embrace the hands on empirical methods espoused. I had known the resistance to altering the way things are done by the subject oriented high school teachers. The college was more a glorified finishing high school than a real college, let alone a teacher training institution. So my approach was to figure out where we were and go from there.

The Ministry of Education was better organized. They were implementing the new curriculum in certain schools at the primary level. Both boys and girls went to these classes. There were kits of mathematics manipulative materials imported from Canada. There were library rooms with banks of computers for kids to use. They were integrating the kids and training the mostly female teachers on the spot. Non of our students and very few faculty ever saw inside these pilot schools.

Nothing of the kind was happening at the teacher training colleges. Half of the faculty were computer illiterate. The text books were way out of date. Worse, many faculty were fully aware they knew nothing about the new methodology but to say so was an admission of failure and a loss of face.

The faculty had no idea that they could order materials as they had never had any and since I had a social studies and science background, I set out to support those department demands for equipment. Few requests came to me. They had no idea what they needed since they had never taught with any aids. They lectured and used chalk. The situation was much the same in other departments.

The students, I learned, were sent to the college. They had limited options. All were rejects from university entrance. They had done some sort of profile test. They did not get sent to a community college to learn to be a medical technician or a trades person. They were sent here to become teachers. I tried to foster some enthusiasm about the value of their new career. It was a noble calling and worthy of their future. They were not easy to convince. They knew full well someone else had chosen their future. The students were deliberately sent to us from all parts of Oman so as to be mixed with different tribes. Ending tribalism and promoting national unity was government policy. Often the student's relocation was far from home and to survive they were given a small pay check or stipend to go to school. The ones from Muscat came with their own cars and video cameras. Others came from tents in the desert. None were sure they wanted to be teachers.

Only one college was mixed and that was Salalah. Apparently the Salalah girls were to go to Rustaq, the all girl school. Their parents objected to them living at the other end of the country so agreed to let them go to school with the boys. The national Sultan Quaboos University and the technical schools were also mixed schools. In all cases girls covered in black sat in one part of the class and the boys dressed in white sat in another . Outside class hours sex separation was expected. However tales from the university proved that Omani youth found ways to surreptitiously fraternize. There was o danger of that in all male Nizwa.

There was a huge upward curve in the facilities. Oman was spending big money on education. I calculated that within a few years they would have produced so many teachers there would be a huge surplus. I wrote a report on this and sent it off to the Director. As usual I got no response that it was ever read although the Sudanese fellow in her office usually read anything I sent but did the DG read it? I had the impression that she didn't read most of the reports. However years after I left, I learned the time lines I had set down had been observed and the colleges were recast to serve other training purposes.

My working days were extremely busy as I was involved in a myriad of diverse activities such as the bidding contracts for the telephone system, ordering all the furnishings, supervising the timetable team of the college, writing and creating of the goals and objectives for the college, ordering other materials, organizing facilities, overseeing that we got decent computers, and many other tasks.

I attempted to organize some staff events based on my theory that pleasing the faculty was the best way to improve the lot of the students. One such event was to take a trip around Muscat harbor on a wooden Arab dhow. A few faculty and office staff decided to go on this day long adventure. It was for me a sedate couple of hours. For several of the group it was high adventure. They had never set foot on a boat before and some were very anxious before we left the dock. The Arab hand made wooden dhow constructed in traditional methods from the Sur shipyards was sturdy and we sailed past the souk and the palace and the Portugese forts of the 15th century. When back on firm soil, several confided it had been wonderful to experience what it was like to ride on a boat.

I had to always be alert to cultural issues. When I was introduced to the head of the Islamic department, I met the stern gaze of a cleric who had come from Al Azar University. It is an ancient revered Arabic school, the oldest university in the world. Surrounded by others, he was caught in a dilemma. The white infidel before him was his boss and had his hand stretched out to shake his hand. He did not really want to shake the hand of an infidel but reluctantly he did as we exchanged steady glares, blue eyes into brown.

The Education department which ought to have been the core of the college was considered by other faculties to be intellectually inferior. It was my position that they were the most important part of the college. This position and my background gave me considerable credibility with them. I ran several workshops on teaching strategies that enabled several of the faculty to alter their programs. Their department head maintained a certain distance from me as he was my next door neighbor the first year and given to lead prayers in the mosque on Fridays. He knew he did not have the grasp of what he was supposed to be doing as the head of the department and not being very fluent in English meant he did not understand my workshops nor what was happening in the schools.

The Mathematics department was full of Coptic Christians from Egypt. They viewed me as something of a compatriot. I never did understand just why it was Christians were the choice for the department. They were an affable lot and I enjoyed their company. Not long after I returned to Canada I was sent word that several had been killed in a head on car crash while returning from Muscat.

I made friends in the Science department whose faculty often had western educations and all spoke very good English. The Science department also had a natural inclination to using the empirical methods and ideas of the new program. Several of them undertook to modify their methods in an effort to meet the new curriculum. Other than the English department the Science faculty proved the most congenial and appreciative of my efforts.

The English department was always sure of being kept abreast of all that was going on. They were the ones with whom we socialized in the after work hours. Britain, New Zealand, Ireland, America and Tunisia provided the English training. The department also provided its fair share of problems as one of the faculty had to be dismissed.

The Arabic and Islamic departments had the most distance between us. My visits to their offices were usually awkward as there was a real language barrier. Nonetheless, I made it a point when doing my rounds to be inclusive with them and solicit their views and needs. Typically these were limited. So there was lots of hand shaking and smiles but not much else. These departments felt more awkward as well because friendly fact finding visits from the boss were not part of their culture. A visit from the boss usually meant trouble.

Impressing the computer department that I knew as much about computers as they did was an unexpected bonus. It seemed all the instructors knew only how to teach COBOL, a computer language. They actually had never had a lot of hands on experience beyond programing nor had they much experience with the operating of computers. I put state of the art materials in their hands. It pleased them greatly that they were getting hardware they needed and that they were expected to come up with appropriate software. We had a good comfort base to carry out our tasks since I was the guy who could give them what they needed. We had many discussions about what to buy, how to implement and how to set up the classes.

As I have said, I ran model instruction classes on methodology for the education department and sorted out the personal problems in the English department. I presented the Geography department with real maps which they had never used. I explained things in broken French to Tunisian faculty members and attended international conferences held in Muscat sponsored by the Ministry.

In addition to the college work I frequently went to Muscat to attend planning meetings for developing the college curriculum.

My peers on the committee were more or less at my mercy as I was the only one who had done what they were expected to plan. Goals were set and objectives laid down and a working blueprint developed for reorganization of the training for the colleges. Only in the last few months did we even get to run a couple of implementation seminars.

I was only one but I was one. I could not do everything but I could do something. I kept telling myself this important information.

Our first class of graduating students were summoned to Muscat to attend their graduation. The minister of Higher Education would present their certificates. One of the other Canadian deans called to see if I had been invited. I had not. None of us had. I broached the topic with the other dean. Naggar, the Egyptian, was not even aware the event was to take place. It was Omanis only. The hired foreign help was not to be present. That pretty much summed up our status. Nassar, the Omani college business agent, went.

During all of this time I kept wondering if I was really making any difference in the way things were being done. On the level of providing facilities and arrangements, I was pretty satisfied. Even seeing that the registrars office finally was able to properly keep track of the 1600 students was satisfying although the registrars did the actual work. Some of our first class of students had no clear trail of their credits and standing until the registrars developed a standardized system of record keeping. It was basic but necessary stuff. Still it was an organizational problem I had to supervise.

The Ministry decided they wanted a stadium built at the college for sports events. We had a fair chunk of property and set out to measure some soccer fields. As I stood with the group contemplating the new stadium, I was looking across the road at the community stadium that we used once or twice for some school or other events. A huge unused modern complex and the Ministry wanted to build another. I argued in vain that we should simply make use of the other stadium that we could walk to in five minutes. I viewed a second stadium so close as a waste of the Sultan's money. The Sultan had all the oil revenue and was owner of the country, a true feudal monarch. The stadium discussion was at the end of my time there. My practical opinion was not important anymore. The college would grow and change without me.

There had been attitude and program changes. We were providing the facilities. But did we actually create a teacher's college that trained real teachers? The answer was a flat NO!

At the end, I had had a wonderful time and put forth a huge effort but the checks and balances I daily confronted meant as an education college we were not going anywhere quickly. Three years had laid the foundations but key elements were not functioning and were not likely to do so for some time.

The End of the Journey

We learned in the spring of 1999 that the ECS representative was having a hard time getting in to speak with the Director General. That did not bode well. Finally on March 17th of 1999 it was known that ECS was not going to have their contract renewed. The reasons were not made known.

ECS owned us, the six Canadian deans. Like every expat in Oman we had a sponsor, in our case, the Ministry of Higher Education. The contract for every expat, be they Indian, Pakistan, Philippino, Egyptian or Canadian included two things, accommodation and a ticket home. We were now to get the ticket home.

With the ECS contract gone the future of the Canadian Deans was in doubt. There was some discussion about working directly for the Ministry. Some deans entered into preliminary talks about direct employment. However, it was widely known, a pay check from an offshore employer was more reliable. In Oman it was assumed you would work for four to five months before you got your first pay if you worked directly for a Ministry. The working conditions were also somewhat unfathomable. Ultimately no one stayed.

We now were in a state of limbo. My contract technically ended the end of July. However considering I had holiday time, my departure could really be the middle of May. Nobody knew but myself when I was to leave. There was no effort made to appoint anyone to fill my job. The other Dean was asked to go to Salalah where he could sit all day at his desk and write huge volumes of material like he did at Nizwa. The new incoming Dean would be one who spoke little English but was fluent in French which posed a serious communication problem if I stayed on. No one was proposing I stay and no one was acting as if I was leaving. There was work to be done and yet there was no replacement coming for me to advise. Was I to go or stay?

This weird scenario went on for a few weeks until I decided that I would put in motion an exit plan. ECS was out but I think they were still hopeful of staying involved with some part of the government. They were offering no information or guidance so in the vacuum I acted in my own best interest. We had a house full of furniture. Some was provided by ECS but some was bought by ourselves. We had a car to sell and goods to pack and send home.

I set a deadline in my head and when that date passed with no word from the Ministry about what was happening, I proceeded to arrange my exit. Nobody knew I was readying to leave or when it was to happen. I chose June 20th because classes had ended for the year and planning had been done for the fall semester. We were definitely going home. We had stayed long enough. A few days before my departure I informed the other Dean and the faculty when I was leaving.

My solution to disposing of the furnishings was to place a single package price on all the stuff I didn't want to take to Canada. Everyone else used a yard sale approach but that was too time consuming for us. I checked with ECS and they agreed on what their share was worth. They devalued everything less than 50% on the rial. Our stuff was priced closer to what we paid for it since the ECS material was going so cheap. Together a whole house full was going for 900 rials. If the scheme worked, I would sell my stuff at almost what I paid for it. I put the word out and a few days later the registrar from the college brought around a student who was getting married to inspect the stuff. He came back the next day with a friend and paid cash. He could pick it up the day I was leaving.

In the meantime ECS had decided they would store the furniture rather than sell it. I quickly told them it had been sold. It was too late. End of conversation! Of course I was still using it all since the deal was contingent on my departure.

The Pajero, our four wheel drive vehicle, created another disposal problem. No one seemed to be interested yet at the very last minute another student arrived with the cash to buy it. I had set a price and arranged for a colleague at the technical college to try and sell it on my behalf if it did not sell before I left. I had the paper work all arranged when the offer came in. My secretary Gamoodi who had helped me get my licence now was helping me sell the car. We had to make a fast trip to Muscat and back in the morning to get the registration transfer. The car was sold at 2 p.m. in the afternoon. I handed the keys to the Omani buyer and had a photo taken of the handshake.

By 5 p.m. we were in a truck with our packed goods and we were waving goodbye to Nizwa. As we passed the college, I looked down the gate lane to see the other Dean walking toward his car. He looked a lonely old man. He had been testy and actually nasty to Donna since I said I was departing and I was put off enough that I never offered to stop to say goodbye. We had worked reasonably well together but were not on the same wavelength at all. He had earned his PhD in Chemistry at Moscow University and had his tank shot up by the Israelis in the war with them. His political views and management methods were totally opposite to mine. I managed by walking around, sitting with students in the cafeteria, going to faculty offices and patrolling the halls. He never ever left his office to see what was going on. He wrote copious reports about how wonderful the college was without taking any interest in changing the college to do the tasks assigned. He needed the pay check and the glory.

When I discovered that two professors were frequently late for class and when they finally did arrive the students had nearly all departed, I hauled them into my office. They explained that they were waiting until the students were all seated and waiting to hear their pearls of wisdom. I said that in my country the teacher arrived before the class and I expected the same. Their option was to go back to Egypt.

However before I could haul them up, I had another issue to solve. We had no clocks in the college. I found some in a shop but they were all our western arabic numbers. None had the current arabic number system. It was no matter and I bought clocks and had them installed. Now classes could start on time. The performance of these two faculty continued as an issue and eventually Naggar reluctantly agreed with me and we recommended one contract be terminated. It had a profound impact on performance. He had qualms about sacking his fellow Egyptians because these contracts were the ticket to prosperity for these men. His interests were career preservation where mine were implementing changes that he knew little about. However, he had bragged that we got along well unlike the other colleges where Canadians had come and gone regularly. It was important he give lip service to collegiality as it enhanced his position. We had joked that as we came together, we should leave together which in fact was the case and a fact I mentioned to him in one of our last conversations.

So as we both were to leave there was to be no leadership continuity. In some ways the college was right where it had been when we arrived. Yet it was functioning fairly well as an institutioneven if it did not meet the objectives of a teachers' college.

Naggar's real authority was due to the fact that with 110 faculty nearly 90 were from Egypt and gravitated to him with their issues while he sat adding two spoons of sugar to his clear tea. It was a minor miracle we never had it out. Mainly I think we both understood the others agenda and shared some common goals. We differed in style but we each knew why the other was there.

Back in Muscat for the last time we had to deliver our goods to the shipping agent. The air freight would arrive in Toronto not long after we did. We shipped Turkish carpets, a fake Xmas tree, a small table, Omani baskets and clay pots along with our clothes and a bottle of desert sand, all treasures of our Omani life. We went on a last shopping trip around the city and bought a silver child's Khanjar. This ornate knife was a carry on item. At the airport the ministry sent a young clerk to ensure our passports and exit visas were correctly completed. The customs officer blanched at the prospects of going through Donna's suitcase of clothes. Touching women's clothing was something he found hard to do. A routine scan turned up the Khanjar and another Omani officer was agitated about what to do. A British air attendant passed by and asked about the problem. The Khanjar went into a paper bag to be given to me once we landed in London. As we went through the boarding line, a flight attendant asked my name, handed me the paper bag, took out the knife and said as the blade was barely six inches long it would pose no problem. It went back into my carry on. That was pre 9/11!

Once we were settled in our seats and the plane began to move, I realized my life in Oman was over. It was nearly midnight, June the 22, 1999. The hectic last few days of organizing to get out had prevented me from absorbing the fact. Now we had no more planning to do. In a few hours we would be back at Curries living the same life we had been living as if nothing had happened at all. Only now we were empty nesters as our kids had moved out, off on their own.

The Optimist club was holding their annual picnic the night we arrived home after 3 years away. After our greetings we stood about with a hamburg and beer chatting. No one seemed very interested that we had been gone for 3 years or where we had been. If we had said we had spent the day at Niagara Falls, I think the reaction would have been about the same. We had not been on a holiday but it seemed that way. Anyone who has lived in another culture must know that it is they who see things differently not those who stayed at home. A neighbor saw us in the grocery store the next day and mentioned he had not seen us around lately. He didn't know we had been gone. It was all so normal yet there were differences.

The toilet seats in the house seemed unusually cold. The fruits and vegetables in the grocery store looked in superb condition and the young women shopping in shorts looked too naked, too fat and too pink. The air was too cool even on a warm day and the trees and bushes seemed dense and luxuriously green. The countryside was neat and tidy. There was a freshness about being home again.

The new Woodstock grocery store was fun to shop in but little did we know it closed early on the day we went shopping. Our cart was piled high with purchases as we had much to buy. We stopped to check out the magazines and after a little went to the check out counter. There was no one there. The store was closed and we were locked inside. After a few minutes a lone employee emerged from the back. He looked surprised but other than to let us out the door could not help us. The groceries stayed behind. Fortunately we did not have to spend our second night home sleeping in the grocery store. Shops in Woodstock don't remain open late like they do in Nizwa. Home was the same but not the same.

Had we stayed in Nizwa it would not have been the same either since many of our new friends also were leaving. Come the next semester things would be very different. I felt that I had made the right choice not to seek to remain in Oman. It was time to depart. I had done what I could and remaining longer even at a different job would have been just another cycle of the wheel. We had been there and done that. Time to go home.

In a few more semesters there would be a surplus of teachers and the college would be recast as a technical school with Omani deans. These new deans were the same people who had worked under me and who I had recommended as worthy of promotion. In retrospect I considered the mentoring of these future leaders the most important role I could have undertaken. Unfortunately I did not have enough time to engage in much mentoring.

In three years I had seen a country emerging from mud huts to cement palaces, transforming before my eyes. The rate of change was amazing. I had met in my first year an expat who had returned to Nizwa after 10 years. He could not believe the changes that had taken place. My students went from beduin camel herders to computer literate college men. I had taken part in this adventure of theirs. I had changed my understanding of the world as much as they had changed theirs. Now fifteen years later I have written of those things which were known to me and I often wonder how things have changed since I was there. I wonder because I still feel part Omani.

"No man can live this life and emerge unchanged. He will carry, however faint, the imprint of the desert, the brand which marks the nomad; and he will have within him the yearning to return, weak or insistent according to his nature. For this cruel land can cast a spell which no temperate clime can hope to match."

Wilfred Thesiger "Arabian Sands"

www.ingramcontent.com/pod-product-compliance
Lightning Source LLC
Chambersburg PA
CBHW031310150426
43191CB00005B/154